Romance Linguistics

Editorial Statement

Routledge publish the Romance Linguistics series under the editorship of Martin Harris (University of Essex) and Nigel Vincent (University of Manchester).

Romance Philogy and General Linguistics have followed sometimes converging sometimes diverging paths over the last century and a half. With the present series we wish to recognise and promote the mutual interaction of the two disciplines. The focus is deliberately wide, seeking to encompass not only work in the phonetics, phonology, morphology, syntax, and lexis of the Romance languages, but also studies in the history of Romance linguistics and linguistic thought in the Romance cultural area. Some of the volumes will be devoted to particular aspects of individual languages, some will be comparative in nature; some will adopt a synchronic and some a diachronic slant; some will concentrate on linguistic structures, and some will investigate the sociocultural dimensions of language and language use in the Romance-speaking territories. Yet all will endorse the view that a General Linguistics that ignores the always rich and often unique data of Romance is as impoverished as a Romance Philogy that turns its back on the insights of linguistics theory.

Other books in the Romance Linguistics series include:

Structures and Transformations
Christopher J. Pountain

Studies in the Romance Verb
eds Nigel Vincent and Martin Harris

Weakening Processes in the History of Spanish Consonants
Raymond Harris-Northall

Spanish Word Formation
M.F. Lang

Tense and Text
Dulcie Engel

Variation and Change in French
John Green and Wendy Ayres-Bennett

Latin Syntax and Semantics
Harm Pinkster

Thematic Theory in Syntax
Robin Clark

Tense and Narrativity
Susanne Fleischman

Comparative Constructions in Spanish and French Syntax
Susan Price

Latin and the Romance Languages in the Early Middle Ages
Roger Wright

Also of interest:

The Romance Languages
Martin Harris and Nigel Vincent

The Rhaeto-Romance Languages

John Haiman
and
Paola Benincà

ROUTLEDGE

London and New York

First published in 1992 by
Routledge
11 New Fetter Lane, London EC4P 4EE

Simultaneously published in the USA and Canada
by Routledge
a division of Routledge, Chapman and Hall, Inc.
29 West 35th Street, New York, NY 10001

Typeset in 10/12 Times by Megaron, Cardiff.
Printed in Great Britain by TJ Press (Padstow) Ltd, Padstow, Cornwall

British Library Cataloguing in Publication Data
Haiman, John
The rhaeto-romance languages. –(Romance Linguistics)
I. Title II. Benincá, Paola, III. Series 450

Library of Congress Cataloging-in-Publication Data
applied for

ISBN 0-415-04194-5

Contents

Acknowledgements

Stephen Leacock wrote that, having once spent a night at the Mitre Hotel in Oxford in 1907, and then revisited the University in 1921, his views on Oxford were based on observations extending over fourteen years.

My relationship with Rhaeto-Romance is even deeper. In 1969, I spent a year as a graduate student in Chur, learning Surselvan and Vallader. Since 1987, I have started to learn (the Passariano di Codroipo dialect of) Friulian from expatriates in Winnipeg. When I add that I have on two occasions gone on hiking trips with my family through the Swiss Alps and the Dolomites, it will be seen that my impressions of Rhaeto-Romance are based directly on observations extending over a period of *eighteen* years. To my teachers, both inside and outside of the classroom 'over' this respectable span, my humble and hearty thanks.

I am grateful to Professor Clifford Leonard, for his careful reading and penetrating criticisms of chapter 1, which amounted almost to a chapter in themselves; and to Dr Christine Kamprath for checking the Surmeiran data and informing me about the latest attempt to create a unified 'Romantsch grischun' on the 2,000th anniversary of the arrival of the Roman legions in Switzerland. For perceptive comments on portions of chapter 4, my thanks to Professors Dwight Bolinger and Knud Lambrecht.

Finally, I am most grateful to my co-author, Dr Paola Benincà, whose collaboration on this project began when she served as the outside reader for the original manuscript. Her comments were so rich and detailed that I asked her to acknowledge them by appearing on the cover of this book. After a satisfying correspondence over two years, I look forward finally to meeting her this year.

John Haiman

This is one of those works which, by its very nature, is certain to attract criticism before it is even begun: due to the vastness of the area dealt with, errors and omissions are almost sure to occur. None the less, I am happy to have contributed to it, because I think that the set of languages described here represents one of the most interesting linguistic groups in the world, for many reasons, some of which we hope will appear to the readers of this book. After a hiatus of many decades, the area is once again described in its entirety, and for the first time equal space is devoted to phonology, morphology, and syntax.

My contribution to Professor Haiman's project was mainly to supply additional information regarding 'Italian Rhaeto-Romance' (i.e. Ladin and Friulian). In the best tradition, we still do not totally agree with each other in our respective interpretation of all the data presented here: I hope, however, our collaboration has proved as pleasant and stimulating to him as it has to me. I thank Laura Vanelli, who kindly read the final version and provided useful comments and encouragement, and Gian Paolo Salvi, who read the proofs and suggested various improvements.

Paola Benincà

Abbreviations

acc.	accusative	*Liv.*	*Livinallongo*
AIS	*see* Jaberg and Jud 1928–40	*Long.*	*Longobardian*
Amp.	Ampezzan	*LRL*	*see* Holtus *et al.* 1989
ASLEF	*Atlante storico-linguistico-etnografico friulano*	m.	masculine
		ME	Middle English
attr.	attributive	MFr.	Middle French
Bad.	Badiot	MHG	Middle High German
c.	common (gender)	n.	neuter
dat.	dative	nom.	nominative
DESF	*Dizionario etimologico storico friulano*	OHG	Old High German
		pl.	plural
dim.	diminutive	poss.	possessive
DRG	*see* Schorta and Decurtins 1939–	p.p.	past participle
		pred.	predicative
Eng.	Engadine	pres.	present
f.	feminine	prf.	perfect
Fr.	French	PRR	proto-Rhaeto-Romance
Frl.	Friulian	RR	Rhaeto-Romance
Gard.	Gardena	*REW*	*see* Meyer-Lübke 1935
ger.	gerund	sg.	singular
Goth.	Gothic	Slov.	Slovenian
i.i.	imperfect indicative	subj.	subjunctive
imp.	imperative	Surm.	Surmeiran
impf.	imperfect	Surs.	Surselvan
ind.	indicative	Suts.	Sutselvan
inf.	infinitive	T	topic
inter.	interrogative	Val.	Vallader
i.s.	imperfect subjunctive	Ven.	Venetian
Lat.	Latin	VL	Vulgar Latin

Introduction

If the Romance languages can be compared to a solar system – with Latin shining in the centre, surrounded by its offspring – then the Rhaeto-Romance (RR) dialects are truly, in D.B. Gregor's vivid metaphor, among the asteroids. Unlike familiar members of the family such as Spanish, French, and Italian, they are not even visible to the layman's naked eye, and their discovery is comparatively recent.

In 1873, the Italian linguist Graziadio Ascoli introduced the study of Romance dialects into the research framework of comparative linguistics, analysing the historical phonology of the present group of Romance dialects. He pointed out that they shared a number of characterizing phenomena and constituted a linguistic group, which he named 'Ladino'.

Since 1883, with the appearance of Theodor Gartner's classic *Raetoromanische Grammatik* on the same topic, the name 'Rhaeto-Romance' has been associated with these dialects. They are spoken in three separated areas located along a narrow strip of land running almost west to east, from the headwaters of the Rhine and along the valley of the Inn in southern Switzerland, over the Dolomitic Alps of northern Italy, to the drainage basin of the Tagliamento river, which flows into the Adriatic Sea between Venice and Trieste. As indicated on map 1, these enclaves are separated by areas where German or northern Italian dialects are spoken. The Swiss or Rhenish and Engadine dialects, known collectively as Romansh, and spoken by no more than 50,000 people, are officially recognized as a single language: in 1938 accorded institutional status as the fourth national language of Switzerland (no doubt to counter Mussolini's pretensions to 'Italian' territories in Switzerland): nevertheless, under the impetus of the Reformation, five separate Swiss dialects (Surselvan, Sutselvan, Surmeiran, Puter, and Vallader) had acquired distinct orthographies and normative gram-

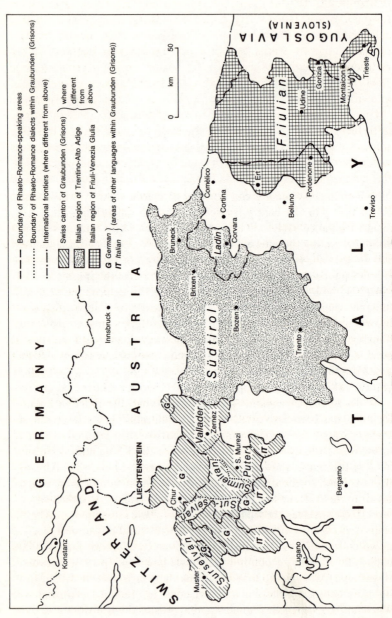

Map 1 The distribution of Rhaeto-Romance

---- Boundary of Rhaeto-Romance-speaking areas

········ Boundary of Rhaeto-Romance dialects within Graubunden (Grisons)

—·— International frontiers (where different from above)

Swiss canton of Graubunden (Grisons)	where different from above
Italian region of Trentino-Alto Adige	
Italian region of Friuli-Venezia Giulia	

G German } (areas of other languages within Graubunden (Grisons))
IT Italian

matical traditions (embodied in pedagogical grammars dating back to the eighteenth century), and attempts to create a single 'Romonsch fusionau' have failed. The half-dozen Dolomitic dialects, herein collectively named Ladin, and spoken by perhaps 30,000 people, have no official or literary status, except in the province of Bolzano, where instruction in Ladin has been given for one or two hours per week since 1948. Even less recognition is accorded to the easternmost dialects, known as Friulian, and spoken by as many as 500,000 people today.

One index of the uncertain and peripheral status of all of these dialects is the fact that there is hardly a single speaker of any of them at this time who is not also fluent in a major local 'prestige' language. In Switzerland and in part of the Dolomites (in the area which was Austrian until 1919), this language is usually German, while in the Friulian plain, it is either Venetian (Francescato 1956; 1966: 8) or (some version of) standard Italian, generally (at least until several decades ago) both.

The first comparative Romanist, Friedrich Diez, mentioned Romansh (Churwaelsch) in his survey of 1843, but decided that since this dialect had no literary language, it could not be accorded status as a full-fledged Romance language. Of Ladin and Friulian (as of the other Rhaeto-Romance dialects, in fact), he said nothing at all. After Ascoli and Gartner, scholars have been careful to enumerate Rhaeto-Romance among the Romance languages. Their descriptive and classificatory efforts have, paradoxically, been far more significant than they had a right to be, and Rhaeto-Romance, like an electron under an electron microscope, has been affected by its scholarly observers in ways that grosser entities like French could never be.

When dealing with such larger entities, scholars may take for granted certain divisions in their subject matter. For example, it is fairly easy to make a straightforward distinction between the socio-political history of a language itself, and the history of its scholarship. The first (at least for the linguist) is primarily an account of how a standard language came into existence: this may have been through the efforts of a handful of great writers, the prescriptive norms established by a committee of lexicographers or grammarians, political and bureaucratic central-ization, or, most frequently, some combination of these.

The second history, the story of the *study* of a language, is generally a meta-topic of decidedly peripheral importance. No 'external history' of Italian, for example, can overlook such facts as the existence of Dante, the foundation of the Accademia della Crusca, or the political unification of Italy. On the other hand, the external history need not concern itself (except perhaps, 'for the record') with even masterpieces of descriptive scholarship such as Jaberg and Jud's (1928–40) monumental dialect atlas of Italy and southern Switzerland, which described, but certainly had no effect on, its subject.

In the case of Rhaeto-Romance, this oversimplified (but surely not outlandish) distinction between the observer and the thing observed, is totally unusable. The Rhaeto-Romance dialects are not now, nor have they ever been, coextensive with a single political unit; some of them have had their (quite separate) Dantes and their Luthers, while others have not; and some of them have had their arbiters of proper usage, and others have not. It is difficult to say whether it is the multiplicity or the partial absence of pedants and poets which have been the more damaging to the creation of an idealized 'standard language', but in the almost total absence of contact among the speakers of the major dialect groups, the lack of political unity or of any unifying cultural centre is decisive.

Mutual intelligibility, the favoured structuralist criterion for grouping dialects together as members of a single language, depends on speaker contact: in the case of Rhaeto-Romance, this is sporadic, infrequent, or totally non-existent. Occasional claims of mutual intelligibility are made: for example, travellers once claimed (in 1805) that Ladin speakers could understand a great deal of Romansh when they went to Switzerland (see Decurtins 1965: 274; the claim was repeated in Micurà de Rü's still unpublished '*Deutsch–Ladinische Sprachlehre*' of 1833, cited in Craffonara 1976: 475). Similarly, an appeal for Romansh volunteers to help victims of the great earthquake in Friul of 1976 added the inducement that language would be no problem (see Billigmeier 1979; in fact, language was a considerable problem, as has been told). For all their anecdotal nature, such claims may be absolutely true: yet they still need to be partially discounted, given the notoriously close resemblances among Romance languages. Any speaker of French, Spanish, or Italian, for example, could probably get the gist of the utterance /in um aveva dus feʎs/, or even /n uəm oa doj fioŋs/ 'a man had two sons', but this would not prove that the Romansh Surselvan or the Ladin Gardena dialects were dialects of French, Spanish, or Italian. Nor would it prove that they were related dialects of the same language. (It is well known, on the other hand, that an Italian dialect, when properly spoken, is not easily intelligible to speakers from a different dialect region: sometimes less intelligible, in fact, than a foreign language like Spanish would be.)

All standard languages are, in a sense, artificial creations. But they are 'real' to their users only if they share a common polity or written language (so that their speakers share a common perception of themselves because of a common history or written tradition). Granting this, we must conclude that there has never been a 'real' basis for the unity or autonomy of the dialects which are the subject of this book. Like French and Italian, Rhaeto-Romance is a fiction. Unlike these, however, it is a fiction which is the creation, not of a handful of great writers, nor of a bureaucracy supported by an army or a navy, nor yet of a people who are conscious of a common history, but of a handful of (great) linguists. 'Consciousness of [Ladin] ethnicity', notes Pellegrini (1972a: 111), 'is entirely the consequence of linguistic researches carried out in the latter half of the nineteenth century, primarily by our own compatriot [G.I.] Ascoli.'

Even more important than this is the fact that (until quite recently) hardly anyone subscribed to this fiction, or even thought about it very much. The qualification is necessary because over the last hundred years there has been a Rhaeto-Romance 'revival', beginning with the formation of philological and ethnological societies such as the Lia Rumantscha in Switzerland, the Società Filologica Friulana in Friul, and the Union dils Ladins in the Dolomites. These activities have culminated in the celebration of the 'bimillennium' of Rhaeto-Romance in 1985, a year that was marked by exchange visits between Switzerland and Italy, and the official launching of a new pan-Romansh language, 'Rumantsch Grischun', among other things. Typically, all of these organizations, projects, and activities, have been spearheaded by linguists. No enthusiast, however, has ever proposed or attempted to design a pan-Rhaeto-Romance language at any time.

The 'external history of Rhaeto-Romance' is therefore almost entirely the story of what linguists have thought and said about it – or about them, since the unity of the group is not surprisingly problematic.

Logically, there are exactly four positions one could adopt concerning the status of any putative language, depending on the answers to two mutually independent questions. First: do the member dialects share enough features to justify their being grouped together? (Perhaps what we thought of as a single asteroid of the Romance solar system is really two or three.) Second, irrespective of whether they constitute a unit, does this unit differ sufficiently from other languages to justify status on a par with them? (Perhaps the 'asteroid' is really a moon of Mars, rather than a sister planet.) Although we may ask questions like these about such languages as 'French', they are really beside the point, for obvious reasons of sentiment and history. On the other hand, for Rhaeto-Romance, they are crucial: for example, in his survey of Romance languages, Walter von Wartburg acknowledges that 'There can be no question of a conscious active unity [among the speakers of the Rhaeto-Romance dialects]. Consequently, [these] dialects underwent no common innovations which are peculiar to them alone' (Wartburg 1950: 148). A more vehement statement defining the problem of using a common label for the Rhaeto-Romance dialects at all is that of the Italian linguist, late-blooming actor (and native speaker of the Nonsberg Lombard-Ladin dialect), Carlo Battisti:

> This supposed linguistic unity which corresponds neither to a consciousness of national unity, nor to a common written language, nor to any ethnic nor historical unity – and the question whether such a unity exists at all – this constitutes 'the Ladin question'.
>
> (Battisti 1931: 164)

In the absence of historical or external criteria, evidence for the unity or independence of the Rhaeto-Romance dialects must be provided by purely structural considerations, which – perhaps surprisingly – are always ambiguous. Depending on the importance that analysts attribute to individual features, it is possible to make an intellectually reputable case for each of the four positions implied by the two questions above.

Position 1: the dialects are united and independent of any other group of languages;

Position 2: the dialects are united but only as members of a larger group;

Position 3: the dialects are not united, but each of them is a language in its own right;

Position 4: the dialects are totally distinct, and in fact belong to different linguistic groups.

(We will say no more about the distinction between 3 and 4 here.) A reasonable inference, given the single name for the dialects, and the fact that this is a single book, is that a great deal of influential scholarship (for example, almost all handbooks of Romance philology) today leans to position 1: the Rhaeto-Romance dialects *do* share enough features to constitute a single entity, and this entity *is* sufficiently different from other Romance languages to merit recognition as a separate group. This position can be considered a trivialized version of Ascoli's theory about language classification: Ladin (or Rhaeto-Romance, like Franco-Provençal etc.) was to be identified as a linguistic group on the basis of the particular combination of specific linguistic features in the area, not necessarily all present in the entire area (see Ascoli 1882–5: 388). (Dealing as he was with structural concepts, Ascoli never spoke about a Ladin *language*.)

Position 2, with a number of competent supporters, does not dispute the unity of Rhaeto-Romance dialects – but recognizes them only as part of a larger linguistic group, generally the northern Italian dialects, excluding southern Venetian. Confusion comes from the fact that these related dialects are referred to as 'Italian dialects' or even 'dialects of Italian', which is absurd. Not surprisingly, many of the adherents of position 2 happen to be Italian – in many cases because they are certainly more familiar with the linguistic and historical reality of the Italian dialects – but it must be noted that they generally ignore the Swiss Rhaeto-Romance dialects when making their arguments and comparisons. Position 2 was most stubbornly articulated during and after World War I in support of Italian claims to the recently awarded South Tyrol, or Upper Adige, where Ladin is spoken. The political mileage which the Mussolini government derived from this position should not be allowed to obscure whatever scientific merits it may have, nor does the position automatically imply a putative Italian ancestry to the group, as many of its opponents seem to believe; in a strict sense they are not 'dialects of Italian', but simply Romance dialects of people who speak Italian – or German – as a second or reference language. Carlo Battisti himself, whose position we will consider later on in detail, denied the very existence of a Ladin (or Rhaeto-Romance) unity, but when speaking of northern Italian, occasionally contrasted Italian with – Ladin.

A notational variant of position 2, adopted, among others, by Rohlfs (1971: 8–9), Kramer (1976, 1977), Pellegrini (1972a, 1987a, etc.), and many of Pellegrini's students and associates, is that all the northern Italian dialects belong to a single group. A supporter of position 2 who identifies all the Rhaeto-Romance dialects as varieties of French (or at least descended from the same ancestral stock) is Leonard (1964: 32).

Considered from a different point of view, positions 2 and 3 are indistinguishable: if there is no Rhaeto-Romance group, then they are coordinate languages within northern Italian, as independent of one another as they are of Milanese or the dialect of Busto Arsizio. In this perspective, we can see as an extreme version of this same position the following statement of E. Pulgram (Pulgram 1958: 49), who brusquely dismisses Rhaeto-Romance as a bunch of not particularly related 'dialects usually classified together (for no good reason of historical or descriptive dialectology) under the heading Raeto-Romanic (for no better terminological reason)'.

Of the four areas of linguistic structure, phonology, morphology, lexicon, and syntax, the first three have been the focus of almost all studies on Rhaeto-Romance. Almost nothing has been written on the syntax of these dialects. In the following pages, we have tried to organize our discussion of these areas in such a way that the questions of unity and independence are constantly before us: necessarily, this will involve some passing reference to neighbouring related languages. The discussion of phonology, morphology, and the lexicon will be a synthesis and reinterpretation of existing classic and contemporary works. The treatment of syntax is relatively new: although the facts discussed are familiar enough, this may be the first time that they have been presented together with a view to either confirming or challenging the conventional wisdom regarding the unity and independence of Rhaeto-Romance.

To anticipate the rather uncontroversial conclusions that may be drawn from this survey, particularly from a study of the syntax: there are no very convincing reasons for grouping together as a single language the various dialects known as Rhaeto-Romance. From the point of view of syntactic typology at least, modern Surselvan and Friulian resemble each other no more than any two randomly selected Romance languages. Even within Italian Rhaeto-Romance, again from the point of view of syntax, Friulian is more distant from Gardenese than from any other northern Italian dialect (see Benincà 1986). So much for unity. As for independence: the Swiss Surselvan dialect exhibits some remarkable independent morpho-syntactic features which set it off from every other Romance language (including Ladin and Friulian!) but a great deal of the word order of Surselvan (as of all Romansh, and part of Ladin) is radically different from what we encounter in the remaining Rhaeto-Romance dialects: the pattern, traceable back to widespread medieval Romance characteristics, is what one would expect of a language which has been under heavy German influence for more than a thousand years. In their treatment of subject pronouns, on the other hand, the Italian dialects, whether spoken in the Dolomites or on the Friulian plain (excluding Marebban, Badiot, and Gardenese), resemble other northern Italian dialects (Piedmontese, Lombard, Ligurian, or Venetian) much more closely than they resemble standard Italian or any other Romance language – or, perhaps surprisingly, given the history of language contact in the Dolomites, much more than they resemble German. It could be argued that Rhaeto-Romance is a classic example of what Kurt Vonnegut in his *Cat's Cradle* called a granfalloon, a largely fictitious entity like the class of 'vitamins', sharing little in common but a name.

Of course, if this should prove to be true, it would hardly make Rhaeto-Romance unique among human languages, or among human cultural concepts or artefacts in general. (Among Vonnegut's examples of granfalloons were 'any nation, any time, any place'.) Whether or not our conclusions regarding the heterogeneity of the dialects in question are correct, you will soon be able to decide for yourselves: but they are certainly not particularly radical.

0.1 HISTORICAL BACKGROUND

The most enthusiastic proponents of Rhaeto-Romance unity can point to only two moments when the 'Rhaeto-Romance peoples' may have constituted a single ethnic or political group. The first was before they were colonized by Rome, that is to say, before they spoke a Romance language at all (or even an Indo-European one), and before we know anything about them. The Raeti are identified by Livy and Pliny as a branch of the Etruscan people, who were pushed northwards by the Gallic invaders of northern Italy. In the period of their maximal expansion, the Raeti were spread over an area extending from the Alps to the Adriatic Sea in the north-east corner of Italy. They were subsequently submerged and absorbed by Indo-European peoples (the Gauls or the Veneti, depending on the area). So, in the region we are dealing with, we can reconstruct three linguistic strata: pre-Indo-European Raeti, pre-Roman Indo-European Gauls and Veneti, and finally the Romans (see Pellegrini 1985).

All our 'data' about the pre-Indo-European Raeti come from a handful of inscriptions written in an Etruscan-type alphabet. Consisting mainly of proper names and obscure terms, these inscriptions are of very little use in determining properties of the 'Raetian' language. Another important fact about these inscriptions, however, is that, although they were called Raeticae, not a single one of them was found in either of the Rhaetic provinces (where the Raeti were still found at the time of Romanization), but only in the neighbouring areas of Noricum and Decima Regio (see Meyer 1971; Risch 1971).

A minority of Rhaeto-Romancers (beginning with Ascoli 1873) seem to find in a Celtic substratum the only basis necessary for the unity of Rhaeto-Romance. A problem for this theory is that a great part of northern Italy, not to mention all of Gaul, was also presumably Celtic, while the Raeti were not.

The second moment of Rhaeto-Romance unity may have been during the massive *Völkerwanderungen* of the fifth, sixth, and seventh centuries, when the depopulated Friulian plain was resettled by immigrants from Noricum (the North Tyrol). This theory, to which we will return later, was proposed by Ernst Gamillscheg (1935) in order to explain the relative scarcity of Longobardisms in the Friulian dialects (compared with e.g. Tuscan).

An effort to write a single historical sketch of the 'Rhaeto-Romance peoples' is, if anything, even more awkward than the attempt to treat the dialects as a unified entity. The following summary does show the complete and enduring absence of any political or social unity for the areas where the languages are spoken today. What it does not show, however, and what needs to be stressed immediately, is how little most of the historical developments outlined below probably affected the people whose languages are in question here. Dynastic successions, and even 'official languages' of church and chancellery, probably had little to do with preliterate subsistence farmers until long after the Rhaeto-Romance dialects had gone their separate ways. By one account (Wartburg 1956: 34) this separation occurred at least 1,300 years ago.

The Romanization of the Friul began in 181 BC, with the foundation of Aquileia. Nevertheless, the year 15 BC is usually given as the birth-date of Rhaeto-Romance, because it was then that Roman legions under Tiberius and Drusus conquered, and the Roman Empire began to colonize or populate, the provinces of Raetia (present-day Romansh, and part of Ladin, territory, very approximately), Vindelicia (present-day Bavaria), and Noricum (present-day Austria). From AD 100 to 250, these provinces were well within the frontiers of the Roman Empire. After the latter date, with the first incursions of the Alemanni, they were on the frontier once again, and during the fifth century they were once again outside that frontier.

Notably, the entire Friulian territory was never a part of Raetia. It has been mooted, however, that the area was settled by refugees from Noricum, who, fleeing from Slavic (Gothic? Hun?) invaders moved back south into the Friulian plain during Langobardic times – that is, over a period of more than two hundred years after AD 568.

At the beginning of the seventh century, Friuli lay open to the Avars, who burned Cividale, the capital, and laid waste the surrounding territory. It was later repopulated by the Langobardic princes. But the new population came not from the neighbouring western region of upper Italy, but from the Alps, primarily from Noricum, where the simultaneous Slavic invasions compelled the Romance population to emigrate (Gamillscheg 1935: 179).

Gamillscheg's very specific claim about the wandering of the Raetic peoples (actually Noricenses) deserves careful notice. It is important as the only attempt in the literature to buttress the putative unity of the Rhaeto-Romance dialects with data from the historical record of the people who speak them. As such, it is loyally repeated by other scholars like von Wartburg. But it is (as far as we are aware) almost entirely conjectural. Gamillscheg himself, at any rate, provides only indirect evidence in support of it (1935: II, 178–80). This evidence, as we have noted, was that there were relatively few Longobard borrowings among Friulian place names. Subsequent research, however, has shown that the apparent absence of Longobard borrowings in the Friul is illusory.

Gamillscheg's theory may have been inspired by a passage from the fifth-century Christian historian Eugyppius (*Vita Severini*, 44.5), which mentioned a proclamation by Odoacer inviting the Roman population to leave Noricum and take up refuge in (northeastern?) Italy. Since the putative 'resettlement' of the Friul began *two hundred years later* (it allegedly occurred between AD 568 and AD 774), this is (like crediting George Washington for winning World War II) somewhat anachronistic.

The separation of Romansh from the Gallo-Romance dialects of present-day French Switzerland probably began with the incursions of the Burgundians and the Alemannians during the period of the *Völkerwanderungen*. Over a period of nearly six hundred years, between ca AD 250 and 800, the Alemanni effectively separated modern Graubünden from the upper Rhone valley. Roughly speaking, the Burgundians occupied what is now French Switzerland and were assimilated by their Latin subjects, while the far more numerous Alemannians occupied, and imposed their language on, what is now German speaking Switzerland. Bonjour *et al.* (1952: 40) speculate that the effect of the Alemannic invasion may have been to 'provoke a Romanization . . . more intense than had been known while Raetia was still a province of the empire', as provincials heading for the hills in flight before the Alemannic hordes (Heuberger 1932: 74, 121) brought with them their 'Romance speech and customs'. Henceforth, Swiss Rhaeto-Romance and South Tyrol Ladin would be steadily diminishing islands in a German-speaking sea. The process of linguistic erosion began with the Germanization of the Lake Constance area by the eighth century; it includes the Germanization of Chur in the fifteenth century, of Montafon and the Praettigau in the sixteenth century, and of Obervintschgau in the seventeenth (Heuberger 1932: 140–1); and slowly continues, in spite of a highly self-conscious Romansh revitalization movement, to this day.

To return to the period of the *Völkerwanderungen*, the migrations of the Ostrogoths and the Bavarian tribes in the fifth and sixth centuries separated Latin-speaking populations of southeastern Switzerland from those of the Tyrol. Roughly speaking, southern Raetia became Ostrogoth territory, while Noricum (Nurich-gau) was now Bavarian (Heuberger 1932: 130, 144). (What this means is that Swiss Romansh was separated from the present-day Ladin dialects of Italy at about the same time as it was separated from French.) This separation was not, however, a permanent one, and was at least temporarily reversed when the Franks conquered both the Ostrogoths and the Bavarians.

Burgundians and Alemannians were conquered, but not physically displaced, in the sixth century by the Franks and the Ostrogoths. Pressing on the Eastern Roman Empire, with its capital of Byzantium, the Ostrogoths in 537 yielded control of what is now Swiss territory to the Franks, who had conquered both the Burgundians and the Alemannians in 534 and 536 (Heuberger 1932: 42). At least until the time of Charlemagne, it is unclear whether the ultimate Frankish overlordship of Raetia had any significant influence 'on the ground'.

During this period, when political control over large areas by semi-barbarian princes was largely fictional, some territories may have been independent in fact from any secular prince. For this reason, possibly, we find that ecclesiastical and political boundaries frequently failed to coincide. In some cases, it may well have been the former that were culturally – and thus, linguistically – decisive. Two notable examples of this are the following:

From 537 onwards, 'Churraetien' was a 'more or less autonomous church state' (Billigmeier 1979: 13) within the Frankish kingdom, and remained so until approximately 800. Although it is probable that German was the language of the aristocracy from this time on (Schmidt 1951/2: 24), it is noteworthy that the bishopric of Chur was incorporated into the diocese of Milan, and it was not until Charlemagne that church and secular power were formally separated. Only after AD 843 was the Bishopric of Chur (the erstwhile capital of Raetia prima), transferred to the archdiocese of Mainz. In 847, the Synod of Mainz, by an enlightened edict, established native language religious instruction, and made German compulsory within churches – alongside the 'rustica romana lingua' (Gregor 1982: 45). This suggests that German, from being the language of the aristocracy and clergy, was now also the language of an increasing proportion of the people in what is now southeastern Switzerland. In this case, it is clear that ecclesiastical boundaries were brought into line with ethnic political boundaries.

On the other hand, the history of Engadine-Vintschgau (comprising the upper Adige, South Tyrol, and the lower Inn regions; Heuberger 1932: 28) reflects a conflict between political and ecclesiastical organization. Geographically a crucial link between (present-day) Romansh and Ladin territories, it was ecclesiastically a part of the medieval bishopric of Säben/Sabiona throughout the seventh and eighth centuries. In 788, it was politically adjoined, under Bavarian control, to the South Tyrol Grafschaft of Trent. Conflicts over its dual status persisted until the Counter-reformation, when the (Protestant) Lower Engadine went over to Graubünden, and the (Catholic) Vintschgau remained in the Tyrol. As was often the case in the later history of Rhaeto-Romance, linguistic identity was identified with religious grouping. The seventeenth-century Austrian Catholic clergy of Vintschgau perceived Engadine Romantsch as the language of Protestantism, identified it with Ladin, and accordingly attempted to suppress the use of Ladin (Wartburg 1956: 36). This bigoted perception may seem to provide some evidence for the linguistic unity of Romantsch and Ladin, but in fact it does not. (Later on, we will see that relatively minor dialect differences which happen to be associated with confessional distinctions are grossly exaggerated: in the same way, it seems likely that profound linguistic differences which are not supported by confessional distinctions may be overlooked.)

In partial contrast with Raetia, the territorial integrity of the Friul remained relatively stable even through the Dark Ages. After the fall of Rome, in order to ensure its northern borders, Byzantium was forced to play the loser's game of making alliances with one barbarian horde in order to fight off another. Over the sixth century, Byzantium formed alliances with the Longobards (Lombards) against the Ostrogoths, and then with the Franks against the Longobards. In 555, Longobard mercenaries under Alboin defeated the Ostrogothic armies, temporarily 'saving' Byzantium. This victory proved Pyrrhic for the Eastern Roman Empire, as the Longobards then invaded northern Italy for themselves in 568 and occupied most of what is now the Piedmont, Lombardy, Emilia, northern Venezia, and Friuli, making Pavia the capital of their principalities (Heuberger 1932: 137). Forum Iulii (modern Cividale, and the origin of the name 'Friuli' for the whole region) remained the centre of the duchy whose extent corresponded roughly to the present-day Friul. Unlike the Huns and the Goths, the Longobards stayed for over two hundred years as the masters of northern Italy (with two important duchies in central Italy (Spoleto) and southern Italy (Benevento) as well), until their defeat at the hands of the Frankish Charlemagne in 774.

Franks and Longobards clashed long before this time, however, and initially, at least, the advantage was to the Longobards. The Franks, who had occupied Venetia between 539 and 567, retreated until 590, by which time the valley of the Adige in the Dolomites became the frontier between Frankish and Longobard territories. Subsequently, the Franks and the Longobards both retreated in the Dolomites before the Bavarians. Over the seventh century, the Bavarians won the territory of present-day Ladin from the Longobards, and held on to Bozen/ Bolzano, Merano, and the easternmost portion of Vintschgau until they too were defeated by the resurgent Frankish armies of Charlemagne (Heuberger 1932: 209).

For roughly two hundred years, then, the three separate enclaves where Rhaeto-Romance dialects are now spoken were under the suzerainty of three separate Germanic controllers: modern Switzerland under the Alemanni, ultimately under the overlordship of the Franks; the Dolomites under the Baiuvarii; and the Friul under the Langobardi.

Friulian, Ladin, and Romansh, whatever their previous history, may well have become established as separate languages during this period of split Frankish/Alemannic, Bavarian, and Longobardic hegemony between 568 and approximately 774.

The subsequent political and ethnographic history of 'Rhaeto-Romania', all observers agree, has no further bearing on the question of the linguistic unity of the dialects which comprise it. Thus, it is essentially irrelevant that, for the brief (800–43) period of the Carolingian kings Rhaeto-Romania was once more under a single government. In any case, this government, like the Roman Empire, embraced a considerably greater area than just that of Rhaeto-Romania. Moreover, unlike the Roman Empire, it was probably never a stable political entity. By 843, the Empire was divided into three kingdoms, whose existence ended when their respective inheritors died without heirs or were deposed.

The Frankish kingdom of Lotharingia (including most of northern Italy and portions of Switzerland) dissolved with the deposition and death of the last of the Carolingian kings, Charles the Fat, at the end of the ninth century. With it, there seems to have ended the last political unity which encompassed all of Rhaeto-Romania, however tenuous and artificial it may have been. Over the next four hundred years, in spite of the re-creation of the (now Saxon, later Austrian) Holy Roman Empire in 962, the dominant political tendency was the greater political independence of local ecclesiastical and temporal authorities (Billigmeier 1979: 27).

It is symbolically significant that the first written attestations of Rhaeto-Romance date from this time of political fragmentation, a fragmentation which for Rhaeto-Romance was to prove to be irreversible.

The first monument of Swiss Romansh is the Einsiedeln Homily, an interlinear gloss of a Latin text of fifteen lines. Dating from the twelfth century, it has been identified as an early form of Surselvan. The first monument of Friulian also dates from approximately 1150. It is a census register, mainly in Latin text with a number of Friulian proper names and place names (Krasnovskaia 1971: 71; D'Aronco 1982).

Very roughly speaking, we can say that political control of the various areas of Rhaeto-Romania became centralized from the fourteenth and fifteenth centuries: the three political centres to which the Rhaeto-Romance dialect areas became attached were Switzerland, the German Habsburg Empire, and the Republic of Venice.

0.1.1 Swiss Romansh

It was over the fourteenth century that the Holy Roman Empire began to assume greater control of the Tyrol, and to threaten Churrätien as well. The Swiss confederation began as a response to this, and although Graubünden did not join the confederation until 1803, the canton had roughly its present boundaries and was totally independent of Habsburg political or Catholic ecclesiastical control by 1650.

The last major influence on the development, or rather, the codification, of Romansh, was the Reformation. Romansh written literature began under its impetus: translations of portions of the Bible and catechisms rapidly began to appear in four major Swiss dialects beginning with Puter, the upper (southern) Engadine dialect (from 1534 onwards). Surselvan, the major Rhenish dialect, was represented by two orthographic traditions, a Protestant (from 1611) and a Catholic (from 1615). This confessional distinction is a clue, perhaps, to the difficulties with establishing a single written standard language. Today, the Surselva is predominantly Catholic, while the Engadine is primarily Protestant, and the strict separation of the two is symbolized by the existence of two major Romansh newspapers, the *Gasetta Romontscha* (with articles in Surselvan), and the *Fögl Ladin* (with articles in Puter and Vallader, the Engadine dialects). G.A. Bühler (1827–97) attempted to create a single written form of Romansh (essentially Surselvan without the morphological feature most peculiar to it, the masculine predicate adjectives in -*s*), but not surprisingly, this creation never found general acceptance. Rather than acting as the moral equivalent of the Académie Française or the Accademia della Crusca, the Societad Retoromontscha (founded by Buehler in 1886), and the Ligia Romontscha (founded in 1919) publish and preserve belletristic literature in all five of the Romantsch dialects, an undertaking which has not been able to halt the continuing decline in the total number of Romansh speakers.

Five dialects are canonized for fewer than 50,000 speakers, somewhat less than a quarter of the population of the canton of Graubünden, and less than 1 per cent of the population of Switzerland. Since a referendum of 20 February 1938, the Romansh language(s) has (have) been accorded official status as national language(s) of Switzerland, and elementary school instruction for the first three years until very recently had to be in Romansh in those districts where it was the majority language (Gregor 1982: 12).

In 1982, Heinrich Schmid, a German-speaking scholar at the University of Zurich, devised a new orthographic Romansh koine called *Rumantsch Grischun*. This purely written language has been accorded some official recognition as the language of government regulations, but is not intended to supplant the spoken dialects. In essence, it is a spelling compromise among the three major Romansh dialects (Surselvan,

Surmeiran, and Vallader). A monumental *Dicziunari Rumantsch Grischun*, under the editorship of Andrea Schorta and Alexis Decurtins and published by the Società Retorumantscha, has been appearing in fascicles since 1939.

0.1.2 Dolomitic Ladin

There are five valleys traditionally forming the territory where Dolomitic Ladin is spoken: Gardena, Gadera, Fassa, Livinallongo, and Ampezzo. These areas have been split apart both ecclesiastically and politically ever since the eleventh century.

We do not possess very detailed information about the early history of these territories. Apparently, they did not belong to the same Regio of the Roman Empire: the Regio of Raetia began north of Sabiona, while the rest of the Dolomitic area was part of the Decima Regio (Venetia et Histria).

Ampezzo, with Cadore, was part of the Bishopric of Aquileia within the Habsburg German Empire. In 1420, Cadore (with Friul) passed to Venice. Ampezzo, briefly contested by Venice (1508–11), remained a fief of the Habsburg monarchy until 1919.

The remaining Dolomitic valleys, since the eleventh century, were divided among the bishopric–principalities of Brixen and Trent. By 1200, the Bishops of Brixen had deeded the northern Gadera and Gardena valleys to the German nobility, who created the Grafschaft of Tyrol. The entire territory passed to the Habsburg family in 1363. Again, Venice contested Habsburg control of both Brixen and Trent throughout the sixteenth century, but Habsburg control was never shaken until the twentieth century.

A very balanced study by L. Palla (1988), published in the German-oriented journal *Ladinia*, gives an idea of the complexity of the factors involved in 'Ladin' linguistic and ethnic consciousness. To the nineteenth-century Austrian government, Ladin was a dialect of Italian, and as such, its use was prohibited in Badia, in an edict of 1886, as a counter to Italian nationalism and irredentism. To the Ladin clergy and laity, however (who strongly protested against this prohibition), Ladin and Italian were Catholic languages, and they opposed the use of German, which they viewed as the language of Protestantism.

Nevertheless, the Ladin population of the Dolomites were loyal Habsburg subjects until 1919. In World War I, many of them fought against Italy on the Dolomitic front, in which 60,000 people died. Of these, only 800 were Ladin speakers, but they constituted perhaps 4–5 per cent of the Ladin population of the time: enough that some observers reckoned World War I to be the greatest tragedy to befall the Ladins since the fall of the Roman Empire (Richebuono 1985: 16).

When Italy was awarded the South Tyrol in 1919, the Ladin valleys were separated into three administrative units: the Gadera and Gardena valleys were included in the province of Bolzano/Bozen; Ampezzo and Livinallongo were included in the province of Belluno; and Fassa is a part of the province of Trent. Given Ladin–Italian hostility, it may not have been surprising that in World War II, by the time that the Italian resistance was fighting against the Germans, the sympathies of most Ladins remained with the German-speaking side (Pellegrini 1987a).

Unlike in Switzerland, the Reformation had no galvanizing effect on Ladin linguistic or ethnic consciousness. Written Ladin in some dialect dates from only 1631 (see Ghetta and Plangg 1987). A Ladin 'revival' began only with the foundation of the Union Ladina in Innsbruck in 1905. In 1919, the Italian government embarked on a vigorous campaign of Italianization of their newly acquired territories: this was directed in the first instance against the German-speaking majority of Brixen, but Ladin, predictably, was submerged as an Italian dialect. It was not until 1948 that the Bolzano provincial government allowed both German and Italian to be used as media of instruction in the public shools, and sanctioned a maximum of two hours of instruction per week in Ladin in the Gardena and Gadera valleys, over 90 per cent of whose populations listed their native language as Ladin. There is still no official government recognition of the status of the Ladin dialects spoken in Belluno province.

A number of periodical publications exist in Ladin, but their circulation is tiny. The largest and most important of these is *La Usc di Ladins*, issued monthly since 1972 with sections in each of the five Ladin dialects. In 1984 it boasted 2,170 subscribers. There is no daily or even weekly publication in Ladin, although both the German-language daily *Die Dolomiten* and the Italian *Alto Adige* have a weekly 'plata ladina' or page in one or more dialects of Ladin. It cannot be said that any of the dialects has the status of a koine.

Two very good journals, devoted to linguistics and popular literature and traditions of the various Rhaeto-Romance areas, are published: the Istitut Cultural Ladin (Fassa) puts out *Mondo Ladino*, and the Istitut Ladin (Val Badia) publishes *Ladinia*. Both institutions are collaborating with the University of Salzburg, Austria, in the preparation of an atlas of the Ladin region, under the direction of Hans Goebl. An attempt to devise a 'common Ladin' is under consideration.

0.1.3 Friulian

In comparison to the Dolomitic Alps, the territory of Friuli has been a relatively stable political and administrative unit since the period of Longobard suzerainty (if not before). The Longobards had made Forum Iulii (present-day Cividale) the capital of a duchy in 568. When they were supplanted by the Franks in 774, the territory was maintained intact. In 1077, the Emperor Henry IV deeded the Friul to the Patriarch of Aquileia, who remained its ecclesiastical and secular ruler until Venetian conquest in 1420. In 1566, the easternmost fringe of Friuli, including the town of Gorizia on the present-day Yugoslav border, was awarded to the Habsburgs by the Treaty of Noyon, and not reincorporated into the Friul (and hence, into Italy) until after World War I. The rest of Friuli remained a part of the Republic of Venice until the latter ceased to exist in 1797. Following the Napoleonic Wars, it was incorporated into the Habsburg monarchy in 1815, and into the Kingdom of Italy in 1866.

The first Friulian glosses, bills, and accounts date from AD 1150, but the first conscious literary productions in Friulian were two fourteenth-century lyric poems (ballads), each attributed to a notary: *Piruç myo doç inculurit* 'My sweet rosy little pear' (or 'little berry' or even 'little Piera': see G. Pellegrini 1987b for discussion) is attributed to the notary Antonio Porenzoni; *Biello dumlo di valor* 'Fair lady of worth', is attributed to the notary Simon di Vittur. Both were written in the latter half of the fourteenth century (see Joppi 1878; D'Aronco 1982). Of all the Rhaeto-Romance dialects, Friulian is the one most exposed to the inroads of a closely related language, Venetian. Possibly because there is an extensive Friulian diaspora (substantial communities exist in Argentina and Roumania), and possibly because of the extreme difficulty of distinguishing between bidialectalism and bilingualism in cases of this sort, estimates of the total number of Friulian speakers vary between 400,000 and 1 million (Krasnovskaia 1971: 6; Marchetti 1952: 16–17; Frau 1984: 8 cites a census of 1975 which gives the total number of native speakers resident in the Friul as 526,649). Many speakers in the town of Udine and in the southern part of the region could also speak a variety of Venetian. This kind of bilingualism has almost disappeared today, in favour of Friulian–Italian bilingualism. No standardized form of the language exists, although the east-central dialect, spoken in the lowland areas between the Tagliamento River and the Yugoslav border, has recognized status as a koine. This is because it was the variety adopted, with some minor variations, by nineteenth-century poets and novelists. One of the most prominent Friulian writers, the poet, novelist, and film director Pier Paolo Pasolini, used a western dialect of Friulian, which, although undoubtedly belonging to the Friulian system, is characterized by a number of peculiarities in all parts of its grammar.

The Società Filologica Friulana publishes two important journals: *Ce fastu?* and *Sot la Nape*. The former, devoted to linguistics and philology, is written mainly in Italian, while the second, which deals mainly with folklore and popular traditions, includes many Friulian texts.

0.2 RHAETO-ROMANCE SCHOLARSHIP

The first reference to a Rhaeto-Romance dialect in what may be called the scholarly literature is the appearance of a fragment of Bifrun's (1560) Puter translation of the New Testament in C. Gesner's *Mithridates*. The first reference linking Swiss and Italian Rhaeto-Romance dialects in any way is in a letter of 1559 by Petrus Paulus Vergerius, who says only that 'the language . . . of the Three Leagues (Romansh) . . . (is) almost worse than Friulian, which itself is so impoverished' (cited in Decurtins, 1965: 261). Vergerius was referring to lexical contamination or impoverishment, it is not clear which. It is in any case extremely unlikely that he considered the dialects particularly closely related, except in their wretchedness.

A somewhat bolder claim was presented by G. Fontanini in his *Della eloquenza italiana* of 1737, where Romansh was genetically related with Friulian and the dialects of 'some districts in Savoy bordering upon Dauphine' (von Planta 1776: 27), and this stock was identified as the 'original' Romance language, or the direct descendant of Vulgar Latin.

J. von Planta's *An account of the Romansh language* of 1776, presented to the Royal Society in London, is the first account in English, and also the first which buttresses its claims with textual attestation – though of a rather unusual sort. Von Planta thought that Rhaeto-Romance approximated the language of Charlemagne, and supported his contention by providing a quintalingual presentation of the Oaths of Strasburg of 842: in the Gallo-Romance original, in Latin, in twelfth-century French, and in two Romansh dialects, of which he identified the first as Ladin (Engadine Romansh) and the second as 'Romansh of both dialects'. It is clear that Planta recognized two Swiss dialects which 'differ so widely as to constitute two distinct languages' (1776: 2): Cialover (Surselvan) and Engadine (Vallader and Puter). Planta was residing in London as librarian (subsequently president) of the Royal Society, but was born in Castegna, Graubünden, of a famous family of the canton. The 'Romansh of both dialects' was identified by H. Lehmann in 1790 as Surselvan (rather than as some precursor of G. Bühler's ill-fated 'Romontsch fusionau').

The Italian economist Gian Rinaldo Carli, in an essay which appeared in 1788 in the journal *Antologia italiana*, and was subsequently cited by

Ascoli, was the first to connect Friulian and Romansh, considering both derived from Old Provençal.

Planta and Carli may have been the sources for Carl Ludwig Fernow's grouping in the third volume of his *Römische Studien* (1808): in this, the first description of Italian dialects since Dante's *De vulgari eloquentia*, Friulian and Romansh were grouped together on the basis of shared archaic Romance features.

Fernow had no clear ideas about the position of Dolomitic Ladin. The first Ladin dictionary was a list of words from Badia contained in the *Catalogus multorum verborum quinque dialectuum*, written before 1763 by the lawyer Simone Petro Bartolomei.

In 1805, there appeared a remarkable monograph by P. Placi a Spescha on *Die Rhaeto-Hetruskische Sprache*, which identified Surselvan as the purest or most archaic dialect of 'RH' – and thus the one most closely related to Etruscan. Modern scholarship agrees with the first part of this assessment (see Prader-Schucany 1970: 18), though, perhaps needless to say, not with the second. Placi's monograph, incidentally, is the one which tells of mutual comprehensibility between Romansh and Dolomitic Rhaeto-Romance (impressionistically no further distant from each other than the geographically corresponding varieties of German: see Decurtins 1965: 278), and is, as far as we are aware, the first and last effort in the literature to justify grouping Rhaeto-Romance dialects together on the basis of this criterion. (To the extent that later scholars have concerned themselves with this question, they tend to emphasize the mutual *in*comprehensibility of the dialects: thus Gruell (1969: 101) insists that Ladin and Romansh speakers require standard Italian as a lingua franca; Pizzinini and Plangg (1966: xxv) discuss the problem of mutual intelligibility among the various Ladin dialects of the Dolomitic Alps of Italy; and Gregor (1982: 25) notes that even Swiss Romansh 'is an abstraction, as there are five 'fourth' languages'. For our part, we can attest that a native speaker of Friulian can neither read nor understand either Surselvan or Vallader – at least as spoken by us).

The collection of translations of the Pater Noster into about 500 languages (initiated by Adelung, and completed and edited in 1809 by Vater), is the first work suggesting a connection of the three Rhaeto-Romance areas (see Goebl 1987: 138).

L. Diefenbach's *Über die jetzigen romanischen Schriftsprachen* of 1831 recognized a group of Romance languages, including French, Romansh, Friulian, and Piedmontese, which shared a number of structural features now identified with Gallo-Romance, among them the 2nd singular and the plural endings in -*s*. He noted, in addition, that Romansh (actually

Surselvan) had peculiarities which linked it now with Italian, now with French, and was apparently the first to comment on how Romansh syntax reflected heavy German influence.

A more explicit attempt to link Romansh, Ladin, and Friulian (the latter only in passing, however) as an exclusive sub-group of Gallo-Romance was J. Haller's *Versuch einer Parallele der ladinischen Mundarten in Enneberg und Groeden im Tirole, dann im Engadin und in dem romaunschischen in Graubuenden* in 1832. Like von Planta, he compared texts in four dialects: Swiss Surselvan and Vallader, and the Tyrol dialects Badiot/Abtei, Marebbe/Enneberg, and Gardena/ Groeden (for which he coined the cover label 'Ladin') and noted the presence, in all four dialects, of the reflexes of Lat. COCCINU 'red', VOLIENDO 'willingly', AMITA 'aunt', and Goth. *skeitho* 'spoon'. Haller's study was followed in 1856 by J. Mitterrutzner's phonological account of the Rhaeto-Ladinic dialects of the Tyrol, and C. Schneller's work of 1870 *Die romanischen Volksmundarten im Südtirol*, which identified the currently recognized extent of Rhaeto-Romance in the following memorable words (Schneller 1870: 9): 'In the Friulian–Ladin–Romansh complex [Kreis], we have a separate and independent branch [Hauptgebiet] of the Romance languages, granting even that its speakers have no common written language or even any consciousness of its inner unity.' Schneller characterized Rhaeto-Romance as a sub-family of Romance rather than a single language: he was the first scholar to adduce a specific grammatical criterion in support of this claim: the Rhaeto-Romance branch of Romance was characterized for him by 'One fundamental and commonly shared distinguishing feature, the palatalization of velar stops before a – that is to say, a feature which is also shared by French' (1870: 10).

All of these authors may be regarded as precursors of the giants of Rhaeto-Romance sholarship, G.I. Ascoli and T. Gartner, whose efforts identified the features and limits of the Rhaeto-Romance languages that are still accepted by almost all scholars today.

Ascoli, himself a native speaker of Gorizian Friulian and one of the foremost Indo-Europeanists of his day, initiated the Archivio Glottologico Italiano in 1873 with a 500-page monograph *Saggi Ladini*. In this, one of the classics of Romance comparative linguistics, he identified Rhaeto-Romance (which he called 'Ladin') on the basis of several shared phonological retentions and innovations (see Ascoli 1873: 337; 1882–5: 102–5). Among these are

(a) the palatalization of inherited velars before *a;
(b) the preservation of *l* after obstruents;
(c) the preservation of inherited word-final -s;

(d) the diphthongization of mid vowels (from Latin E, O) in checked syllables;

(e) the fronting of A to *e*;

(f) the diphthongization of tense *e* (Latin E, I) to *ei*;

(g) the fronting of tense *u* (Latin U) ;

(h) the velarization of *l* after *a* before a consonant.

Concerning this list, it should be noted, first, that many of these features are shared by languages outside Rhaeto-Romance. For example, (a), (b), (c), (e), (g), and (h) are common to much of Gallo-Romance. More remarkable, they do not seem to be shared by all the dialects within Rhaeto-Romance. Thus Ascoli noted Friulian did not undergo changes (e) (1873: 484ff.) or (g) (1873: 499). Second, the *Saggi* were rigorously limited to phonology. Ascoli meant to return to Ladin and evaluate the morphological, lexical, and syntactic evidence in favour of this putative group, but never had a chance to do so. What he might have said on these subjects is unknown (and, in many respects, difficult to imagine). While he is customarily credited with the invention of Rhaeto-Romance, it is notable that later scholars who deny the existence of this language are careful to insist that Ascoli's pronouncements on Ladin are by no means dogmatic (see Pellegrini 1987a). In fact, Ascoli identified a 'linguistic family' in the sense familiar to historical–comparative linguistics, rather than a 'new Romance language' in the usual sense.

Elsewhere, Ascoli acknowledged the aberrant status of Friulian, as attested by the absence of front rounded vowels (*vocali turbate*) and the absence of a 'three-syllable rule' which deleted the post-tonic vowel of words stressed on the inherited antepenult (1873: 476).

Ascoli's great study is now almost certainly unread by all but a handful of specialists, but it exerted a unique historical influence. No subsequent survey of the field fails to list essentially the same phonological characterizing features of Rhaeto-Romance as those noted by Ascoli. And not one fails to group the Rhaeto-Romance dialects into three groups exactly as Ascoli did.

Theodor Gartner had already made his name as a Romanist in 1879, with the (private) publication of his intensive study of the Ladin dialect of Gardena/Groeden. This was the first of several dozen such works of historical phonetics, which still constitute the majority of original research monographs on Rhaeto-Romance today by scholars, many of whom are native speakers of the dialects described. Gartner's work was based exclusively on field research using adolescents of both sexes as his subjects. But his masterpiece was his *Rätoromanische Grammatik* of 1883, which was based on a full year of fieldwork in over sixty communities, from Tavetsch (Surselvan) to Pordenone (Friulian), and buttressed by familiarity with, and citation of, what seems to have been almost every published work in any of the vernaculars from the Travers battle song onwards. This was a work of stupendous erudition, but is even more interesting to us as a pioneering example of fieldwork in a local language. Some of Gartner's observations on the methodological pitfalls of working with naive or oversophisticated informants deal with canonical problems of field researchers (debated at that time, for example, by the French dialectologists Jean Psychari and l'Abbé Rousselot in the *Revue des patois Galloroman* I: 18 (1887) and II: 20 (1888)). In his later *Handbuch der rätoromanischen Sprache und Literatur* (1910), Gartner enunciated his version of what is now familiar to us from the writings of William Labov as the observer's paradox. While there are problems working with uneducated people (who may not be perfectly bilingual and thus fail to provide accurate translations from German or Italian), the problems of dealing with educated people are almost infinitely worse, as the investigator will usually record 'an unnaturally refined diction or pronunciation, with purisms or other whimsical turns [Liebhabereien]' (Gartner 1910: 10). Gartner's two overviews of 1883 and 1910 constitute the last major surveys of the domain of Rhaeto-Romance as defined by Ascoli up to the present day.

Pioneering and original studies of everlasting value, these works are also striking in their faithful enumeration of the distinctive features of Rhaeto-Romance, enlarging on the checklist provided by Ascoli, but not questioning any of its conclusions. For Gartner (1883: xxiii) as for Ascoli, the major features of Rhaeto-Romance included:

(a) retention of (word-initial) C*l*- clusters;
(b) palatalization of velars before inherited /a/;
(c) retention of the -*s* plural
(d) retention of the -*s* 2sg. verbal desinence;
(e) syncope of proparoxytones

To this list of phonological features, Gartner added

(f) retention of the pronouns *ego, tu*;
(g) use of the pluperfect subjunctive in counterfactual conditionals.

Not much has been added to this skimpy and questionable list by later scholars. Walther von Wartburg (1950: 12; 1956: 36) notes a conservative phonological trait which distinguishes (some) Romansh from both French and Italian: this is the preservation of the original difference between /j/ and palatalized /g/, attested in the dialects of Bravuogn/Bergün and Müstair. That this conservative trait is also shared by Sardinian does not affect its usefulness as a diagnostic for

Rhaeto-Romance; on the other hand, the fact that it is also shared by the geographically contiguous northern Italian dialects of Bergell and Livigno (Wartburg 1950: 13), while it is not shared by putative Rhaeto-Romance dialects like those of Moena (Heilmann 1955: 97) and Gardena (Gartner 1879: 61, 64) seems to vitiate its effectiveness.

We may add, finally, one last defining feature noted by (among others) H. Kuen (1968: 54): both standard French and standard Italian have eliminated the inherited distinction between indicative and imperative in the second-person plural. In contrast to both standard French (which has generalized the inherited indicative form) and standard Italian (which has generalized the inherited imperative through the operation of phonological changes), the Rhaeto-Romance languages maintain the inherited distinction between indicative and imperative in the second-person plural.

The last survey of Rhaeto-Romance, by the great Romanist G. Rohlfs, is a digest of these earlier classics, in which, again, the basic defining features of Rhaeto-Romance are listed pretty much unchanged (Rohlfs 1975: 8). Like Gartner, Rohlfs sought to extend the list of features, but with indifferent success, inasmuch as the features he adduced were either not shared by all the Rhaeto-Romance dialects, or were shared by languages outside of Rhaeto-Romance, or both. Thus, for example, the fronting of long /u/ was shared by Romansh and several Ladin dialects (those of the Non and Gadera valleys), but failed to establish Rhaeto-Romance unity, since it was not shared by Friulian; and it failed to establish its independence, since it was also shared by Piedmontese and Lombard.

This raises, of course, the question already addressed in Schneller's work of 1870: were the other defining characteristics of Rhaeto-Romance – such as the palatalization of velars before inherited /a/ – any different? And, if not, what basis is there for arguing for a Rhaeto-Romance language, or sub-group, within Romance? This question was taken up with considerable polemical vigour, but also great scientific acumen, by C. Battisti, in a number of publications, of which the most comprehensive summary is his 1931 monograph *Popoli e lingue nell'Alto Adige*. It is tempting to dismiss this and other works by Italian scholars as merely 'expounding the Italian irredentist doctrine that Ladin and the other Rhaeto-Romance languages do not constitute a separate unity' (thus Hall 1974: 42 fn.), but this temptation should be resisted. (As Benincà-Ferraboschi (1973: 126) observes, Battisti first wrote in 1910, when he was still an Austrian subject, honoured by the Austrian government, teaching at the University of Vienna.)

Battisti's conclusion may be too strong that the 'Ladin dialects must be considered to be peripheral forms of other Italian dialects' (Battisti 1931: 211; for concurrent assessments by other scholars, see Bühler 1875, anthologized in Ulrich (1882: 136); and now Pellegrini (1972a, 1987a), Rizzolatti (1981), and Benincà-Ferraboschi (1973)). But there is more than one way to refute the position that the Rhaeto-Romance dialects are an independent unity. Battisti argued that they were united, but only as peripheral dialects of northern Italy, and provided compelling evidence that they shared no more than many other Romance dialects north of the Spezia–Rimini line. For Battisti, alone among scholars dealing with all of Rhaeto-Romance, the fundamental question was always this: do the undeniable features which link Romansh, Ladin, and Friulian form a tighter bond than the features which link each or all of these to other geographically contiguous languages or dialects? Battisti's position was that the structural similarities between Romansh and Lombard, between Ladin and Trentino, between Friulian and Venetian, were more pervasive and more archaic than the similarities between the three putative Rhaeto-Romance dialects. Of the defining characteristics of Rhaeto-Romance enumerated by Ascoli and Gartner, he admitted only one – Schneller's law of the palatalization of velars before inherited /a/: and this one also he attempted to belittle. He did not do this, as Schneller had already indicated that one might, by showing that the innovation was shared far beyond the confines of Rhaeto-Romance. Rather, he tried to show that the palatalizations occurred in the three putative dialects at different times, and thus could be dismissed as independent parallel innovations (Battisti 1931: 185).

Diagrammatically, Battisti's position (1931: 193) could be represented as in the diagram,

where the vertical links are stronger than the horizontal ones. The lower three dialects are separated from standard Italian by one of the major isoglosses within Romance, the line from La Spezia to Rimini.

With the exception of works like Prader-Schucany 1970 and Luedtke 1957 (which showed, respectively, the existence of several isoglosses between Romansh and Lombard, and isoglosses between Venetian and Friulian, but did not address themselves to the unity of Rhaeto-Romance as a whole), no scholar has attempted a refutation of Battisti's position, and in fact hardly any have tried to deal with more than a single dialect at a time.

Special mention, however, should be made of two recent works by American scholars. The first is Leonard's ingenious and subtle reconstruction of a proto-Rhaeto-Romance (PRR) phonemic system distinct from that of Vulgar Latin (Leonard 1972). Although Leonard assumed the unity of Rhaeto-Romance, rather than attempting to prove it, the reconstructed system he proposed, to the extent that it is distinct from that of Vulgar Latin, is implicitly a powerful argument for proto-Rhaeto-Romance, and will be extensively cited and challenged in the immediately following chapter. The second notable work is Redfern's (1971) use of Jaberg and Jud's monumental dialect atlas (1928–40) in an attempt to prove Rhaeto-Romance unity in the domain of the lexicon. But this study, which will be examined in chapter 3, does almost exactly the opposite of what its author claims, and shows the lexical heterogeneity of Rhaeto-Romance to be exceeded only by its syntactic diversity.

More recent contributions to the debate are Pellegrini's (1972a, 1987a), essentially an endorsement of Battisti based in the first instance on studies of the lexicon. Pellegrini argues that Ladin claims of a pervasive lexical divergence between Ladin and common northern Italian are unfounded, and most probably motivated by a snobbish distaste for the uncouth peasantry of Lombardy by a would-be *Kulturvolk* who were first loyal to the Habsburgs (see Kramer 1963/4), and then enthusiastic allies of the Fascists.

No survey of previous scholarship in Rhaeto-Romance would accurately reflect its scope and nature, without a mention of the atomistic works of historical phonetics of the various dialects, which, as we have noted, constitute the bulk of descriptive studies in this area. Among these, one of the greatest is undoubtedly Lutta's magnificent study of the phonetics of the Surmeiran dialect of Bravuogn/Bergün (Lutta 1923), which is also a survey of the historical phonetics of all the Romansh dialects. Another is W. Theodor Elwert's masterly work on the dialects of the Fassa valley (1943), which compares these dialects with other varieties of Rhaeto-Romance, and with Venetian and Lombard as well. The term 'phonetics' is the correct one: so painstaking and precise are the descriptions of the dialects in Lutta's and Elwert's work, that it is difficult to infer what the distinctive phonemes might be.

In a structuralist framework, Heilmann 1955, a study of the Ladin dialect of Moena, and Francescato 1966, a survey of the entire Friulian diasystem, are milestones of dialectology.

While there are also structural phonemic descriptions of Surselvan, and several Ladin and Friulian dialects (Kramer 1972a, for Surselvan; Urzi 1961, Plangg 1973, and Politzer 1967, for varieties of Ladin; Bender *et al.* 1952, and Iliescu 1968–9 for Friulian), no similar work has been done on most Rhaeto-Romance dialects, for all their standardized orthographies. Consequently, answers to a number of questions (for example, as to the phonemic status of long vowels) are uncertain.

1 Phonology

The most convincing case for the unity of Rhaeto-Romance can be made in the domain of shared phonological innovation, as scholars since Schneller have agreed. We shall divide our discussion of phonology into two parts: first, a synchronic statement of the systematic phonemes in the principal dialects; and second, a survey of the sources of these sounds, tracing their development from Vulgar Latin.

For ease of exposition, we will adopt the fiction that there are only (!) fifteen dialects of Rhaeto-Romance:

Swiss	Ladin	Fruilian
Surselvan	Nonsberg	Ertan
Sutselvan	Badiot-Marebban	Western
Surmeiran	(Gadera Valley)	Carnic
Puter	Gardenese	East-Central
Vallader	Fassan	
	Livinallongo-Fodom	
	Ampezzan	

No more eloquent admission of the significance of a standardized orthography is possible. The Romansh dialects, with fewer than one-tenth of the speakers of Rhaeto-Romance, constitute a third of our data base. (This distortion will be inconsistent: where the data warrant, we will disregard some dialect divisions, and introduce others.)

In this study the symbols { } will be used to indicate orthographic representations in older texts of the modern standardized languages; the square brackets [ ], as is customary, will be used for phonetic transcriptions, and the obliques / /, for more abstract representations, generally corresponding to a fairly low-level phonemic transcription which includes archiphonemes. Angle brackets ⟨ ⟩ will be used in chapter 3 for reconstructions of 'proto-Rhaeto-Romance' forms.

1.1 THE PHONEME INVENTORIES

1.1.1. Surselvan

This dialect with approximately 18,000 speakers has two orthographic traditions dating back to the seventeenth century. The vowels are:

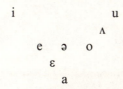

where phonetically, /o/ = [ɔ] (Nay 1965: viii–ix, Kramer 1972a: 354). The phone /ə/, as well as being the unstressed alternant of /a, ɛ, e/ (see Kramer 1972a: 356), must be accorded independent status for invariably unstressed vowels. In addition, the diphthong sequences which are permitted are:

iə, iw	uə	ju	
ɛj, ɛw			wɛ
aj, aw		ja,	wa
Falling		Rising	

There are, in addition triphthongs /jaw/, /waw/. After palatals or before /n/, /aw/ is raised to [əw]: thus {jeu} [jəw] 'I', {clavau} [klavaw] 'barn', {tgaun} [cəwn] 'dog' are phonemically /jaw/, /klavaw/, /cawn/.

The inventory of syllabic nuclei in unstressed syllables is /i,ə,u/ (see Huonder 1901: 518; Kramer 1972a: 355–6). Synchronically, in verbal paradigms, the choice of unstressed vowel corresponding to a given stressed vowel is not entirely predictable: stressed /o/ corresponds to either unstressed /ə/ or unstressed /u/, and stressed /ɛ/ corresponds to either unstressed /ə/ or unstressed /i/.

The consonants (Kramer 1972a: 346; Leonard 1972: 63) are as follows:

p	t	c	k
b	d	ɟ	g
	ts	tʃ	
f	s	ʃ	h

$$
\begin{array}{ccc}
\text{v} & \text{z} & \text{ʒ} \\
\text{m} & \text{n} & \text{ɲ} \\
 & \text{l} & \text{ʎ} \\
 & \text{r} &
\end{array}
$$

The above are pretty nearly identical with what we may call the consonantal skeleton of all Rhaeto-Romance dialects, as we shall see.

Consonant alternations include the following:

Voicing assimilation:
(a) C → − voice/____$
(b) C → αvoice/____ − sonorant
$$\qquad\qquad\qquad\qquad\quad αvoice$$

T-epenthesis:
null → t/n, l, ʎ____s (Leonard 1972: 64)

Casual cluster simplification:
C → null/Nasal____#

Nasal Assimilation:
n → ŋ/____K

Note that in Surselvan, unlike English, cluster simplification and nasal assimilation apply in the (transparent) order given. Thus /ɛwnk/ 'even' becomes, in careful speech [ɛwŋk] (where nasal assimilation only has applied), and, in casual speech [ɛwn] (where casual cluster simplification pre-empts or bleeds nasal assimilation) (Kramer 1972a: 353).

1.1.2 Sutselvan

This is the most marginal and endangered Romansh dialect, with fewer than 4,000 speakers, all of them by this time probably more fluent in German than in Sutselvan. In spite of a written 'tradition' dating back to a catechism in the Domleschg dialect which appeared in 1601, Luzi reported in 1904 that the dialect was usually written in the Surselvan orthography (1904: 760) and that the language of education was universally German. The homogeneity, and hence the survivability, of the dialect was further threatened by the fact that there was a major dialect split within Sutselvan between Catholic and Protestant varieties, which contributed to boundary maintenance: 'the confessional difference between the dialects probably also played a role in making the [one] dialect seem even more comic and uncouth' (Luzi 1904: 759) to the speakers of the other. Himself a native speaker, Luzi predicted the ultimate disappearance of Sutselvan within a matter of decades. The following description, from his work, thus resurrects a virtually extinct system, the ruins of which are described in works like Cavigelli 1969.

The vowels included:

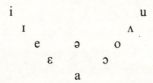

Although phonetically [ɪ], the sound /ɪ/ was perceived as a 'kind of e'. Its phonemic status is confirmed by minimal contrast pairs like /lec/ 'lake' vs. /lɪc/ 'read (p.p.)' (Luzi 1904: 762).

Among the permitted diphthongs, the most notable is /ɛə/, unique to Sutselvan, and constituting a 'signature' for this dialect (as the front rounded vowels are a signature for the Engadine dialects and Badiot Ladin, and the *Verschärfung* of postvocalic glides (i.e. their change to stops) is a signature for Surmeiran).

The consonant inventory was the same as in Surselvan. The velar nasal [ŋ] occurred as a syllable-final allophone of /n/ after back vowels (Luzi 1904: 810).

1.1.3 Surmeiran

This again is one of the endangered dialects, with perhaps 5,000 speakers, and less of a written tradition than either the Rhenish or the Engadine dialects. On the other hand, Lutta (1923) has ensured its immortality in at least the scholarly literature. The vowels are structurally, although not phonetically, the same as in Surselvan:

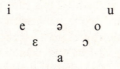

They also occur in the following diphthongs:

	ij			uw	
	ej			ow	
	ɛj		ɔw		
		aj			

and in the triphthongs /jow/ and /wej/. A peculiarity which Surmeiran shares (to some extent) with Puter, is the rule of *Verschärfung*, whereby diphthongal off-glides (not only /j/ and /w/, but also /ə/) become velar stops before a following consonant: thus /krejr/ becomes [krekr] 'to believe' (see Kamprath 1985, 1986). A similar, contextually more restricted *Verschärfung* occurs in word-final position of pronouns in some of the Friulian dialects (see Gartner 1883: 72–3; Francescato 1963). In Belluno, MEI > (>mjej) > /mjek/ 'mine (m. pl.)'; *ILLEI > (>ljej) > /ʎek/, etc. While this is scarcely a Rhaeto-Romance, or even a Romansh, feature, it is shared by not widely separated dialects of Franco-Provençal spoken in the Rhone valley. Whether this similarity constitutes particularly cogent evidence for a 1,500-year-old Franco-Rhaeto-Romance unity, as von Wartburg (1956: 30) and Rohlfs (1972: 125 fn.) seem to intimate, is highly questionable.

Thöni (1969: 16, 275) lists several cases of minimal contrast pairs from which it seems that length may be phonemic for vowels. Among them are [er] 'also' vs. [eːr] 'field'; [got] 'drop' vs. [goːt] 'forest'; [bot] 'hill' vs. [boːt] 'early'. Leonard (p.c.) adds some near-minimal contrast pairs like [ʃtaːt] 'summer' vs. [jat] 'cat' for the Cunter dialect.

The inventory of consonantal phonemes is the same as in Surselvan. As in Surselvan, the sound [ŋ] occurs, but may be a syllable-final allophone of /n/: thus *staziun* [ʃtatsiuŋ] 'station' (Thöni 1969: 15 and *passim*), but it may be that the phonetic contrast [n]/[ŋ] is in the process of becoming phonologized as a result of the pressure for paradigm coherence. Note the phonetic contrasts [buŋ] 'good (m.sg.)' vs. [buna] ~ [buŋa] 'good (f.sg.)', (Thöni 1969: 41). If [buŋa], motivated by paradigm coherence, becomes established, the distribution of the phone [ŋ] will no longer be contextually predictable. Leonard (p.c.) notes that inherited -*nn*- yields final [n], thus phonologizing the contrast between [n] and [ŋ] in pairs like [ɔn] 'year' (< annu) vs. [maŋ] 'hand' (< mano).

As in almost all Romansh and many Ladin dialects, the opposition between /s/ and /ʃ/ is neutralized before a consonant within the same morpheme in favour of [ʃ] ~ [ʒ], with voicing agreement before a non-sonorant consonant, but invariable [ʃ] before nasals and liquids. (We may therefore posit an archiphoneme /S/ in this position. Thus /Sminar/ [ʃminaːr] 'feel', /Snaer/ [ʃnaɛkr] 'deny'.) The fact that this neutralization *fails* to occur in the 2nd singular ending -*st* (Thöni 1969: 12) is evidence that the final consonant here originated – very recently, in all likelihood – as a copy of the personal pronoun cliticized to the verb, most probably originally in inverted word order: thus *te ast* [te ast] 'you have' derives, by this analysis, from /te as + t/. The enclisis of 2nd singular (and 2nd plural) subject pronouns is widespread in the Lombard dialects (see Rohlfs 1968: 149) – as it also is in the German 2nd singular -*st* and medieval English 2nd singular -*st*.

1.1.4 Puter

The vocalic systems of the Engadine dialects are marked by the presence of the front rounded vowels /y/ and /ø/. In addition, the issue also arises here whether length in vowels is phonemic: it seems that in Puter and Vallader, length is largely, if not entirely, predictable, while there are Ladin dialects where it is not, and that, finally, in Friulian length is totally phonemic. However, vowel length in the Engadine dialects has an origin analogous to its origin in Friulian, while in Dolomitic Ladin, vowel length has completely different origins and distribution.

The vowels are as follows:

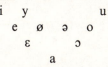

Most long vowels occur before syllable-final /r/ or /ʃ/. The productivity of *Verschärfung* is much lower than in Surmeiran, and Scheitlin (1962: 15), in his pedagogical grammar of Puter, simply lists several dozen words where – in lower register speech styles (!) – non-phonemic velars appear after the high vowels /i, y, u/: among them are /trid/ [trikt] 'ugly', /bryt/ [brykt] 'ugly', /ura/ [ugra] 'hour', and /Skrivər/ [ʃkrigvər] 'to write'. (Leonard (p.c.) reports that in the Silva Plana dialect, *Verschärfung* is apparently independent of both vowel height and register, but seems to occur only in final syllables.)

The consonant inventory is that of Surselvan, enriched by the palatal fricative /ç/ , a dialect-particular reflex of inherited /k/, after /i/: thus /amiç/ 'friend'.

1.1.5 Vallader

The vocalic inventory is nearly the same as for Puter, except the phonemic status of long vowels is a little firmer: there are some near-minimal contrast pairs cited in Arquint's pedagogical grammar (1964: xiii), and in Ganzoni (1983b: 18), among them /tʃel/ (<ECC-ILLE) vs. /tʃeːl/ < CAELU, and /fətsøːl/ 'kerchief' vs. /føʎ/ 'leaf'. Most long vowels occur before syllable-final /r/, although Leonard (1972: 65, and p.c.) notes the minimal contrast pair /car/ 'wagon' (< CARRU) vs. /caːr/ 'dear (m.sg.)' (<CARU) and near-minimal pairs like [naːs] 'nose' (< NASU) and [pas] 'step' (< PASSU). Given such pairs, it is reasonable to reconstruct the process of phonologization of length in Vallader as essentially parallel to the more general process in Friulian: stressed vowels are phonetically lengthened before inherited single consonants (or, if we consider a stage before the loss of most word-final vowels in proto-Romance, in open syllables). Length is recognizably phonological after the simplification of word-final consonant clusters. Compare Friulian /fat/ < FACTU with /fini:t/ < FINITU, /na:s/ < NASU with /nas/ < NASCI(T).

Diphthongs include falling /ɛj, ɛw, ow, aj, aw/, rising /je, wa, we, wo, wi, yo/; the lone triphthong is /jew/.

The consonant inventory is the same as in Surselvan. Leonard notes two consonantal alternations, of which the first is quite general throughout Romansh, and the second is peculiar to Vallader (Leonard 1972: 65):

'Sonorant' syllabification:
$\emptyset \rightarrow$ V/C ____ n, l, r, ʃ $ (except for /rn, rʃ/)

Gemination:
C → geminate/V ____ V
+ stress
− long

These rules must apply in the order given: /krɛʃ + r/ → /krɛʃr/ → /krɛʃər/ (syllabification) → [krɛʃʃər] (gemination) 'to grow'.

1.1.6 Ladin

There is tremendous phonemic variation among these dialects. The major split among them is roughly geographical. On the west is the Lombard-Ladin dialect of the Val di Non (Nonsberg) between Trento and Bolzano/Bozen, the phonetics of which were described exhaustively by the youthful native speaker and future polemicist Carlo Battisti (1908), and restudied by Politzer (1967). On the east are Ampezzano (Appollonio 1930), with approximately 3,000 speakers, and the dialects spoken in the valleys radiating from the Sella massif south-east of Bressanone/Brixen: these include the dialects of the Gardena valley/ Gröden (Gartner 1879; Urzi 1961), with perhaps 8,000 speakers; Livinallongo/Buchenstein/Fodom, with 3,000 speakers; the Fassa valley (Elwert 1943; Heilmann 1955), with 7,000 speakers; and the Badia-Gadera valley (Alton and Vittur 1968; Plangg 1973; Pizzinini and Plangg 1966; Belardi 1965; Craffonara 1971–2), with as many as 10,000 speakers. The works of Urzi, Heilmann, Plangg, and Politzer are explicitly phonemic structural descriptions, while those of Gartner, Battisti, and Elwert are of the familiar historical-phonetic kind. Appollonio's description of Ampezzan, and Alton-Vittur's description of Badiot and Marebban, are both synchronic pedagogical or reference grammars. Craffonara's dissertation is both a structural and a diachronic description of Marebban and Badiot.

Linguistically, if not geographically (von Wartburg 1956: 48), Marebbe-Badiot counts as a 'western' dialect with respect to one important feature: the presence of the phoneme /y/. In Nonsberg Ladin, as in Swiss Romansh, inherited long /u/ was fronted to /y/. The trait is shared by the Lombardic dialects to the south, and was identified by Battisti as a borrowing from Trentino (1908: 9) into Nonsberg rather than a feature common to Romansh and Western Ladin. Badiot and Marebbe have both /y/ and /ø/, but the sources of both sounds are heterogeneous, and sometimes quite recent. In Fassa and other varieties of Ladin, /y/ > /i/ and /ø/ > /e/. In Friulian, no fronting of long *u occurred.

We will arbitrarily select the Badiot dialect described in G. Plangg (Pizzinini and Plangg 1966; Plangg 1973) as the exemplar of 'western' Ladin, and the Moena dialect of the Fassa valley (Heilmann 1955) as the exemplar of 'eastern' Ladin, with asides for the other dialects from time to time.

The vocalic inventory of Western Ladin is exactly the same as for Vallader and Puter. In addition, Plangg (1973: 15) notes the existence of an Upper Badiot dialect with a phonemic length contrast for /a, ɛ, i, ɔ, o/. The origins of this distinction are totally different from the origins of phonemic length in the Engadine dialects or Friulian.

On the other hand, front rounded vowels tend to be missing from the phonemic inventories of the eastern Ladin languages: according to Heilmann (1955: 267), Moena lacks /y/. Other eastern dialects, among them those of Gardena, also lack /ø/. In one recent description, the Ladin dialect of Gardena has the stressed vowels /i, e, a, ɔ, o, u, ə/, and the unstressed vowels /i, a, ə, u/ (Leonard 1972: 66). This inventory is remarkable not only for the absence of the front rounded vowels, but for the phonemic status of /ə/, distinct from /a/, in both stressed and unstressed syllables.)

As the vocalic inventory gives hints of expanding, moving eastward, so the consonantal inventory hints of imminent reduction. While the canonical consonantal inventory in Nonsberg Ladin is the same as in Surselvan, there is a middle Nonsberg dialect in which there is no phonemic contrast between [c] and [tʃ], nor between their voiced counterparts (Politzer, 1967: 19). 'Standard Badiot' as described by Plangg maintains a phonemic /c/ vs. /tʃ/ distinction (Pizzinini and Plangg 1966: xxxvi) for word pairs like /tʃamp/ 'left' vs. /camp/ 'field'. Leonard (p.c.) points out that in both Badiot and Marebbe, the distinction was maintained only by older speakers as long ago as 1958 and is by now entirely extinct, as attested by Craffonara (1971–2). In addition, Iliescu (1968–9: 279) notes the absence of this phonemic contrast in several other Ladin dialects, among them those of Livinallongo, Cortina d'Ampezzo, and Fassa (made famous by Elwert; see Elwert 1943: 67).

The status of [ŋ] in Ladin is fairly complicated. In Fassa, as in most of northern Italian, [ŋ] is simply the syllable-final allophone of /n/ (Heilmann 1955: 159–62; Belardi 1965: 190). Moena differs phonetically from Fassa in that [n] occurs syllable-finally; phonologically, however, the two neighbouring dialects are alike in that [ŋ] is a predictable allophone of /n/, occurring in Moena before velar stops only.

One Ladin dialect may reflect redistribution of the phone [ŋ]. In Gardena, Gartner (1879) consistently recorded [ŋ] as the syllable-final allophone of /n/. In her restudy of 1961, Urzi finds syllable-final [n], with [ŋ] occurring as the conditioned alternant of /n/ before velar stops only. At neither stage does [ŋ] seem to have phonemic status.

Another Ladin dialect may have lost the phoneme /ŋ/. Battisti (1908) found minimal contrasting pairs like /an/ 'year' vs. /paŋ/ 'bread' in Nonsberg, but noted the tendency to replace all final non-palatalized nasals with [m], a tendency which he attributed to the influence of Trentino. In his restudy of 1967, Politzer found no occurrences of syllable-final [ŋ]: hence there is no phonetic basis for a phoneme /ŋ/ in Nonsberg. Belardi (1965: 188) concurs, alleging that in the Avisio valley dialect (also western Ladin, and closely neighbouring Nonsberg), [ŋ] has no phonemic status.

Only the Badiot and Marebban dialects, among those Ladin dialects spoken today, still definitely retain the contrast between inherited syllable-final /n/ (from *-mn-*, *-nn-*, *-n*C-) and syllable-final /ŋ/ (from *-n-*, *-m-*) (see Belardi 1965: 190; Pizzinini and Plangg 1966: xxxv; Craffonara 1971–2. Thus /an/ < ANNU contrasts with /faŋ/ < FAME.

The status of the phone [ʃ] is equally various. Throughout Romansh, as we have observed, all preconsonantal /s/ are [ʃ]. The same is found in the Ladin dialects of Fassa and Gardena, and the Carnic varieties of Friulian. In Moena, on the other hand, the palatalization of /s/ before consonants is optional (Heilmann 1955: 15). Finally, in Nonsberg, there is no phonetic difference between prevocalic and preconsonantal /s/, both being rendered by a sound that is intermediate between [s] and [ʃ] (Battisti 1908: 139).

Pizzinini and Plangg (1966: xxxvi) note a phonological rule of *t*-epenthesis, which converts underlying /ls/, /ms/, and occasionally /ns/, to [lts], [mts], and [nts]. A similar rule exists in Surselvan, but it is also attested in many non-Rhaeto-Romance dialects of central and southern Italy.

1.1.7 Friulian

According to the standard sources (Marchetti 1952; Francescato 1966; Iliescu 1972; and, partially disagreeing, Frau 1984), the vowel inventory is the canonical five-vowel set /i, e, a, o, u/, with phonemic length. Generally, long vowels are tense, short vowels are lax. Some Friulian dialects, for example the east-central dialect of Mortegliano, also have a phonological contrast between lax and tense mid vowels (see Frau 1984: 18–19). Illustrating this are minimal contrast pairs like /mɛs/ 'usher' vs. /mes/ 'month', /fɛde/ 'ewe' vs. /fede/ 'faith', /soj/ 'I am' vs. /sɔj/ 'his/her (m.pl.)', /soːs/ 'you are' vs. /sɔːs/ 'his/her (f.pl.)', /veris/ 'glasses' vs. /vɛris/ 'true (f.pl.)'.

Minimal pairs contrasting for length include /laːt/ 'gone' vs. /lat/ 'milk', and /miːl/ 'honey' vs. /mil/ 'thousand', /peːs/ 'weight' vs. /pɛs/ 'fish', /voj/ 'I go' vs. /voːj/ 'eyes', /kroːt/ 'I believe' vs. /krɔt/ 'frog', and /bruːt/ 'daughter-in-law' vs. /brut/ 'ugly'. The contrast (which is generally only observed in final stressed closed syllables) is neutralized in favour of the short lax form in unstressed syllables, in favour of the long tense form before tautosyllabic /r/ (in some varieties: see Bender *et al.* 1952: 221; Iliescu 1968–9: 287), and in favour of the short lax form before tautosyllabic nasals (in all varieties: Francescato 1966: 7; Vanelli 1985: 370).

Friulian can be divided into two major dialect groups depending on whether or not the phonemic contrast between /c/ and /tʃ/ is maintained (see Francescato 1966: 11). The dialect of Udine described by Bender, Francescato, and Salzmann (Bender *et al.* 1952) is one in which the opposition has been lost.

Here, the consonants are:

```
p  t      k
b  d      g
       tʃ
       dʒ
f  s
v  z
m  n   ɲ
   l
   r
```

Not only the palatal stops, but the palatal fricatives /ʃ, ʒ/, the palatal lateral, and /h/ are entirely missing, at both the phonetic and the underlying phonological levels. On the other hand, in the northwestern (Carnic) dialect of Pesariis, described in Leonard (1972: 66), the /c/ vs.

/tʃ/ contrast is maintained, and there also exist the palatal fricatives /ʃ, ʒ/. Iliescu (1968–9: 276–7) maintains that the /c/ vs. /tʃ/ distinction survives in Northern and Western Friulian (her dialect groups A and B), and is lost in the areas east of Udine and at Cormons (her groups C and D). For a more thorough discussion, see Francescato (1959, 1966). The exact boundary, after Francescato (1966: 47) as adapted by Frau (1984: 42) is given in map 2.

Frau (1984: 42) identifies the isogloss as the one between Western Friulian (no distinction between [c] and [tʃ]) and east-central koine, with the exception of Udine (where a phonological distinction is maintained). But this isogloss only partially coincides with the Tagliamento river, which marks the other isoglosses that separate these two dialect groups.

1.1.8 Common features

The common consonantal structure of the Rhaeto-Romance dialects is clear enough. Moreover, the differences in the vowel inventory, while often spectacular, are – at least in some cases – the result of fairly recent changes, as the survey of historical phonetics below will shortly demonstrate.

Beyond these similarities, almost all Rhaeto-Romance dialects (with the exception of the Ladin and Friulian dialects just noted above) have in common the archiphoneme /S/ (with phonetic values [ʃ] and [ʒ]), representing a neutralization of the four phonemes /s/, /z/, /ʃ/, and /ʒ/, occurring before consonants within the same morpheme and (essentially) agreeing with this consonant in voicing.

The most ambitious and careful reconstruction of a proto-Rhaeto-Romance ancestor language distinct from Vulgar Latin is that of Leonard (1972). The chart below reproduces the vowel system of proto-Rhaeto-Romance that Leonard reconstructs, contrasting it with those of Latin and Vulgar Latin:

Latin	Vulgar Latin	Proto-Rhaeto-Romance
iː	i	i
i		
eː	e	ə
e	ɛ	$\begin{cases} e/\text{\_\_\_\_umlauting environment} \\ \varepsilon \end{cases}$
aː		
a	a	fronted a
o	ɔ	$\begin{cases} ø/\text{\_\_\_\_umlauting environment} \\ \mathfrak{I} \end{cases}$

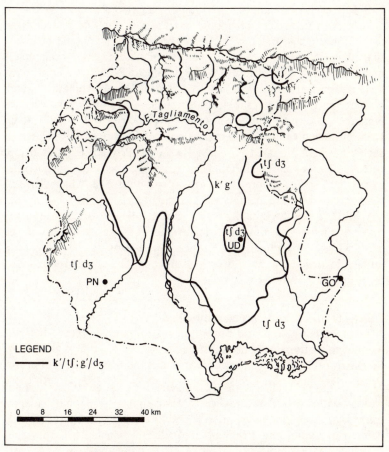

Map 2 The /tʃ/ ≠ /c/ isogloss within Friulian

Latin	Vulgar Latin	Proto-Rhaeto-Romance
oː		
u	o	o
uː	u	y

In addition, Leonard postulates the phonemicization of length in proto-Rhaeto-Romance.

Before even summarizing this claim in a cursory fashion below, or dealing with its specific claims in detail (as we shall do in piecemeal fashion in our discussion of historical phonetics), we should be aware that Leonard's claim of proto-Rhaeto-Romance unity is not one that is made in support of position 1 (in which Rhaeto-Romance is considered an independent unit). Rather, the proto-Rhaeto-Romance which Leonard reconstructs, as well as being the ancestor of just Rhaeto-Romance, is very possibly the ancestor of French as well: 'The Friulian, Dolomitic, and Grisons dialects are not much more closely related to each other than they are to French.' (Leonard 1964: 32). (To this group, we suggest, many northern Italian dialects could also be added.) In other words, Leonard is arguing in favour of position 2 (in which Rhaeto-Romance dialects are members of a larger unity).

While Leonard accepts the reality of proto-Rhaeto-Romance rather than treating it as a construct which requires explicit justification, the existence of the innovations outlined above provides very powerful implicit evidence for proto-Rhaeto-Romance. The crucial innovations from the chart above are

1   e > ə
2   umlaut of ɛ, ɔ and the resulting splits;
3   u > y;
4   the innovation of phonemic length;
5   the fronting of a.

The synchronic evidence for the universality of some of these innovations within Rhaeto-Romance is relatively spotty. In particular, it seems that some innovations (like 1 and 2) are not only shared outside Romansh, Ladin, and Friulian (a conclusion which Leonard would anticipate: for example, in Leonard (1978), change 2 above is explicitly located within proto-Romance), but that some of them (like 3, 4, and 5) define isoglosses within it.

1.2 HISTORICAL PHONETICS

Some of the striking phonological differences among the Rhaeto-Romance dialects are of demonstrably recent origin. Among these are the treatments of inherited /u/, which establish what may seem at first to be massive boundaries within Romansh. (On the other hand, it may be that some of the striking common innovations are also independent of each other, and that the similarities they lead to are similarly recent.)

The cursory survey which follows relies entirely on some of the classic descriptions of the phonological development of various Rhaeto-Romance dialects. The reader should be aware that the 'dialects' which constitute the units of discussion here do not correspond to idealizations like 'Surselvan' or 'Ladin', but to the speech of individual villages or small areas. We have restricted ourselves to descriptions of 'typical' rather than deviant dialects within each group (thus relying on Pult's description of the Vallader of Sent, rather than on Schorta's more extensive discussion of the Müstair Vallader of Santa Maria, and so forth), but even so, there is a tension between the incorrigible particularity of the sources, and the generality which the reader is entitled to expect from a crude survey such as this. For Surselvan, the classic survey of the Disentis and Tavetsch dialects is Huonder 1901 (with full treatment of vowels, and only passing mention of consonantal developments); for Surmeiran, and for Romansh generally, the classic source is Lutta 1923; for Sutselvan, Luzi 1904; for various Ladin dialects, Gartner 1879, Battisti 1908, Elwert 1943; and for Friulian, Francescato 1966 and Iliescu 1972. The latter surveys four Friulian dialects, all spoken by expatriate communities in Roumania. Useful recapitulations of the Friulian developments are also provided by Rizzolatti 1981, Frau 1984, and Benincà 1989.

1.2.1 The evolution of stressed vowels

The inherited Vulgar Latin vowel system of /i, e, ɛ, a, ɔ, o, u/ is the basis of the phonemic systems of all Rhaeto-Romance dialects, and is reproduced in the phonemic systems of some of them. Most of the characteristic Rhaeto-Romance changes involved the mid vowels (particularly the low mid vowels), which were diphthongized.

The phonologization of vowel length in the Friulian dialects is explained (by Francescato (1966), as revised by Trumper (1975) and Vanelli (1979), briefly restated in Rizzolatti (1981: 20) and Frau (1984: 31)) as the outcome of four well-attested diachronic processes:

1. intervocalic lenition of voiceless consonants;
2. non-distinctive lengthening of stressed vowels before all voiced consonants but the nasals;

3.   loss of final non-low unstressed vowels;
4.   devoicing of final obstruents;
(5.   consonant-cluster simplification).

Following these changes, it would seem that 'length' has become phonologized in stressed vowels in inherited open syllables which are now closed final syllables: 'length' subsumes a number of phonetically distinct but clearly related features: length, raising, and diphthongization. There are two important qualifications to this general principle, which we shall consider after the unmarked cases have been reviewed.

Thus, the regular developmental histories of (AMBU)LATU 'gone' and LACTE 'milk':

	LATU	LACTE
1.	ladu	—
2.	laːdu	—
3.	laːd	lact
4.	laːt	—
5.	—	lat

Each of these processes is plausible, and the only problem with the mechanism proposed is that it is so natural that we should expect to encounter the phonologization of vowel length not just in Friulian, but throughout Rhaeto-Romance. On the other hand, length is phonologized in other Rhaeto-Romance dialects besides Friulian, and this mechanism might account for how this came about. The orderly sequence of events postulated by Vanelli (1979) is certainly compatible with Leonard's contention that proto-Rhaeto-Romance had phonologized vowel length, and we are then left with the task of identifying the processes whereby this distinction was pretty generally lost.

The first major qualification to the general principle that length was phonologized in inherited open syllables is forced upon us by contrasts like /laːt/ 'go (p.p. m.sg.)' vs. /lade/ 'go (p.p. f.sg.)'. Apparently, lengthening occurred only in stressed syllables which became *final* syllables as a consequence of change 3, the loss of unstressed final non-low vowels. From the synchronic perspective of the Friulian speaker, lengthening occurs only in stressed final syllables which are closed by an obstruent that is voiced in paradigmatically related forms. Thus, while there is length alternation in /laːt/ vs. /lade/, there is none in /lat/ 'milk' vs. /lataruːl/ 'milkman' (no voicing alternation). There is no need, as yet, to impute to the speaker a knowledge of the phonological history of Friulian.

Here we come to the second qualification. One relative implausibility in the model above is that rule 2 is apparently sensitive to the historical origin of voicing. Vowels lengthen before voiced consonants which are voiced by intervocalic lenition, but not those which were voiced to begin with. Thus, no lengthening occurs in PANE, which becomes /pan/ 'bread', or in TARDU, which becomes /tart/ 'late'. In fact, no lengthening takes place before nasals, ever. The case of the remaining sonorants /l/ and /r/ is more complex. Diachronically, stressed vowels are lengthened in inherited open syllables: thus /vaːl/ < VALET vs. /val/ < VALLE, and /caːr/ < CARU vs. /car/ < CARRU. There is no phonetic implausibility to the initial non-distinctive lengthening in open syllables, but there is no productive length contrast for consonants in Friulian. We must therefore assume that speakers have simply learned contrasts like /caːr/ vs. /car/ by rote.

1.2.1.1 *i

The high front vowel was generally maintained in the Italian Rhaeto-Romance dialects (see Francescato (1966: 195) and Iliescu (1972: 42) for Friulian; Elwert (1943: 47) for Ladin), and in Vallader, the easternmost Romansh dialect. In Surmeiran and in Puter, diphthongization yielded /ij/, with subsequent *Verschärfung* before a following consonant to [iK] (Gartner 1883: 48; Lutta 1923; *passim*). That this *Verschärfung* is automatic is hinted in its non-existence in the standard orthographies, and in the totally productive way stressed /ij/ ([ik] ~ [ig]) alternates in the spoken language with unstressed /i/ [i]. Lutta (1923: 315–16 drew attention to how the [iK] ~ [i] alternation was sensitive not only to word stress, but also to phrase and sentence stress in pairs like (the night is) [ʃcigra] 'dark (f.sg.)' vs. [la ʃcira nwets] 'the dark night'. The status of glide obstruentization as a 'familiar' or 'uncouth' pronunciation is indicated in Scheitlin (1962: 15), and Rohlfs (1975: 19). For a phonological account, see Kamprath (1986).

In Surselvan, Sutselvan, and Surmeiran, there was a tendency to lower /i/ in closed syllables. In Surselvan, all /i/ underwent lowering to /ɛ/ before tautosyllabic consonants: thus PRIMU > /(əm)prɛm/ 'first'. In Sutselvan, /i/ lowered to /ɪ/ syllable-finally, before /n/, and before /ʎ/ (Luzi 1904: 766–8), thus DICTU > /dɪc/, FINE > /fɪn/ ([fɪɲ] ~ [fɪŋ]) 'end', and FAMILIA > [fəmɪʎa] 'family'. In Surmeiran, /i(j)/ lowered syllable-finally to /ɛ(j)/, thus DORMIRE > /durmɛ(j)r/ ([durmɛkr]) 'sleep'.

That the lowering process is very recent can be seen from the form of fourth-conjugation infinitives in Surselvan and Sutselvan. In these dialects (and, in Sutselvan, not consistently), final /r/ of the stressed infinitival desinence is lost: DORMIRE > /durmi/. The non-existence of

Table 1.1 Some reflexes of *u

Source	Friulian	Ladin	Vallader	Puter	Surmeiran	Surselvan
UNU	uŋ	uŋ	yn	yn	ɛɲ	in
PLUS	pluj	plu	ply	py	plɛ	pli
OBSCURU	skuːr	ʃkur	ʃcyr	ʃcyr	ʃcikr	ʃcir
DURU	duːr		dyr	dykr	dɛkr	

infinitives like */durmɛ/ suggests an ordering

(a) loss of infinitival -r;
(b) lowering of /i/ to /ɛ/ before consonants.

1.2.1.2 *u

This vowel is also maintained in the Italian dialects (Iliescu 1972: 43; Elwert 1943: 53), but undergoes a series of changes in Romansh. In all Romansh, as in French (and as in Lombard and Piedmontese, see Battisti 1931: 140; Rohlfs 1972: 125), /u/ originally was fronted to /y/. Over the seventeenth century, this high front rounded vowel was unrounded in Surselvan, Sutselvan, and Surmeiran to /i/. While Old Surselvan texts of the seventeenth century still have {ün} for modern /in/ 'one (m.sg.)', there is evidence that this change may have begun much earlier, perhaps as early as the eighth century, thus the toponym /flɛm/ < FLUMEN 'river' (Prader-Schucany 1970: 58). In any case, /i/ derived from inherited *u was able to undergo the subsequent lowering (to /ɛ/ in this example), and regularly to /ɪ/ in Sutselvan (Luzi 1904: 791), thus FUMU > /fɪm/ 'smoke'. In Surmeiran, /i/ diphthongized to /ij/ or /ɛj/, with *Verschärfung* to [iK] or [ɛK] before a following consonant. Some idea of the complexity of the correspondences may be given by table 1.1. Perhaps in the fluctuations between [e] and [i] in Surmeiran, we see the traces of the (Sutselvan) phoneme /ɪ/.

Leonard (1972: 73–4), as we have seen, views the change *u > y* (possibly under Celtic influence?) as a common proto-Rhaeto-Romance or 'Gallo-Italian' (see Leonard 1964: 32) innovation. Leonard's Gallo-Italian, like Rohlfs' Gallo-Romance, includes not only French and the Rhaeto-Romance dialects of Grisons, the Dolomites, and Friuli, but also the dialects of northern Italy above the ideal line from La Spezia to Rimini. In fact, however, there is no evidence whatever that Friulian ever participated in such a fronting (Leonard 1964: 30), and the u/y isogloss splits Rhaeto-Romance in two. To be sure, the phone [y] occurs in some Ladin dialects, like that of Nonsberg. But the geographical distribution of this sound suggests recent Trentino, rather than ancient Celtic, influence on the Lombard-Ladin dialect of Nonsberg (see Battisti 1908: 57). In Badiot, /y/ derives from Latin long U, and also from Latin short (lax) O in inherited open stressed syllables. Since Latin lax O in this position yields Friulian /uː/, we may be justified in generalizing, and saying that Badiot */uː/ (whether directly from Latin U, or indirectly, from Latin lax O) yields /y/. Examples include /pyɲ/ 'fistful' < PUGNU, /ɲy/ 'come (p.p.m.sg.)' < *VENIUTU, /ʒyk/ 'game' < IOCU, /ny/ 'new (m.sg.)' < NOVU.

1.2.1.3 *e

All the Rhaeto-Romance dialects are said to have undergone some kind of diphthongization, whether to /aj/, to /əj/ (Huonder 1901: 468), or to /ej/. Some of these dialects, at least in some contexts, exhibit /e/ or /eː/, which, if Huonder is correct, must be interpreted as an inhibition of the inherited change, or a later development. Vallader seems to be the most conservative dialect, retaining /aj/ throughout. Puter orthography is identical with Vallader pronunciation, indicating that the restoration of /e/ in this dialect (or the monophthongization *aj* > *e*) is a very recent development. Ladin has retained /ej/ in open syllables, but has /e/ in closed syllables.

In Friulian, tensed *e in inherited open syllables results in a diphthong in some varieties, and simply a lengthened vowel in others: Carnic Friulian has /ej/; east-central koine has /eː/; northwestern Friulian, typified by Clauzetto, has a so-called 'reverse diphthong' /íə/, where ə has the same pronunciation as final unstressed -*a* in this dialect (/a/, /e/, or /o/):

Source	Carnic	East-central	Clauzetto	Gloss
NIVE	nejf	neːf	níəf	'snow'
ACETU	adzejt	azeːt	azíət	'vinegar'

Tensed *e in other positions in Friulian generally results in /e/ or /ɛ/: /strɛt/ 'narrow' < STRICTU, /fɛde/ 'ewe' < FETA.

Surselvan has /e/ almost everywhere. Sutselvan in general changed /ej/ to /ɪ/, but retained a diphthong /aj/ (Domleschg dialect) or /ɔj/ (Bonaduz dialect) before nasals, or /ɛə/ before /rC/ (dialects of Domleschg and Schams (Luzi 1904: 771–3). In Surmeiran, once again, the diphthong /ɛj/ is subject to preconsonantal *Verschärfung*, particularly in syllables closed by /r/ (Grisch 1939: 24). The range of variation is exemplified in the reflexes of the second-conjugation infinitival desinence -ERE: Surselvan /e/, Sutselvan /ɪ(r)/, Surmeiran /ɛjr/ ([ɛkr]), Puter /er/,

Vallader /ajr/, Ladin /aj/, Friulian /e(j)/, /íə/, /eː/.

Leonard (1972: 82–4) insists on a proto-Rhaeto-Romance innovation *e* > *ə*, the reflex being maintained in the Ladin dialects of Gardena and Livinallongo. Even granting the (considerable) plausibility of this reconstruction within Rhaeto-Romance, it should be noted that some of the best evidence for its existence comes from outside Rhaeto-Romance in the narrow sense we are adopting for this study, as Leonard himself points out. Among the languages and dialects which exhibit a phonetic reflex which directly supports earlier *ə* are the Italian dialects of Bologna and the Piedmont, and Franco-Provençal; among those where indirect arguments for its existence may be constructed are Friulian and Catalan.

1.2.1.4 *o

In inherited open syllables which are now closed and word-final, the vowel *o* is lengthened in Friulian koine (Iliescu 1972: 41), diphthongized to /ow/ in Carnic Friulian, and diphthongized to /úə/ in the northwest (Rizzolatti 1981: 21–2):

Source	Carnic	Koine	Clauzetto	Gloss
FLORE	flowr	floːr	flúər	'flower'
LUPU	lowf	loːf	lúəf	'wolf'

In other positions in Friulian, the reflex is /o/: /tos/ 'cough' < TUSSIM, /sola/ 'alone (f.sg.)' < SOLA.

In Gardena, *o* > *ɛw*. In Fassa, *o* > *ow* in originally open syllables (Elwert 1943: 52). Simplifying the very complex case of Badiot, *o* > /u/ in inherited open syllables, and /o/ elsewhere (Craffonara 1971–2: 214ff.). The Swiss dialects, on the other hand, are in agreement in undergoing the following changes: diphthongization to /uə/ before /rC/ or /Cr/ (Prader-Schucany 1970: 23 n. 5 notes the same change in Provençal); and raising to /u/, possibly via an intermediate /ou/, everywhere else.

These complementary changes resulted in a regular paradigmatic alternation in the Engadine dialects for nouns in final -*or*, as the singular in -ORE (later /ur/) diverged from the plural in -ORES (later /uərs/). Thus, AMORE > /amur/, but AMORES > /amuərs/. In the western Romansh dialects, this alternation was levelled in favour of /u/ throughout. However, where there is no paradigmatic alternation, the regular change takes place: in all Romansh dialects, CULPA > /kuəlpa/ 'fault'.

In Surmeiran, the diphthong /uə/ underwent *Verschärfung* to [uk] before consonants. Thus LUPU > [lukf] (compare Fassa Ladin, Carnic Friulian /lowf/, Friulian koine /loːf/, northwestern Friulian /lúəf/,

Surselvan, Vallader /luf/) 'wolf' (see Lutta 1923: 109).

1.2.1.5 *E

Throughout Romansh, this lax vowel is said to have diphthongized, first to /ɛə/, then to /ja/ (see Huonder 1901: 463), but the present dialects exhibit considerable divergence.

The most conservative of the Romansh dialects may be Sutselvan, which retains /ɛə/ (corresponding to sixteenth-century Surselvan and Engadine orthography) in the (Vulgar Latin) environment before C + non-high vowel, but umlauts this to /iə/ before (inherited) C + high vowel: compare /iəStər/ < EXTERU 'foreign', with /fənɛəStrə/ < FENESTRA 'window', or /əntiər/ < INTEGRU 'entire', with /ɛərə/ < ERAT 'was (3sg.)' (Luzi 1904: 774).

This alternation has paradigmatic consequences in nominal roots ending in the suffix -ELLU. AUCELLU > *utʃiəl > /utʃi/ 'bird' (the latter changes morphologically conditioned), contrasting with AUCELLOS > /utʃɛəls/ ([utʃɛəlts]) 'birds'.

While Surselvan regularly has /ja/ as the reflex of inherited *E, there are a number of (no longer phonologically conditioned) alternations in this dialect which reflect a state of affairs similar to that of Sutselvan. First, the paradigmatic alternations among nominal stems in -ELLU is the same as in Sutselvan: BELLU > *biəl > /bi/ 'beautiful (n.sg.)', but BELLUS, BELLOS > *bɛlos > *bɛəls > /bjals/ 'beautiful (m.sg., m.pl.)'. Similar are the singular/plural pairs for /kaSti/ 'castle', /kunti/ 'knife', /riSti/ 'rake', and /marti/ 'hammer'.

Assuming that the alternation between /iə/ and /ja/ was originally 'motivated' as a kind of umlaut, frozen alternations like Surselvan

Source	Singular	Plural	Gloss
CASTELLU	kaʃti	kaʃcals	'castle'
VERBU	viərf	vjarfs	'word'

may be said to be caused by the umlauting environment -U (< Lat. -UM) in the singular (see Schuchardt 1870; Luedtke 1965; Leonard 1978). But the alternation has obviously become morphologized as a redundant index of number in those cases where the putative conditioning environment is not even in the following syllable:

Singular	Plural	Gloss
ʃpiəgəl	ʃpjagəls	'mirror'
dumiəʃti	dumjaʃtis	'servant'

(In fact, the phonetic alternation [iə] ~ [ja] has become morphologized in adjectives – including adjectives of non-Latin origin – as well as in nouns, and as the index of a more general opposition, to be discussed in greater detail in the morphology: essentially, [iə] represents neuter singular or attributive masculine singular, while [ja] represents all other genders and numbers, and also predicative masculine singular. Thus, for the adjective /Sliət/ (< OHG *sleht*) 'bad', we have the contrast between [in ʃpiəgəl ʃliət] 'a bad mirror' (with 'bad' as an attributive masculine singular adjective), and [(iʎ ʃpiəgəl ej) ʃʎats] 'the mirror is bad' (with 'bad' as a predicative masculine singular adjective). (Tekavčić (1974: 382) provides a complete list of the forms in which the alternation occurs.)

In the Engadine dialects, /ja/ has recently remonophthongized to /ε/ or to /e/ (Lutta 1923: 68 n. 1; Elwert 1943: 39).

In the Italian Rhaeto-Romance dialects, it is perhaps better to start from the assumption that the lax mid front vowel ε (like its counterpart ɔ) was affected by the Romance rule of diphthongization, originally yielding /je/ (Elwert 1943: 39; Francescato 1966: 196; Iliescu 1972: 35; Craffonara 1971–2). In Fassan, diphthongization is apparently confined to inherited paroxytone open syllables: thus /grjef/ 'heavy' < GREVE vs. /tera/ 'earth' < TERRA (inherited closed syllable) and /tebek/ 'warm' < TEPIDU (inherited proparoxytone). Final -I and -U, as in Romansh, could induce umlauting diphthongization also, however. Thus, while /petra/ < PETRA is regular, /pjer/ < PETRU is a result of umlaut.

In Badiot and in Friulian, ε seems to have yielded /je/ in both open and closed syllables, and in both paroxytones and proparoxytones. Thus Friulian /fjeste/ < FESTA, /spjete/ < EXPECTA(T), /mjedi/ < MEDICU.

In Friulian, three further changes affect inherited */je/.

1   Before inherited tautosyllabic /r/, /je/ lowers to /ja/ or /jε/ depending on the dialect: PERDERE > /pjεrdi/ (western Friulian) or /pjardi/ (east-central koine).
2   In inherited open syllables which are now final in Friulian, /je/ raises to /iː/ or becomes /ej/, depending on the dialect again: PEDE > /pejt/ (western Friulian) or /piːt/ (east-central koine).
3   Before tautosyllabic nasal, /je/ raises to /i/: TEMPUS > /timp/.

1.2.1.6 *O

The development of *O in most Rhaeto-Romance dialects is a long eventful story. The only near-generalization possible seems to be that originally, *O > *uə, though even to this, there are exceptions; for example, the vowel seems to have remained throughout Romansh /ɔtz/ < HODIE 'today' (Luzi 1904: 784).

Friulian developed *o > *wi* before *n*C, *o > *wa* before *r*, and *o > *we*
elsewhere. It seems Friulian is the only Rhaeto-Romance dialect which
never umlauted the resulting sound before inherited -u or a front vowel.

The status of the Erto dialect, on the westernmost fringes of Friulian,
has been contested. Against Battisti and Gartner, who considered Erto
to be a Dolomitic Ladin dialect, Francescato (1966) concluded that Erto
is Friulian, citing as evidence the peculiar development of *o in the
dialect. The claim is particularly striking when we note that the reflexes
of *o coincide neither with those of Ladin, nor with those of Friulian:

$$o, ɔ > \varepsilon w/\_\_\_\$$$
$$ɔ > uə/\_\_\_C\$$$

Thus, FOCU > /fɛwk/ 'fire', *CORE > /kɛwr/ 'heart', NOVU > /nɛwf/
'new', CRUCE > /krɛwʃ/ 'cross', NOCTE > /nuət/ 'night', COXA > /kuəsa/
'haunch', COCTO > /kuət/ 'cooked'. What is at issue is the purely
structural fact that in Erto, the sound o has different reflexes depending
on whether or not it occurred in an originally open syllable.
Francescato's argument, then, is only as strong as the claim that in
Dolomitic Ladin, the development of inherited o is not sensitive to
inherited syllabic context. As we shall see in a moment, by this criterion,
the Ladin dialect of Marebbe is also equally 'Friulian'!

Fassa Ladin regularly has some mid rounded back vowel, except
before a palatalizing environment or a tautosyllabic nasal, where the
reflex is /e/. Elwert (1943: 48) postulates a chain of phonetic changes *ɔ
> *wɔ > *we > *ø > *e. Before inherited /ʎ/, no umlaut occurred, and the
attested reflex is tense /o/.

There is some unclarity as to whether the sequence of changes outlined
by Elwert actually represents an -*U* desinence-conditioned umlaut. If it
is not, then the claim of Battisti (1931: 146–8), citing an earlier opinion of
Gamillscheg, that the umlaut of inherited *E* and *O* before -*U* is a
strictly Romansh phenomenon, at least within Rhaeto-Romance, must
be considered valid. On the other hand, there is evidence from other
Ladin dialects which strongly supports umlaut before -*U* and before -*lj*.
Consider the correspondences in table 1.2 from the Ladin dialects of
Marebbe and Moena, contrasted with the non-umlauting dialects of
Nonsberg and Gardena. The Marebban forms, incidentally, show
sensitivity to syllabic context. In inherited open syllables, (?) umlauted ɔ
> /y/, while in originally closed syllables, it becomes /e/. This contrast is
reminiscent of similar contrasts in Carnic Friulian and Erto. But it seems
to us that (unless we wish to call Marebban a Friulian dialect), such
alternations cannot be used as a diagnostic to distinguish Ladin from
Friulian.

Table 1.2 Some ladin outcomes of *ɔ

Source	Nonsberg	Gardena	Marebbe	Moena	Gloss
FOCU	fwɛx	fuək	fy	føk	'fire'
LOCU	lwɛx	luək	ly	løk	'place'
OVU	wɛw	uə	y	øf	'egg'
FOLIA	fwɛja	fuəja	feia	føa	'leaf'
OC'LU	ɔkjel	uədl	edl	ølje	'eye'

Table 1.3 Diphthongization of *ɔ in Surselvan

Source	Singular	Plural	Gloss
PORCU	piərc	por(k)s	'pig'
MORSU	miərs	mors	'bite'
HORTU	iərt	orts	'vegetable garden'
NOVU	niəf	nofs	'new'
BONU	biən	buns	'good'
GROSSU	griəs	grɔs	'big'

Vallader underwent the changes *ɔ > *uó* > *úa* > *óa* > *o* (Pult 1897:
97). The first stage in this progression is orthographically attested in
sixteenth-century texts for most closed syllables: thus {nuof} 'new'. The
second-last is attested in the same sources where the syllable is closed by
a liquid cluster: thus {moart} 'dead'. (Compare Carnic Friulian /núof/,
/mwart/.) Modern Vallader has /nof/, /mort/. Umlauted *o gives /uə/
before liquid clusters, /ø/ elsewhere.

Puter has [ok] in closed syllables, possibly by *Verschärfung* of
intermediate (*oa*>) *oə* > *ow* (see Lutta 1923: 98).

Sutselvan in umlauting environments, has /iə/ (before high or front
vowels), or /ɪ/ (before palatalized consonants; see Luzi 1904: 784–5).

Surselvan generally has /ju/ before velars, /e/ before /ʎ/, /iə/ before
umlauting environments, and /ɔ/ ∼ /o/ elsewhere. In both Surselvan and
Sutselvan, umlauted /iə/ (or Sutselvan /ɪ/) arose by unrounding of prior
/uə/ (or /uəi/; see Luzi 1904: 784).

The umlauting (and palatalizing) effect of accusative masculine
singular/neuter singular -U, in contrasting with non-umlauting
masculine plural -OS, (nominative) masculine singular -US, feminine
singular -A, resulted in some nominal and adjectival alternations in
Surselvan, as indicated in table 1.3 of common examples. (Again, for
nouns, the phonetic alternation [iə] ∼ [o] corresponds to singular vs.
plural, while for adjectives [iə] is neuter singular or attributive masculine
singular.) The alternation is clearly morphologized in the examples in
table 1.4, where the conditioning environment is not in the next syllable

Table 1.4 Analogical extensions of diphthongization of *ɔ

Source	Singular	Plural	Gloss
NOBILE	niəbəl	nobəls	'noble'
COCCINU	ciətʃən	kotʃəns	'red'
APOSTOLU	apiəʃtə,	apoʃtəls	'apostle'
CORPU	ciərp	kɔrps	'body'
CAECU	tʃiək	tʃoks	'blind'

(thus, the first four examples), the conditioning environment never existed (as in CORPU, the second-last example) or where we are dealing with an analogical formation (thus, the last example).

Tekavčić (1974: 384) provides a complete list of the forms affected by the [iə] ~ [o] alternation. The vast majority of Surselvan forms manifest no umlauting alternation for the singular/plural (or neuter singular/all other) distinction. Most have generalized the umlauted /iə/ form throughout, thus /ɟiəvɟa/ < *JOVIA 'Thursday', /siəmi/ < SOMNU 'dream'. Others (mostly later Latinate borrowings) have generalized /o/, thus /gloria/, /solid/ (see Sutselvan /siəli/ < SOLIDU 'fresh, dry, strong (said of wood)'; Lutta 1923: 100); but note also the backformation /korf/ < CORVU 'crow', almost certainly not an archaicized Latinate borrowing.

Diminutives in inherited -EOLU are interesting, because it is with these alone that we encounter traces of morphologized umlaut in any Rhaeto-Romance dialects other than Surselvan. Consider the singular and plural forms of LINTEOLU '(bed)sheet' in Surselvan and Vallader:

	Surselvan	Vallader
LINTEOLU	lentsiəl	lintso:l
LINTEOLOS	lentsɛwl(t)s	lintso:z (< lintso:lz)

Similar are /barɟiəl/ 'pimple', /kaʒiəl/ 'cheese', /piɲiəl/ 'pine tree', and a very few others. For most nouns of this, as of other classes, the paradigmatic alternation has been levelled in favour of the umlauted (singular) form.

The correspondences shown in table 1.5 summarize the main points of the discussion of the reflexes of inherited *ɔ in Rhaeto-Romance dialects.

The extent of umlauting induced by final -ʊ within Rhaeto-Romance is unclear. Rohlfs (1972: 126) regards it as a 'Gallo-Romance' phenomenon, citing alternations like *nøv* 'new (m.sg.)' ~ *nova* (f.sg.) in Ticinese, and *grøs* 'big (m.sg.) ~ *grossa* (f.sg.) in Piedmontese in support of this. Leonard (1972: 79) postulates the change ɔ > ø in umlauting environments as a characteristic innovation of proto-northern

Table 1.5 Summary of major Rhaeto-Romance outcomes of *ɔ

Source	Sursel	Sutsel	Surmeiran	Vallader	Ladin (Fassa)	Friulian Koine	Friulian Western	Glosses
CORE	kɔr	kɔr	kokr	koːr	ker	kuːr	kowr	'heart'
ROTA	rɔda	rɔda	rogda	roːda	rɔda	rwede	rwɛda	'wheel'
NOVU	niəf	niəf	nof	nof	nef	nuːf	nowf	'new'
FOCU	fjuk	fiək	fi	fo	fek	fuːk	fowk	'fire'
CORNU	ciərn	ciərn	korn	cyrn			kwar	'horn'
FOLIA	feʎ	fiʎ	fiʎ	føʎ	foa	fweje	fweja	'leaf'

Romance. While there is evidence for this development from Surselvan, Vallader, and possibly some Ladin dialects, as we have seen, there is none from Friulian, where Leonard is forced to posit a development *ɔ > ø > o* (a kind of development elsewhere dismissed by him as a typologically 'incredible, pat regression' (Leonard 1972: 76). To one who is not committed to the burdensome task of defending Rhaeto-Romance unity, a more sensible approach is to assume that Friulian never participated in this change, and that the *o/ø* isogloss splits Rhaeto-Romance, just as the *u/y* isogloss seems to do.

1.2.1.7 Mid vowels before nasals

As we have already noted, the nasals are a neutralizing context for a number of distinctions. It may be opportune to review some of these contrasts at this time.

In all the Rhaeto-Romance dialects, the contrast between lax and tense mid vowels was neutralized before nasals.

In the Swiss dialects, the back mid vowels before /N/ were raised to /u/: this happened regularly in the western dialects, less regularly in the Engadine dialects (Pult 1897: 114–15). The mid front vowels were diphthongized to /aj/; they remain so in open syllables, but are remonophthongized to /e/ in closed syllables, except in Vallader (Lutta 1923: 85–7).

In the Friulian dialects, the length contrast is suspended before nasals for all vowels. In addition, the contrast between reflexes of Latin lax E and O is suspended before a tautosyllabic nasal in favour of /i/: PONTE > /pwint/ 'bridge', CONTRA > /kwintre/ 'against', GENTE > /int/ 'people'.

1.2.1.8 *a

A number of scholars posit a fronting of inherited stressed *a* in all northern Romance languages (see Schuerr 1938: 19; Leonard 1962: 23; Rohlfs 1972: 125). The indirect evidence for such a change, of course, is the palatalization of velar stops before inherited *a. If this development occurred, then dialects like those of Moena and Nonsberg in the Ladin group, and Friulian, are not conservative in apparently retaining the vowel [a] unchanged in most environments (Battisti 1908: 4; Heilmann 1955: 19–32; Iliescu 1972: 35). Rather, we are forced to assume a series of changes *a > *æ > a.

There is some direct phonetic evidence for some intermediate front vowel, to be sure. In Fassa, for example, inherited *a survives as /a/ in final position, and before /m/, but is raised elsewhere to /e/ (Elwert 1943: 26ff.). In Gardena, *a remains /a/ in closed syllables, but in final open syllables becomes /æ/ (as in the first-conjugation masculine singular perfect participle ending), or /e/ (as in the first-conjugation infinitive; see Gartner 1879: 40). The change A > /e/ is also attested in a narrow area of northeastern Carnia (Francescato 1966: 386–7; for more on velar palatalization in Friulian, see Benincà and Vanelli 1978: 251 n. 1).

The Swiss dialects are opposed to the Italian dialects in having diphthongized /a/ to /aw/ before nasals. The resulting diphthong then underwent the following changes:

(a) aw > o/____m
(b) aw > o/____n$C (where $ = syllable boundary)

(For rule (b) to make the correct predictions, it is necessary to analyse the single phoneme /ɲ/ as a cluster /n$j/ at the time of the application of the rule: thus, in all Romansh, *MALESANIA > /maltsɔɲa/ 'sickness'.

The central Swiss dialects (by which we intend to refer here to Sutselvan, Puter, and Surmeiran), are further characterized by the following innovations, which are not equally shared:

(a) a > ɛ/____ $C   (Puter and Surmeiran only; Lutta 1923: 42)
(b) awN > ɛN   (Puter only)
(c) a > ɔ/____#   (Puter and Surmeiran)
(d) ɔ > a/____m   (Puter only; Lutta 1923: 47)
(e) ɔ > o/____m   (Sutselvan only; Luzi 1904: 779)

The correspondences shown in table 1.6 exemplify the major developments enumerated up to here.

1.2.1.8.1 *aw (< *aw *and* < *al/____c)

In Gallo-Romance and Rhaeto-Romance, /aw/ > /o/ occurred following the palatalization of velars before inherited a (thus CAUSA >

Table 1.6 Summary of major Rhaeto-Romance outcomes of **a*

Source	Friulian	Ladin (Fassa)	Vallader	Puter	Sutselvan (Bonaduz)	Surselvan	Gloss
ANNU	aŋ	aŋ	ɔn	ɛn	ɛwn	ɔn	'year'
CANE	caŋ	tʃaŋ	caŋ	cɛːm	cɛwn	cɛwŋ	'dog'
CLAVE	klaːf	klef	klaf	klef		klaf	'key'
FLAMMA	flama	flama	flɔma	flama	floma	flɔa	'flame'
HABET	a	a	a	ɔ	a	a	'has'

/cosa/, and so on). Throughout Rhaeto-Romance there are many cases of retained /aw/, not only in learned words (for which the influence of Church Latin may be held responsible), but also popular terms like /awca/ 'goose' < AVICA in Fassan and Friulian and /tawr/ 'bull' < TAURU in Friulian.

Evidence that modern /aw/ and /al/ corresponding to Latin {au} and {al} are often restorations rather than retentions comes partly from cases of hypercorrection, attested throughout Rhaeto-Romance and much of northern Italy, where we encounter etymologically unmotivated /al/ or /ol/ corresponding to Latin {au} (see Ettmayer 1902: 357–8).

Notable is the backformation /polsa/ < PAUSAT in three of the four Friulian dialects investigated by Iliescu (1972: 46n.). Similar is Surselvan /ɟolt/ 'enjoys' < GAUDET 'rejoices' (the /ɟ/ reflecting palatalization of inherited */g/ before stressed */a/: compare the infinitive /galdér/ with no palatalization).

Fassa has /aw/ virtually throughout (Elwert 1943: 38), and again, there are a handful of hypercorrections to /al/. Gartner (1883: 55, noted /(l)alda/ for LAUDAT 'praises', and Pizzinini and Plangg (1966: xlvi, 4) report /aldi/ for AUDIRE in Badiot. Nonsberg has /ɔ/ (Battisti 1908: 26), except for the common northern Italian hyper-restoration of /polʃare/ for PAUSARE. Gardena has /ɔ/ before liquids, /aw/ elsewhere (Gartner 1879: 40). Moena has /aw/ in a handful of cases, including /pawsa/ < PAUSAT (Heilmann 1955: 75–6).

In Fassa (and, to some extent, in Moena), the resulting monophthong was subject to Ladin *ɔ > ø/____UM umlaut.

Source	Fassa	Moena	Gloss
PAUCU	pek	pok	'few, little'
PAUPERU	pere	pere	'poor'

Such examples suggest either a diachronic succession

(a) monophthongization;
(b) umlaut.

or else the need to identify umlaut as a persistent change.

Table 1.7 Sutselvan outcomes of *al*

Source	Bonaduz	Ems	Schams	Domleschg	Gloss
ALTU	awlt	awt	ɔlt	olt	'high'
FALSU	fawlts	fawts	fɔlts	folts	'false'
CALDU	cawlt	kawt	cɔlt	colt	'hot'
BALD	bawlt	bawt	bɔlt	bolt	'soon'

With the exception of Surselvan and Sutselvan (of which more in a moment), the Romansh dialects fairly consistently have /o/ < AU. Vallader has /a/ before velars, thus PAUCOS > /paks/ 'few (m.pl.)', and also has hypercorrect /al/ in /(d)alda/ < AUDIT 'hears' (Gartner 1883: 55). Surmeiran also has a sprinkling of etymologically unmotivated hypercorrections, among them /galdɛjr/ < GAUDERE 'to rejoice' (Grisch 1939: 82).

Sutselvan monophthongized /aw/ to /o/ (Domleschg dialect) or to /ʌ/ (Schams dialect), preserving or restoring the original diphthong in the Bonaduz dialect (Luzi 1904: 793). Original /al/ before a consonant had at least three Sutselvan reflexes, none of them identical with the outcome of /aw/. In the Ems dialect /al/ > /aw/, while in the other dialects, the liquid was retained, and /a/ > aw/____l (thus Bonaduz), with further monophthongization of /aw/ in the dialects of Schams and Domleschg to /ɔ/ and /o/ respectively (Luzi 1904: 783) (see table 1.7).

Surselvan has *aw > /aw/ throughout, a state of affairs that is considered to be an unambiguous (possibly Latinizing) innovation (see von Planta 1926: 15). Evidence in favour of von Planta's claim is the absence of velar palatalization in forms like /kawsa/ < CAUSA 'cause, matter, thing'. (A similar preservation or restoration of the inherited velar characterizes at least one Sutselvan dialect, that of Ems; see Luzi 1904: 780.) Like Sutselvan, Surselvan distinguishes inherited *al from inherited *aw, in that *al > /awl/.

We find, then, that in peripheral Rhaeto-Romance areas, an ancient distinction (between inherited *al and *aw) is maintained, while in the central areas (Surmeiran, Puter, Vallader, and Ladin) it is lost. The traditional explanation for this sort of pattern is that the peripheral areas represent the most archaic stages of development. In this case, however, another explanation is generally offered: in the western dialects, at least, the inherited contrast has been restored rather than retained. What impulse lies behind this restoration is unclear: Gartner proposed the influence of Church Latin, an explanation which Luzi (1904: 802) treated with some scepticism. We share this scepticism. Not only do we encounter /aw/ in low-register vocabulary items: Church

Table 1.8 Paragogic final vowels in Friulian and Ladin

Source	Badiot	Friulian	Fassan	Gloss
SOLICULU	sorɛdl	soreli	soreje	'sun'
PATRE	pɛre	pari	pere	'father'
MATRE	mɛre	mari	mere	'mother'
VETULU	vɛdl	vjeli	vɛje	'old'

Latin could have had no effect on Germanic borrowings like /bawlt/ < bald 'soon' or /vawlt/ < *Wald* 'forest', whose development is completely parallel to that of words of Latin origin like /cawlt/ < CALDU 'hot' or /awlt/ < ALTU 'high'.

1.2.2   Unstressed vowels

Throughout Rhaeto-Romance, in final position all unstressed vowels with the exception of /a/, disappeared except in hiatus (Huonder 1901: 518; Lutta 1923: 120; Elwert 1943: 53–4; Heilmann 1955: 82; Vanelli 1985: 370 finds in this a characteristic of Friulian which most sharply distinguishes it from the neighbouring southern Venetian dialect). Apparent systematic exceptions to this are of two sorts: first, in Friulian and some Ladin dialects, a paragogic final vowel (Friulian -*i*, Ladin and Venetian -*e*) arose in word-final position after some inherited consonant + liquid clusters (Rizzolatti 1981: 27; see table 1.8). Second, morphologically conditioned exceptions also arose in the reconstruction of inflectional suffixes for nouns and verbs; for example, (Surselvan) subjunctive -*i* (Huonder considers here the possibility that final unstressed /i/ could remain in Surselvan, deriving subjunctive -*i* from ILLUD, thus /aʝi/ < HABEAT ILLUD 'that 3sg. may have (it)'; Huonder 1901: 520); these forms and various speculations about their origins will be treated separately in the morphology.

Although all Rhaeto-Romance retained final unstressed *a, there is a major split within Friulian in the treatment of this vowel (which must have originally been reduced to schwa, and remains [ə] in Clauzetto). In the east-central koine, the vowel has been reconstituted as [e], while in the Western dialects, it is reconstituted as [a]. The different treatments of final *ə are exactly parallel to the different treatments of the offglide in the diphthongs /iə/ and /uə/ (Rizzolatti 1981: 22, 26; Frau 1984: 32).

Much more regularly and thoroughly than the Italian Rhaeto-Romance dialects, Romansh eliminated antepenultimate stress on words by virtue of two functionally related rules:

(a) V > $\emptyset$/V ____ C____CVC#
    [+stress]   (see Lutta 1923: 122)

(b) V > $\emptyset$/VC____C V   C#
    [−low]   [+stress]   (see Lutta 1923: 125)

In the Italian Rhaeto-Romance dialects, in spite of a general tendency to avoid antepenultimate stress, involving actual stress shift in some cases like /se'mena/ < SEMINAT 'sows' (Elwert 1943: 104), rule (a) does not usually occur (it does in Gardena, but not in either Fassa or Badiot; see Elwert 1943: 55; Plangg 1973: 19), and there are a number of words in both Ladin and Friulian of the form /'fɛmena/ 'woman' (contrast the development of FEMINA > /fana/ in Gardena, or of DOMINA > /duəna/ in Romansh).

A possible synchronic consequence of this distinction in the realm of syntax is the different treatment of postverbal pronominal clitics in the Swiss and Italian dialects. Generally speaking, Swiss dialects like Vallader do not permit stress to shift back to antepenultimate position in verb + clitic combinations, even in those cases where the verb by itself already has penultimate stress: following such a verb form, an otherwise non-null clitic may surface as phonetic zero, or either the verb or the clitic may undergo apocope. In Vallader, for example, /vɛndan + a/ 'Do they sell?' becomes [vɛndna] (by rule (a)), and /plova + i/ 'Is it raining?' becomes [plova] (see Haiman 1971). No such reduction seems to affect postverbal subject clitics in the Italian dialects; see Fassa /ke 'faʒe-la/ 'What is she doing?' and /pərke 'tɛʒes-te-pa/ 'Why are you quiet then?' (Elwert 1943: 147, 133). Particularly revealing is /'mene-me-la so'bito/ 'Fetch me her at once!' (Elwert 1943: 264): here in the same sentence we encounter toleration of antepenultimate stress on a verb + clitic cluster, but stress shift from antepenultimate to penultimate position on the adverb [so'bito] < /'subito/.

Another distinction between the two dialect groups which is compatible with this one, although unlikely to have been caused by it, relates to the possibility of stringing a number of object clitics after the verb. In the Italian Rhaeto-Romance dialects, as in Italian, sequences of *verb + clitic + clitic* are easily constructed, where one of these is the direct, the other the indirect, object, as in /daʒe-ne-ne/ 'give us some' (Elwert 1943: 136). In the Swiss dialects (with marginal exceptions to be noted later) only one postverbal object clitic may appear with any verb, a syntactic constraint which inhibits the possibility of antepenultimate stress.

We see, then, that the three-syllable rule invoked by Gartner as a characteristic trait of Rhaeto-Romance in general, rather than defining it may serve to mark an isogloss within it. (See Battisti 1931: 184, for a characteristically vehement statement of this view. Battisti goes further, in that he points out that while the loss of proparoxytones, *pace* Gartner, does not characterize Rhaeto-Romance as a whole, only its Romansh portion, this development is shared outside Rhaeto-Romance by a number of unambiguously Italian dialects, among them those of the Piedmont, Lombardy, the Emilia, and Trento.)

Here, as everywhere else, it is important to distinguish between the diachronic process and the present-day structure of the language in which this process may have once occurred. In Surselvan, for example, the loss of proparoxytones was general, and rules (a) and (b) may be said to have conspired to eliminate cases of antepenultimate stress: but the present-day language has systematic antepenultimate stress in several well-defined contexts (Tekavčić 1974: 379 fn.), among them the following:

1 borrowed feminine nouns in final {-ica}: /'fizika/, etc.;
2 2nd and 3rd person forms of the present subjunctive: /'kontiəs/, etc.;
3 2nd person forms of the imperfect subjunctive: /kan'taviəs/, etc.;
4 2nd person forms of the imperfect conditional: /kan'tasiəs/, etc.

It is also important to distinguish between the diachronic process which is reflected in a grammaticalized and now unmotivated residue, on the one hand, and the totally productive and regular synchronic process which has the same predictable and generally non-distinctive results in the currently spoken language, on the other. For example, Surselvan has a [ə] ~ [*null*] alternation in a large number of phonetically specifiable words like [ʝuvən] 'young (m.sg.)' vs. [ʝuvna] 'young (f.sg.)' exactly comparable to the English alternation in pairs like *possible* ~ *possibly*. In many cases, the fleeting [ə] is the reflex of an inherited vowel, and we have a process which seems to mirror the diachronic process (a), yet in a synchronic analysis, it is probably justifiable to posit underlying zero, with the quality and appearance of the fleeting [ə] predicted by a rule very similar, if not absolutely identical, to the rule we have in English: adjectival stems in final C + sonorant insert [ə] (or syllabify the sonorant) unless the stem is followed by a vowel (see Leonard 1972: 64). The contrast between synchronically motivated rules and diachronic residues of similar processes in past stages of the language is particularly clear in the stress-conditioned vocalic alternations of verb stems, to which we address ourselves next.

Unstressed vowels in initial syllables are generally retained in all Rhaeto-Romance dialects although undergoing a number of reductions: typically, diphthongs become monophthongs, and mid vowels lose their markedness by becoming either high or low (Iliescu 1972: 48–53; Elwert 1943: 58–63; Lutta 1923; 126–35; Huonder 1901: 526). Here

Table 1.9 Stressed-conditioned vowel alternations in Surselvan

Type	Example	Total number	Usual source
ε ~ i	frɛc 'bear fruit'	133	*i, *u
o ~ u	port 'carry'	67	*ɔ
ro ~ ər	lahroɲ 'laugh'	41	*əR/____ɲ
uə ~ u	kuər 'run'	35	*o
ej ~ ə	tʃejn 'dine'	35	*e
o ~ ə	klom 'call'	24	*a/____m
o ~ i	akumpoɲ 'accompany'	18	*a/____ɲ
re ~ ər	fred 'smell'	17	?
aw ~ u	lawd 'praise'	16	*aw
aw ~ ə	sawlt 'jump'	15	*aw, *al
a ~ i	caɹ 'defecate'	13	*a/____Ci
ja ~ ə	Spjard 'lose'	13	*ε
ra ~ ər	brah 'work hard'	13	?
rε ~ ər	krɛʃ 'grow'	8	*Rε

again, we are dealing with a kind of alternation which is nearly universal in the synchronic phonology of stress languages (see Haiman 1972), but which has become conventionalized in a number of Romance languages, among them – although in varying degrees – the Rhaeto-Romance dialects. For example, when Huonder (1901: 518) or Kamprath (1985) reports that in Surselvan or Surmeiran, the seven-vowel system of stressed syllables reduces to /i, ə, u/ in unstressed syllables in general, it is clear we are dealing with a productive set of alternations which we could expect to find in almost any stress language, and which are of typological rather than historical interest. A partially frozen and no longer productive residue of this potentially universal and phonetically motivated process is the alternation of vowel quality in verb stems which typically lose stress in the first- and second-person plural of the indicative. (Notably, this is not the case in the Surmeiran dialect of Bravuogn, which Kamprath describes, where the first-person plural of the present indicative is rhizotonic: /'pεvlən/ 'we feed', but /pəv'leks/ 'you all feed' (see Lutta 1923: 326; Kamprath p.c.): the non-stressed 1st plural desinence here, as in some Lombard dialects, probably derives from HOMO (see Rohlfs 1968: 252–3).)

Surselvan has the greatest number of these alternation types. The data in table 1.9 are derived entirely from Tekavčić's thorough taxonomy (1974: 453–75, but see also Huonder 1901: 546–7). The stressed form is given first under 'type', and the verb stem is given in the root form. We can recognize in some of these alternations stages of the diachronic progressions already treated above. For example, the change *i* > ε is limited to stressed syllables, and forms like [fricejn] 'we procure' reflect a stage in the development of FRUCT-. Similar is the change $a > o/\_\_\_m$, so that the unstressed stem in [akumpaɲejs] 'you all accompany' again reflects an etymologically prior form. On the other hand, in the reduction of [ludejn] 'we praise', it is clearly the stressed root [lawd] which reflects the inherited stem. The general pattern of alternations is compatible with the originally phonetically motivated principle that the vowel inventory in unstressed syllables be diminished relative to the inventory in stressed syllables, and that those unstressed vowels be relatively unmarked. Thus, there are no diphthongs, no /o/, and no /e/, only the set /i, ə, u/ in unstressed syllables.

Surselvan also has several dozen bisyllabic verb stems which undergo stress-conditioned alternation in both syllables. The most productive class (with twenty-eight members) exhibits the alternation [Cə'Cu] ~ [CuCə -'], as in /Skar'vun/ ~ /Skurvan -'/ 'blacken'. Diachronically, [Cə'Cu] may have arisen via dissimilation (Lutta 1923: 135) from *[Cu'Cu], as in the nominal stems COLORE > /kəlor/ 'colour', RUMORE > /rəmor/ 'murmur'. Alternatively, */ə/ may have become /u/ in the neighbourhood of a labial consonant (Huonder 1901: 526), as in MALEDICERE > /Smuldi/ 'curse', INFANTE > /ufawn/ 'child' (Tavetsch dialect only).

Admitting a synchronic rule of palatalization and raising of unstressed /ə/ to /i/ before /ɲ/, we may generalize two alternations: first, the class of alternations $o \sim i$ may be assimilated to the class of alternations $o \sim ə$ for monosyllabic verbs; and second, the class of bisyllabic verbs which exhibit the alternation [Cə'Cu] ~ [CuCi -] (including /mər'muɲ/ ~ /murmiɲ -/ 'murmur') may be assimilated to the most productive class.

The cases of apparent metathesis , where [Ro], [Ra], or [Rɛ] seem to alternate with [əR], may be reducible to a basic vowel ~ zero alternation, with the independently motivated rule of sonorant syllabification applying quite generally, as in [ɟuvən]:

$$\emptyset \rightarrow ə/C\_\_\_R \ \$$$

(see Leonard 1972: 64)

We have seen that such a rule is productive in Surselvan, and an exactly analogous rule is reported for Surmeiran (Lutta 1923: 121) and for Ladin (Elwert 1943: 146), where we observe the alternation [kree] 'believes' vs. [kərdoŋ] 'we believe'.

Whatever the regularities we may extract from these and other correspondences, however, these are now lexically, rather than phonetically conditioned alternations. We note, first, that the alternations, and the verb stems which participate in them, differ even among the

Table 1.10 Stress-conditioned vowel alternations in Surmeiran

Type	Example		Probable (Vulgar Latin) source
e ~ ə	bev	'drink'	*e
	neʃ	'be born'	*a
	redʒɹ	'saw'	*ɛ
o ~ u	romp	'break'	*ɔ
	kor	'run'	*o
e ~ i	ʃpec	'wait'	*ɛ
ej ~ i	salejd	'greet'	*u
	marejd	'marry'	*i
o ~ ə	solt	'dance'	*al/____C
	klom	'call'	*a/____m
aj ~ ə	pajns	'think'	*ɛ/____n
ej ~ ə	pejs	'weigh'	*e

Romansh dialects. Thus, the most common alternations in Surmeiran are shown in table 1.10 (culled from Thöni 1969, a pedagogical grammar; as with the Surselvan examples, the types are presented in roughly decreasing order of frequency, although we lack an exhaustive enumeration). Of the handful of bisyllabic alternation patterns, the only one with more than a single common example is [Cə'Co] ~ [CuCə -], as in the stems /kə'noʃ/ 'know, be acquainted with', /sə'vot/ 'fetch in', and /Skə'zoːl/ 'skate'.

In Surmeiran again, the unstressed vowel seems to reflect an earlier stage in the development of the stressed vowel. This is particularly true in the standard orthography, where /ə/ is usually spelled {a}. Nevertheless, it is impossible (in a synchronic description) to posit the unstressed vowel as the basic one, since no consistent predictions are possible. For example, corresponding to the four unstressed stems [kərɹ] 'load', [rədʒɹ] 'saw', [fən] 'hay', and [kləm] 'call' (occurring with the 1st plural stressed present indicative desinence -['aɲ]), we find the following diverse forms in the 3rd singular: [karɹ-a] (no alternation), [redʒɹ-a] ([e] ~ [ə] alternation), [fən-ɛʃ-a] (use of the *-isc- augment to avoid stress alternation), and [klom-a] ([o] ~ [ə] alternation).

To the extent that predictability is possible, it is clear that the stressed form must be taken as basic. Given the stressed form, and some information about the etymological origin of the verb form in question, the following predictions are frequently correct.

If the stressed syllabic nucleus is

(a) [i, a, u], the unstressed vowel will be 'the same' (granting that [ə] is the unstressed equivalent of /a/);

(b) [aj], the unstressed vowel will be [ə];

Table 1.11 Stress-conditioned vowel alternations in Puter

Type	Example		Probable source
ɛ ~ ə	lɛv	'wash'	*a
	bɛv	'drink'	*e
	sɛnt	'feel'	*ɛ
ɔ ~ u	pɔrt	'carry'	*ɔ
o ~ u	od	'hear'	*aw/____C
	sot	'dance'	*al/____C
uə ~ u	muəs	'show'	*o
ɛ ~ *null*	tʃɛn	'dine'	*e
	mɛn	'lead'	*ɛ
ɛ ~ i	mɛr	'look'	*i

(c) [e], the unstressed vowel will be:
    (i) [ə] if the source was a low vowel;
    (ii) [i] if the source was a high vowel;
(d) [o], the unstressed vowel will be:
    (i) [u] if the source was a mid vowel;
    (ii) [ə] if the source was a low vowel;
(e) [ej], the unstressed vowel will be:
    (i) [i] if the source was a high vowel;
    (ii) [ə] if the source was a mid vowel;
    (iii) Zero if the source was null.

The patterns in the Engadine dialects are almost but not quite identical to each other. In each, there is a perceptible falling off in the productivity of the vocalic alternations, probably as the outcome of levelling. The Puter alternations shown in table 1.11, again in probable order of declining frequency, are culled from Scheitlin (1962), and the following examples from Vallader are culled from Arquint's (1964) pedagogical grammar of that dialect.

It is evident that these alternations, however productive they may once have been, are undergoing various kinds of levelling. As we proceed to Ladin, we encounter only a handful of them (see table 1.13, based on Elwert 1943: *passim*): and Gardena *pro-* ~ *purv-* 'try', *raʒun-* ~ *ruʒn-* 'talk'. Finally, in Friulian, there seem to be very few: *wa* ~ *u*, as in *dwar-* ~ *durm-* 'sleep'; and *we* ~ *o*, as in *pwes-* ~ *pod-* 'be able'. (Recall that /wa/ is the alternant of /we/ before tautosyllabic /r/. Both derive from VL *ɔ.)

The most thoroughgoing levelling process, at least in the Romansh dialects, is the general adaptation of the originally inchoative enlargement -ISC-, which follows the verb stem and takes stress in those persons and numbers where the personal desinence does not bear stress.

Table 1.12 Stress-conditioned vowel alternations in Vallader

Type	Example		Probable source
uə ~ u	kuər	'run'	*o
oː ~ o	kroːd	'fall'	*o
oː ~ u	moːr	'die'	*ɔ
o ~ u	dorm	'sleep'	*ɔ, *aw
o ~ ə	kumond	'order'	*a/___nC
ej ~ *null*	ʤhejl	'freeze'	*e
ej ~ ə	rejzɟ	'saw'	*ɛ
aj ~ a	bajv	'drink'	*e
aj ~ ə	ajntr	'enter'	*ɛ
aj ~ *null*	tʃajn	'dine'	*ɛ
aj ~ i	s'impajs	'think'	*ɛn/___C
a ~ *null*	kusaʎ	'advise'	*e
ɛ ~ *null*	fəvɛl	'speak'	*ɛ, o
i ~ *null*	tir	'drag'	*null*

Table 1.13 Stress-conditioned vowel alternations in Fassa

Type	Example		Probable source
e ~ a	lev	'wash'	*a
ej ~ e	bejv	'drink'	*e
ow ~ u	dowr	'use'	*ɔ
ej ~ i	pejs	'think'	*ɛn
aə ~ u	laər	'work'	*aə
e ~ o	mev	'move'	*o

Tekavčić (1974: 475n.) reports that there are now slightly more verbs in Surselvan with this enlargement than are without it (1,180 to 1,166), and explicitly accounts for this generalization in functional terms as a means of avoiding mobile stress and the resulting alternations of vowel quality (Tekavčić 1974: 477; see also Zamboni 1982–3 for a thorough review and bibliography).

1.2.3 The evolution of consonants

At least three features of the consonantal system are cited as distinguishing features of Rhaeto-Romance as a whole. These are

(a) the common *retention* of word-initial /C + l/ clusters;
(b) the common *innovation* of the palatalizing of velars before inherited /a/;
(c) the common *retention* of word-final /s/ in noun and verb inflection.

Each of these unites Rhaeto-Romance with Gallo-Romance and various conservative northern Italian dialects, while separating these dialects from standard Italian and dialects of central and southern Italy. To these we could add the following:

(d) the common *innovation* of leniting intervocalic stops.

But this feature, which is no more or less peculiar to Rhaeto-Romance than the first three (it defines western Romance, including the northern Italian dialects above the La Spezia–Rimini isogloss; see Rohlfs 1971: 44, 246), is – quite correctly – never cited as a Rhaeto-Romance feature.

Concerning the retention of /C + l/ clusters, there is little that need be said. Even if retention were general throughout Rhaeto-Romance and nowhere beyond, common retentions count for little in establishing close genetic relationships. But in any case, retention of the cluster unites some Rhaeto-Romance dialects with non-Rhaeto-Romance languages, while separating them from other Rhaeto-Romance dialects.

Word-initially, all Rhaeto-Romance dialects are consistent in the retention of /l/, with the very late exceptions of the neighbouring Ladin dialects of Fassa and Moena. In the latter dialects, the palatalization of /l/, on the model of Venetian (rather than of Italian; see Repetti and Tuttle 1987: 82, n. 34) may have taken place as recently as 1900 (see *AIS*: 889; Elwert 1943: 70–1; Heilmann 1955: 119–24): CLAVE > common RR /klaf/, but Fassa /kjef/, Moena /kjaw/ 'key'. In the three Ladin dialects of Gardena, Badia, and Livinallongo, initial *kl > /tl/ (see Gartner 1879: 63; Heilmann 1955: 124).

It would seem, then, that the common retention of inherited /Cl/ is certainly one of the most consistent isoglosses separating Rhaeto-Romance from other dialects of the Italian peninsula and southern Switzerland. But this criterion yields different groupings, depending on the time selected for comparison. If we take the languages spoken today as our comparanda, we will have to regard standard French as Rhaeto-Romance, and the Fassa and Moena dialects as non-Rhaeto-Romance. On the other hand, if we compare the languages spoken around AD 1400, most of the northern Italian dialects are – or 'were' – Rhaeto-Romance. Battisti (1931: 144) has argued that the retention of word-initial /kl/ and /pl/ was also characteristic of Venetian until the fourteenth century, citing Ascoli (1873: 460). (Compare also Rohlfs 1949: I; 287.) If so, either Rhaeto-Romance needs to be redefined to include Venetian, or it needs to be recognized as a language which came into existence later than 1400. Battisti also claimed (1931: 130, 144) that the retention of /C + l/ clusters up to the present time was characteristic of all the dialects of eastern Lombardy, including Lago di Garda, Val Vestino, Val Camonica, and

Bormio. Again, for concurrent findings, see Ettmayer (1902: 657). Moreover, Rohlfs (1966: 240) reports an area of /C + l/ conservatism in the Abruzzo territory, well south of the La Spezia–Rimini line.

Admittedly, modern Venetian has [Cj], and the Cl/Cj isogloss is used by Luedtke (1957: 122) to separate Venetian from Friulian. But if relatively modern developments are to be included, then the same isogloss which separates Friulian from Venetian must also separate conservative Ladin from Fassa and Moena. The *Cl/Cj* isogloss then defined 'Rhaeto-Romance' as an entity which existed between 1400 and 1900: since its alleged component dialects had split apart some nine hundred years before diverging in this way from Venetian, the isogloss seems entirely fortuitous.

Word-internally (intervocalically), the Cl cluster was reduced, except in Nonsberg, Gardena and Badia, to /(l)j/ (*AIS* 103, 360; Battisti 1908: 201): VETULU > Gardena /uədl/, Badiot /vɛdl/ 'old', common RR /vɛʎ/; SOLICULU > Gardena /suradl/, Badiot /soredl/, common RR /suleʎ/; ECCLESIA > Gardena /dlieʒa/, Badiot /dliʒi/; OCULU > Gardena /wɛdl/, Badiot /ødl/, Nonsberg /ɔːkjel/; SPECULU > Gardena /Spiədl/. The young Battisti (1908: 6) drew attention to the extraordinary conservatism of the Nonsberg dialect in retaining intervocalic -C*l*-, and called this trait the most important attestation of the Ladinity of that dialect. (Compare the less conservative Fassan, where intervocalic C + *l* clusters are reduced to /j/: SOLICULU > /soreje/ 'sun', SPECULU > /spjeje/ 'mirror'. Or compare Friulian, where intervocalic C + l is retained before a stressed vowel, and reduced to /l/ before an unstressed vowel: /soreli/ 'sun' , but /sore'gla/ 'to sun-dry', /spjeli/ 'mirror', but /spje'gla/ 'to mirror'.)

A very detailed description of the evolution of C + l clusters has been recently given by Repetti and Tuttle (1987).

1.2.3.1 Palatalizations in Rhaeto-Romance

One of the notable features of the common consonantal system of Rhaeto-Romance, which seems to distinguish it most sharply from that of Sardinian (and no other modern Romance language!), is the existence of a fully developed series of palatal consonants /c, ɟ, tʃ, dʒ, ʃ, ʒ, ʎ, ɲ/. Although some of these sounds may have had common diachronic origins (for example, /ʃ/), others did not, and the generality of some processes which created this inventory (for example, the velar palatalizations), and of subsequent mergers which subsequently reduced it (for example, that of palatal stops and affricates), define clear isoglosses which separate the Rhaeto-Romance dialects from each other. A comparison of northern Italian and Rhaeto-Romance systems of palatal affricates and sibilants in given in Tuttle 1986.

(a) The palatalization of velars before /a/

The palatalization of inherited *k goes hand in hand with the change *$kw > k$, a fact which has led some scholars to posit a purely functional push-chain motivation for this development (see Rizzolatti 1981: 35). But a phonetic motivation, specifically a fronting of *a to *$æ$, is more commonly cited as the impetus for this change.

The change which led from Lat. CANE to RR /can/, probably via intermediate *[kæn] (see Schuerr 1938: 19; Rohlfs 1972: 125; Leonard 1972: 71) is almost certainly not the first Rhaeto-Romance palatalization; but in it we have a feature which has served as the 'signature' of Rhaeto-Romance since the pioneering work of Schneller in 1870. There is, however, some evidence to support Battisti's contention that the common process $k > c$/____a occurred in the different Rhaeto-Romance dialects at different times (Battisti 1931: 152), beginning with Friulian, accomplished in Romansh by ca 1500 (and possibly not even in all of Romansh), and occurring in Ladin even later than this. This evidence is a major isogloss separating Surselvan and Sutselvan (Western Romansh) from all the other Rhaeto-Romance dialects.

Originally, the palatalization may have occurred only before stressed /a/ (Meyer-Luebke 1899: I; 409; Huonder 1901: 454; Luzi 1904: 802; Lutta 1923: 149–52), and this is the state of affairs in 'western Romansh', or Surselvan, Sutselvan, and some of Surmeiran (thus, for example, the village of Cunter in Oberhalbstein; see Leonard 1972: 72) today. In the other Rhaeto-Romance dialects, however, it occurred before unstressed /a/ as well:

	Source	*Eastern Rhaeto-Romance*	*Western Romansh*
	CANE	can	can
	CAPUT	caw	caw
but:			
	CADENA	cadejna	kadejna
	CABALLU	cavaʎ	kavaʎ
	VACCA	vaca	vaka

This may suggest that the process took place last where it was most restricted. It should be noted, however, that scholars do not entirely agree on what the domain of the original rule of palatalization may have been. Against Meyer-Luebke, Huonder, Luzi, and Lutta, Gartner (1883: 68; 1910: 191–4) maintained that palatalization originally occurred before both stressed and unstressed /a/, and that Western Romansh /k/ before unstressed /a/ was the result of a later (possibly Latin-influenced) restoration. In favour of Gartner's position (which was known to, and explicitly repudiated, by both Luzi and Lutta), is the clear evidence from at least one Sutselvan dialect, that of Ems, where the velar /k/ was restored before both stressed and unstressed /a/ in what Luzi himself admitted to be a 'secondary development' (Luzi 1904: 802). Here was a clear case of restoration observed, although the motivation for it was perhaps unclear. Further evidence that the western Romansh forms may be artificial restorations of some kind is provided by forms like /kawsa/ 'matter', which have already come up in connection with our discussion of the development of /aw/. In Rhaeto-Romance, as in French, the palatalization of velars before /a/ was a relatively early process, antedating the monophthongization of /aw/ to /o/ (see Meyer-Luebke 1899: I; 409): thus, French /ʃoz/, common RR /cosa/ < CAUSA. Surselvan /kawsa/ then, represents the undoing of not one but two processes which had to occur in a certain order:

(a) palatalization;
(b) monophthongization.

That this kind of 'unravelling' of historical processes occurred by natural means is much less likely than that a Latin doublet of the native form was simply borrowed.

The different degrees of generalization of velar palatalization suggest that the Italian Rhaeto-Romance dialects may have undergone the change relatively early. On the other hand, an argument has been made by Anton Grad (1969) that the Italian Rhaeto-Romance dialects underwent the change relatively late. Grad cites Slovenian borrowings from Friulian that he confidently dates no earlier than the twelfth century, and in which there is no sign of any palatalization. (But the borrowings could have been from Venetian.)

Finally, it is worth noting that at least one scholar (Leonard 1972: 72) believes that velar palatalization before */a/ (that touchstone of Rhaeto-Romance) in Surselvan – that arch-conservative Rhaeto-Romance dialect – was a borrowed feature there. This, it seems to us, is extremely unlikely, particularly given Surselvan paradigmatic alternations like ['ɹolda] < GAUDET 'enjoys' vs. [gal'dɛr] < GAUDERE 'to enjoy' (Huonder 1901: 467).

Much more problematic is accounting for the spread of palatalization to unstressed syllables (the majority view), or its restriction to stressed syllables (Gartner's view). In deciding between Gartner and the majority view, our problems are of a different sort. If we accept Gartner's opinion that velar palatalization occurred before all inherited */a/, and assume that the change was phonetically motivated, then we must assume that unstressed */a/ was still phonetically a front vowel at the time the shift occurred. In view of the widespread reduction of unstressed /a/ to [ə] in the modern dialects, this is perhaps typologically implausible: but it is by no means the only typological implausibility which we are called upon to believe. Recall that final unstressed -UM > -*u (> *y?) was supposedly an umlauting environment throughout Romansh (see Luedtke 1965) before it vanished. That is, there are (at least) two postulated changes which assume an unattested stage in the development of Rhaeto-Romance where the inventory of unstressed vowels was larger than it now seems to be. So we cannot reject Gartner out of hand. Nevertheless, the existence of pairs like [ɟolda] ~ [galdɛr] is as much an embarrassment to Gartner as to Leonard. If the velar stop is a restoration, why is it sensitive to stress?

Conversely, the majority view requires us to assume an extension of the original velar palatalization, which may have been either phonetically motivated, or analogical. If phonetically motivated, we have to make the same assumptions as we do for Gartner. If analogical, we have to assume a sensitivity to etymological origins (only [ə] derived from */a/ caused palatalization) which seems incredible in the absence of alternations. The least implausible reconstruction is that of the majority view: phonetically motivated palatalization of velars in stressed syllables, followed by phonetically motivated palatalization in unstressed syllables, both occurring before the neutralization of unstressed */a/ to [ə].

(b) The palatalization of velars before front vowels

Before front vowels, /k, g/ palatalized to /tʃ, dʒ/ throughout Rhaeto-Romance (and throughout all Romance, with the present exception of Sardinian). In modern Romansh, in some Ladin dialects, and in some Friulian dialects, the outcome of this palatalization is still phonetically distinct from that of velar palatalization before /a/: CERCARE > (Vallader) /tʃɛrca(r)/ 'look for'; palatalization has proceeded further before /i, ɛ, e/ than before inherited /a/.

Along the Friulian perimeter, the phonemic opposition between /c/ and /tʃ/ has been lost (Bender *et al.* 1952; Francescato 1966: 47) for both voiceless and voiced palatals: thus, Iliescu (1972: *passim*) records (apparently) free phonetic variation between [(d)ʒ] and [ɟ] for reflexes of velar before inherited /a/, and consistent [ʒ] for reflexes of the velar stop before front vowels: GATTU > [dʒat] ~ [ɟat] 'cat', MANDUCARE >

[maŋʒa] 'eat', GENTE > [ʒent] 'people'.

Whether or not the phonemic contrast between /kj/ and /tʃ/ is lost, the inherited contrast between *ka and *ke is always maintained in Friulian. Francescato (1966: 49) points out that in exactly the same areas where *ka > kja > tʃa, *ke > tʃe > se ~ the.

Elwert consistently retains different spellings for original /c/ and /tʃ/ in his phonetic transcriptions of Fassa Ladin, although his practice is to be consistent only before inherited front vowels. Before inherited /a/, he fluctuates between both spellings, and we encounter CANTARE > [tʃanta] 'sing', CANTO > [cant(e)] 'I sing', CANE > [tʃaŋ], CARU > [cɛr] 'dear', PECCATU > [petʃa] 'sorry', and CAPUT > [cef] 'head'. Both Politzer (1967) and Plangg (1973), in their phonemic analyses of two Ladin dialects, maintain the /c/ ~ /tʃ/ distinction, which may still exist, but is clearly threatened by interference from Italian.

(c) Later palatalizations

The first palatalization was followed by a number of processes affecting vowels which created other palatalizing contexts. Among these, we must include the pan-Rhaeto-Romance fronting of /a/ to *[æ], which led to the defining Rhaeto-Romance palatalization, and at least two other changes which are not shared throughout Rhaeto-Romance:

(a) the fronting of /u/ (< Lat. *uː*);
(b) the transition of the inherited neuter singular -U (< Lat. *-um*) to some vowel which could induce palatalization of the preceding consonant, and umlaut a preceding stressed vowel.

(It should be noted that these sounds were distinct in Vulgar Latin, and so the two changes cannot be attributed to the same development.)

The Swiss dialects agree on palatalization of velars to palatal stops before reflexes of VL /u/. It may be observed from the two examples below, that although the phonetic outcome of inherited /i/ and inherited /u/ may have been virtually identical in some dialects, the palatalization that they induced was different, *prima facie* evidence that the fronting of /u/ followed the first palatalization:

Source	Surselvan	Surmeiran	Puter	Vallader	Gloss
CENTU	tʃiən	tʃjent	tʃiːənt	tʃient	'hundred'
CULU	cil	cikl	cyl	cyl	'arse'

The dialects differed in their response to palatalizing -U. In Surselvan, palatalization occurred only if the preceding vowel was also a front vowel, while in the other dialects, palatalization occurred irrespective of the nature of the preceding vowel:

Source	Surselvan	Sutselvan	Surmeiran	Puter	Vallader	Gloss
AMICU	amic	amic	ami	amiç	ami	'friend'
LACU	lak	lec	lec	lɛj	laj	'lake'

In most of Surmeiran (the example in the chart above is from the dialect spoken in the single village of Stalla), and in the Engadine dialects, /c/ in final position was lenited to /j/ some time after the sixteenth century, when the orthography of old Puter and Vallader texts still has {ch}, as in {leich} 'lake', {amich} 'friend', and {föch} 'fire' (see Lutta: 180–1).

The development of the inherited cluster /kt/ split the Romance dialects, among them those of Rhaeto-Romance, into two major areas: in Surselvan, Sutselvan, and (most of) Surmeiran (as in Lombard, Piedmontese, French, Spanish), the result was some palatal or affricate (/ts/, /tʃ/, /c/). In the Italian Rhaeto-Romance dialects (as indeed in standard Italian), we encounter only /t/. In the Engadine dialects of Romansh, geographically in a transitional area – but only if the unity of Rhaeto-Romance is assumed – we encounter mainly /t/, with a handful of words (more in Puter than in Vallader) exhibiting /c/, (see Lutta 1923: 205–9). Thus, for example, FACTU > /fac/ ~ /fats/ ~ /fatʃ/ (Surselvan, Surmeiran, Sutselvan), or /fat/ (all other dialects) 'fact'.

Common to much of the Rhaeto-Romance area were two processes which provided sources for the new phoneme /ʃ/. The first palatalized /s/ before inherited /i/; this change is attested outside Rhaeto-Romance throughout Tuscany (Rohlfs 1949: I, 280; 1966: 224). The second change palatalized /s/ before any consonant (Luzi 1904: 804–6; Lutta 1923: 164; Gartner 1879: 60; Elwert 1943: 69; Iliescu 1972: 58). The latter change is shared throughout Rhaeto-Romance with the exception of Nonsberg, Moena, and some dialects of Friulian; and it is shared outside Rhaeto-Romance in the Ticino, Piedmont, northern Lombardy, and the Romagnol region, as well as various regions of central and southern Italy (Rohlfs 1949: I, 313–14; 1966: 257). Thus PASTA > most RR (and Ticino) /paʃta/, Italian (and some Friulian) /pasta/ (*AIS*: 236). It should be noted that /ʃ/ became recognizably phonologized only as the conditioning environment for the first rule above became obscured.

Common again to all of the Rhaeto-Romance area was the creation of the palatal nasal /ɲ/, which derived from two sources, /gn/ and /n + i/, and the palatal liquid /ʎ/, deriving from /l + i/ and /i + l/.

1.2.3.2 *Intervocalic lenition*

As in Gallo-Romance languages and northern Italian dialects, all intervocalic stops were affected by two lenition processes in Rhaeto-

Table 1.14 Lenition, apocope, and strengthening of *p, b, d,*

	PIPERE	LUPU	DEBE(T)	*VIDERE	VIDIT
1 lenition	*pebər	*lobo	—	*veder	*vede
2 lenition	*pevər	*lovo	*deve	*ve(ðə)r	*veðe
3 apocope	—	*lov	*dev	—	*ved
4 strengthening	—	*loːf	deːf	—	vejt

Romance. First, all voiceless stops became voiced. Then, voiced intervocalic stops were further lenited, in some cases disappearing altogether. Following on from these processes was the apocope of final unstressed vowels.

Preceding apocope of the final syllable (recall that all unstressed final vowels but /a/ are subject to deletion in the history of Rhaeto-Romance), the voiced stop lenited further, in some cases disappearing altogether. But following apocope, the lenited stop was now word-final, and it was devoiced. Table 1.14 shows the idealized histories of the words for 'pepper' and 'wolf' (from Friulian), and 'must (3sg.)', 'to see', and 'sees' (from Fassan). The word for 'pepper' is thus in most of Rhaeto-Romance, (see Lutta 1923: 173; Elwert 1943: 72; Iliescu 1972: 64); the paradigm for the verb 'see' is common to Romansh and Ladin (see Lutta 1923: 182; Elwert: 74–5. Leonard (1972: 87) reconstructs */ð/ as a phoneme in *proto-Rhaeto-Romance on the basis of Surselvan (Tavetsch) [vazajr], Ladin (Moena) [veder]. It seems to us that this may not be necessary, but it is clear that lenition of intervocalic */d/ yielded results different from lenition of intervocalic */t/, and that an intermediate fricative must have had at least a phonetic reality, except in Friulian.)

Essentially, intervocalic /s/ is always lenited to /z/, thus CASA > /caza/ 'house'. Intervocalic /t/ is lenited to /d/ (see Lutta 1923: 175; Elwert 1943: 73; Iliescu 1972: 66), thus ROTA > /roda/ 'wheel', the resulting segment being strengthened back to /t/ after apocope; thus for example VERITATE > (Surmeiran) /vərdet/ 'truth'. The general loss of intervocalic /t/ in the 2nd plural of the verbal paradigm, and in the masculine singular of the perfect participle in -ATU, is morphologically conditioned, and takes place irrespective of whether the deletion site remains intervocalic or becomes word-final, thus CANTATIS > /cantajs/ 'you all sing', CANTATU > /canta(w)/ 'sung'. What appears to be the conservative retention of /t/ in this position in Friulian is probably an analogical extension of the athematic 2nd plural imperative, as in FACITE > /fajt/ (see Benincà and Vanelli 1976). Intervocalic /d/, as we have shown in the examples in table 1.14, lenites to null ultimately, but we must progress through an intermediate *[d], which sound strengthens to /t/ in final position after apocope. Intervocalic /p/, /f/, and /b/ all lenite to /v/; thus the rhyming of [pɛjvər] 'pepper' and [bɛjvər] < BIBERE 'drink', cf. [bevorca] 'fork' < BIFURCA. All /v/, irrespective of its origins, strengthens word-finally to /f/, thus the rhyming of [lo(w)f] 'wolf' and [nɔːf] < NOVU 'new'.

Although resisting the lenition of *C*l*, Ladin dialects are exceptionally leniting in their recent tendency to entirely delete intervocalic post-tonic /v/. This is particularly apparent in the case of the imperfect indicative suffixes:

	Fassa	*Marebbe*	*Badiot*	*Ampezzan*	*Other RR*
*ABAT	ɛ	aa	aa	a	ava
*EBAT	e	oa	oo	e	eva
*IBAT	i	ia	ii	i	iva

Other examples from Ampezzan: /tsiil/ 'civil', /inaante/ 'ahead', /noo/ 'new (m.sg.)', all most probably directly borrowed from Venetian. (The latter is a dialect in which lenition is very widespread.)

The fate of the intervocalic velar stops is complicated by the palatalizations before inherited A (> æ). Inherited /k/ before a back vowel lenites intervocalically to /g/ (Lutta 1923: 178; Elwert 1943: 74–6; Iliescu 1972: 62). The resulting sound did one of the following:

(a) strengthened back to /k/ in final position after apocope: thus INTEGRU > *intregu* > (Ladin) /intriek/ 'entire' (Elwert 1943: 76) is parallel to FOCU > Fassan /fowk/, Friulian /fuːk/ 'fire';
(b) disappeared, particularly after front vowels (we may perhaps infer progressive palatalization as part of the lenition process here). Thus AMICU > Friulian /ami/ 'friend' (but see Puter /amiç/), LACU > Marebban /le/ (but see Fassan /lek/, Friulian /laːk/ 'lake').

Inherited intervocalic /g/ sometimes lenites further to /v/, or null (Elwert 1943: 75–6; Iliescu 1972; 63): AUGUSTU > /avost/, /aost/ 'August'.

Velars before front vowels neutralize the voice distinction intervocalically, all becoming /ʒ/ (Lutta 1923: 177; Elwert 1943: 74), strengthening in final position after apocope to (Romansh) /ʃ/, (Ladin) /tʃ/, as Ladin /letʃ/ < LEGIT 'reads'. The strengthening */ʒ/ > /tʃ/ is suspect, as this process typically involves no more than devoicing. This suggests that primary lenition of palatalized velars is to an intermediate *[dʒ], and that final attested /ʒ/ is the outcome of a secondary lenition. Thus:

	VICINU	*COCERE*	*COQUINA*	*LEGIT*
Palatalization	vitʃinu	kotʃere	kotʃina	ledʒe
Lenition	vidʒinu	kodʒere	kodʒina	ledʒe

Apocope	vidʒin	kodʒer	——	ledʒ
Strengthening	——	——	——	[letʃ]
Lenition	[viʒin]	[keʒer]	[kuʒine]	

With hypothetical reconstructions for all stages but those in square brackets ([viʒin] 'neighbour' in Romansh, [keʒer] 'cook', and [letʃ] 'reads' in Ladin, and [kuʒine] 'kitchen' in Friulian).

While no fixed date can be assigned for primary lenition, it is considered a very early phenomenon in the Romance languages in which it is attested. The process, like the palatalization of velars before /a/, must have occurred before the monophthongization of /aw/, that is, at a time when the second element of this diphthong was acting as a consonant. Note the failure of lenition to occur in cases like /cosa/ < CAUSA 'matter', /uton/ < AUTUMNU 'fall' in many Rhaeto-Romance and northern Italian dialects.

Intervocalic post-tonic *Cl was lenited to /l/ throughout Rhaeto-Romance except, as noted above, in some Ladin dialects like Fodom (where *kl > gl) and Gardenese (where *kl > dl). Thus, for example, Fodom /ogle/, Gardena /úedl/, Friulian /voli/ < OCULU 'eye'. As noted earlier, Friulian exhibits a frozen /gl/ ∼ /l/ alternation between pre- and post-tonic inherited intervocalic *kl. Thus /vóli/ 'eye', but /voglláde/ 'glance'.

Intervocalic *Cr was generally lenited to /r/ throughout Rhaeto-Romance, but there are exceptions in all the dialects. Thus CAPRA > Surselvan /kawra/, Friulian /kja(v)rə/ 'goat'.

A totally unrelated strengthening process in initial position, now no longer productive, converted inherited /j/ to /(d)ʒ/ in the Italian Rhaeto-Romance dialects (Elwert 1943: 70; Gartner 1892: 1879: 64; Iliescu 1972: 58), but to Surselvan /ɟ/, Sutselvan /ɟ/ or /ʒ/ (Luzi 1904: 803), other Romansh /dʒ/ (Lutta 1923: 168): thus JUVENE > (Surselvan) [ɟuvən], (Ladin) [ʒown], (Friulian) [(d)ʒovin] 'young'.

1.2.3.3 Other changes

All final consonants of Classical Latin except /s/ were lost, this change preceding the loss of unstressed final non-low vowels. The retention of final /s/ was morphologically conditioned, and different dialects proceeded in different ways.

First, the retention of final -s in the 2nd singular and the plural of the noun, as we have noted, is a frequently cited signature of Rhaeto-Romance as a whole. Second, many of the Italian Rhaeto-Romance dialects fail to retain final -s of the feminine plural in some nominal syntagms. Finally, Surselvan is unique among the Rhaeto-Romance dialects, and within Romance generally, for retaining final *-s* of the nominative singular of second-declension nouns. These matters will occupy our attention in chapters 2 and 3.

There is a strong and shared tendency to neutralize distinctions of place of articulation for nasals in syllable-final position. In Sutselvan and Puter, syllable-final /n/ assimilates to the preceding vowel (Luzi 1904: 810; Lutta 1923: 196–7); in Ladin, syllable-final /N/ becomes [ŋ] in Fassa (Elwert 1943: 79), [n] in Moena (Heilmann 1955: 159–62), or [m] in Nonsberg (Battisti 1908: 9); while in Friulian, /n/ becomes [ŋ] syllable-finally, and before all consonants other than dentals (Francescato 1966: 16; Iliescu 1968–9: 280). Productive alternations in most Rhaeto-Romance dialects suggest that [ŋ] is still an automatically conditioned variant of /n/ without phonemic status. Thus Gartner (1892), in his grammatical sketch of the transitional dialect of Erto on the western fringes of Friulian, observed paradigmatic alternations between [boŋ] (m.sg.) ~ [bona] (f.sg.) 'good', [uŋ] (m.sg.) ~ [una] (f.sg.) 'one': changes absolutely parallel not only to the alternations in Surmeiran noted in Thöni's pedagogical grammar of that dialect (1969: 41), but generally shared by northern Italian dialects.

A trivial, but characteristic signature of Ampezzan and Lower Gadera Ladin is the change of non-final *l* > *r*, which, however, is shared with non-Rhaeto-Romance Italian dialects such as those of Liguria and Lombardy (see Rohlfs 1966: 306ff.) In Badiot, ILLE > (*v*) ɛl 'he', but ILLA > (*v*) ɛra 'she', PARABOLA > /parora/ 'word', MALATTIA > /maratia/ 'sickness'.

1.2.4 Summary

The shared phonological developments outlined above constitute the best possible evidence for the unity and independence of Rhaeto-Romance. There are several lines which separate Rhaeto-Romance dialects from the other northern Italian dialects (albeit not from Gallo-Romance, or, for that matter, from Sardinian). On the other hand, there is not a single phonological development which is characteristic of all and only the Rhaeto-Romance dialects as a whole.

The situation when we examine morphology is, if anything, even less satisfying, as the morphological cleavages between the various dialects are frequently truly profound. In fact, doing justice to some of the most striking features of 'Rhaeto-Romance' morphology will necessarily entail ignoring most of Rhaeto-Romance to concentrate on a single dialect, as we shall see.

2 Morphology

The morphological features which supposedly help define the Rhaeto-Romance languages include:

(a) -s plural on nouns;
(b) -s 2nd singular desinence on verbs;
(c) non-identity of indicative and imperative 2pl.

In addition, there are morphological features which separate the various Rhaeto-Romance dialects. Up to now, we have been assuming that Ladin and Friulian are distinct, although the evidence for this separation has been primarily geographical. We can, however, point to a number of areal morphological features which distinguish the Ladin group from Friulian, among them:

(a) identity of 3rd singular and 3rd plural in verbal paradigms;
(b) mobile stress on personal desinences which are not adjacent to the verb root.

These criteria define an area which includes not only the dialects spoken in the valleys radiating directly from the Sella massif, but also dialects spoken a considerable distance to the east, in some cases on the western and northwestern fringes of the Friulian-speaking area. Among these are the dialects of Erto (Gartner 1892), and Carnic Friulian as typified in Cedarchis, Paularo, and Lovea (Frau 1984: 123).

Whether or not these and other features provide evidence for the unity of Rhaeto-Romance will be a recurring issue in the following pages. We believe that they do not, sometimes because they are clearly areal rather than genetic features, and sometimes because they are cases of common retention, which demonstrate no more than a common Latin origin.

Ideally, it should be possible to discuss morphology and syntax in the same way as phonology, that is, from both a synchronic and a diachronic perspective. With relatively few exceptions, however, our ability to reconstruct Rhaeto-Romance morphology and syntax is limited, and there exists an enormous gap between Vulgar Latin and our earliest coherent texts. By the time most of the Rhaeto-Romance languages have entered into the light of recorded textual attestation – essentially, no earlier than the fourteenth century – the majority of the morphological distinctions among them have already come into existence. Wherever possible, we will show the changes that we know occurred, particularly in the development of the Romansh and Friulian dialects.

2.1 MORPHOLOGICAL CATEGORIES OF THE VERB

It is convenient (although semantically unmotivated) to distinguish between those categories which are expressed as verbal affixes, and those which are expressed as auxiliary verbs or by means of other periphrastic constructions. There are considerable differences among the dialects here; inasmuch as some categories like the future tense are typically expressed periphrastically in some dialects, synthetically in others, and by a combination of the two in yet others.

2.1.1 Synthetic categories

Verbs in Rhaeto-Romance consist of a root followed by a number of suffixes. Finite verbs consist of the root followed by as many as three non-personal suffixes and one personal desinence. Non-finite verbs consist of the root followed by no more than a single non-personal suffix.

Remnants of the inherited four-conjugation system survive (diminished or elaborated) in only one set of morphemes: those which immediately follow the verb root, whether these are personal desinences or non-personal suffixes. That is, given the basic structure

V + (suffix) + desinence

the same set of desinences may exhibit allomorphy if the suffix is absent, or fail to exhibit allomorphy if the suffix is present.

Usually, only those personal desinences which are immediately adjacent to the root exhibit movable stress (already mentioned in our discussion of stress-conditioned vocalic alternations), where typically the 1st plural and 2nd plural desinences alone are stressed and rob the root of its stress. Generally speaking, personal desinences not immediately adjacent to the verb root are unstressed throughout the paradigm. This suggests a useful division of primary and secondary personal desinences, where the features of adjacency to the verb root, allomorphy, and movable stress are linked as in the chart below:

	Primary	Secondary
Adjacency to verb root	+	−
Conjugational allomorphy	+	−
Movable stress	+	−

By this criterion, a handful of personal desinences are highly marked in exhibiting a mixture of primary and secondary features:

(a) in the Engadine dialects, the present subjunctive personal desinences are adjacent to the verb root but otherwise secondary;

(b) in Fassan Ladin, the imperfect desinences (both indicative and subjunctive) are characterized by movable stress but are otherwise secondary;

(c) in Surmeiran and all dialects to the east of it, future tense personal desinences are secondary in all respects, but are invariably stressed throughout the paradigm.

(d) in modern Friulian (and Old Romansh), the past definite endings are adjacent to the verb stem, exhibit conjugational allomorphy, and nevertheless do not exhibit stress shift, being invariably stressed.

Non-personal suffixes may be divided into two major groups: those which may, and those which may not, co-occur with a personal desinence.

These we may call the *finite* and the *non-finite* suffixes:

Finite	*Non-finite*
augment	infinitive
imperfect	gerund
imperfect subjunctive	perfect participle
future	present participle
past definite	
conditional	

All of these, without exception, exhibit some conjugational allomorphy. (In fact, in the infinitive, one dialect, Surmeiran, has actually elaborated and expanded on the inherited four-conjugational pattern.) Basically, however, the tendency has been to reduce the distinction to a two- or a three-way opposition.

2.1.1.1 The Infinitive

The infinitive is the only form in which all four conjugations are still distinguished in each of the major Rhaeto-Romance dialects. The

Table 2.1 Rhaeto-Romance infinitives

Source	Rhenish	Engadine	Fassa	Gadera	Ampezzan	Friulian
-ARE	-a	-ar	-ar	-e	-a	-a
-ERE	-e	-ajr	-er	-ej	-e	-e
'-ERE	'-Vr	'-Vr	'-Vr	'-e(r)	'-e	'-i
-IRE	-i	-ir	-ir	-i	-i	-i

Table 2.2 Rhaeto-Romance perfect participles

Source	Surselvan	Surmeiran	Puter	Vallader	Fassa	Friulian
-ATU	aw	o	o	a	a	aːt
		eə(/ʃ____)				
-ITU	iw	iə	iw	y	u	uːt
*-ETU	iw	iə	iw	y	u	uːt
-ITU	iw	iə	iw	i	i	iːt

suffixes in all the major dialects with the exception of Surmeiran are
presented in Table 2.1 (here, Rhenish means Surselvan and Sutselvan,
while Engadine, as before, refers to Vallader and Puter). In Surmeiran,
-ARE has had three reflexes: /ar/ after dentals, /er/ after palatal fricatives
and the glide /j/, and /iər/ after the palatal affricates /tʃ, dʒ/; -ERE and -IRE
conflated to /ɛjr/, and '-ERE resulted in /ər/ (see Sonder and Grisch 1970:
Introduction; Thöni 1969: 36).

2.1.1.2 The perfect participle

In the case of the perfect participial endings (at least in some dialects),
three contrasting endings survive, and the inherited second and third
conjugations are identical. Generally, however, there are only two
contrasting forms, corresponding to the inherited first and fourth
conjugations, with the second and third conjugational endings assimilated to either the first or the fourth conjugation, depending on the dialect
in question. Finally, in the personal secondary desinences, all conjugational distinctions are neutralized.

Table 2.2 summarizes the maximally unmarked forms of the perfect
participle endings in the major dialects. In the case of all of these but
Surselvan, the given forms are masculine singular, while in Surselvan,
the cognate form is neuter singular or attributive masculine singular.
(Plural formation for all nominal categories, including derived nominals
like the perfect participle, will be dealt with separately.) All are stressed.
In one respect Surselvan is innovative here, while in another sense it is

immensely conservative. Like Sutselvan, Surmeiran, and Puter, but unlike all the remaining Rhaeto-Romance dialects, it has levelled the inherited distinction between -ETU and -ITU participles, so there is only the contrast between first conjugation /aw/ and all other /iw/. On the other hand, Surselvan endings, by all accounts, reflect an ancient accusative singular or neuter singular form in -U(M), while a contrasting participle in /aw + s/ or /iw + s/ (the present predicative masculine singular), reflects an inherited nominative singular in -(U)s. While there are traces of such a distinction in Sutselvan and the Engadine dialects (inherited -U(M), unlike inherited -(U)s, caused palatalization of the preceding consonant, and umlaut of the preceding vowel), no other Rhaeto-Romance dialect actually preserves final nominative -*s*. We return to this morphological feature, which still links Surselvan with Old French, in the nominal morphology.

Friulian is conservative in another way, maintaining final /t/ (in fact, a devoiced /d/) (see Francescato 1966: 204; Iliescu 1972: 180). This consonant is now lost not only in the other major dialects, but in the transitional West Friulian dialects, including that of Erto (see Gartner 1892: 198). However, the loss may have been comparatively recent. In Old Vallader, at least, we still encounter masculine singular participles {it} 'gone', {vgnüd} 'come' in the 1679 Bible of Vulpius and Dorta, and the modern dialect still has /Stat/ 'been'. Finally, in some of the Ladin dialects, for example that of Gardena, there seem to be a number of irregular verbs which retain final /t/ not only in the masculine singular form of the perfect participle (where it could be interpreted as a devoiced /d/), but also in the feminine forms: /Stat/, /Stata/ 'been', /dat/, /data/ 'given', /ʒit/, /ʒita/ 'gone'. This is phonologically regular only in the case of /fat/ < FACTU: non-alternating /t/ in the other verbs must be attributed to an analogical process (see Kramer 1976: 88–9).

In all Rhaeto-Romance dialects, the /t/ of -ATA (f.sg.) and -ATAS (f.pl.) lenites to /d/; thus, for example, Vallader /cantada/ 'sung (f.sg.)', Friulian /finida/ 'finished (f.sg.)'. In both Ladin and Puter, the first-conjugation theme vowel becomes /ɛ/ before /d/:

Source	Puter	Ladin	(*Vallader*)
-ATU	o	a	a
-ATA	ɛda	ɛda	ada

Puter /o/ may derive from */aw/. On the other hand, the regular development of inherited */a/ to /ɛ/ supports Leonard's (1972) conjecture that a common innovation of *PRR is the fronting of this vowel to something like /æ/.

2.1.1.3 The gerund

The gerund is absent in the spoken form at least of some Ladin dialects, where concurrent activity by the same agent is expressed by an infinitival construction (Elwert 1943: 156, for Fassa; Pizzinini and Plangg 1966: xliii, for Badiot; Appollonio 1930: 54, for Ampezzan). In the dialects which maintain some reflex of -ANDU for the expression of this relationship, only a maximum of two forms survive. First, the Ladin dialects of Gardena and Moena have only a single form: Garden -[aŋ], Moena -[an]. In the remaining dialects, some conjugational allomorphy survives. In Surselvan, the first form derives from -ANDU and is used for all first-conjugation verbs, while the second form seems to derive from II/III -ENDU and is used with all other verbs. In the other dialects, the reflex of -ANDU is used for all verbs but those of the fourth conjugation. The second form, on the other hand, is more likely descended from either IV -IENDU or from a possible offspring *-INDU. In many of the dialects where it survives, the gerund is bookish (the colloquial preference is for a finite clause introduced by a conjunction). Nor is it exclusively a same-subject clause. Where the subject of the gerundive clause is different from that of the main clause, it follows the gerund, and usually translates into a 'since' or 'because' clause. Consider the example from Surmeiran below:

(1) purt-on   ɛl ɛna capɛla n-iʎ   vain-sa bec kunaʃ-iə
     wear-ing he a   hat   not-him have-we not recognize-p.p.
     'Since he was wearing a hat, we didn't recognize him.'

Friulian has a well-developed use of the gerund which is similar to that of standard Italian. It occurs with the auxiliary /Sta/ to mark the durative or progressive aspect, as in /stas tu durmint/ 'Are you asleep?' or /al stave murint/ 'He was dying.' It is used to mark concurrent activity, as in /ɛ vɪɲive kurint/ 'She came running'. Preposed, gerundive clauses generally have the same subject as the main clause. Otherwise, the subject can only be understood as indefinite or impersonal: /ɛsint tart, lu invidarin a bevi/ 'Since it was late, they invited him for a drink'; /kantant, il timp al pase prest/ 'When one sings, time passes rapidly' (see Nazzi Matalon 1977: 143–5).

The following chart recapitulates the occurring forms in the major dialects:

Source	Surselvan	Surmeiran	Puter	Vallader	Gardena	Moena	Friulian
-ANDU	on	on	and	an	ang	an	ant
-ENDU	en	–	–	–	–	–	int
-INDU	–	in	ind	in	–	–	int

2.1.1.4 *The present participle*

The present participle, now distinct from the gerund only in Surselvan and Surmeiran, is (in the unmarked, masculine singular form) phonetically identical with the gerund, and interchangeable with it in marking concurrent activity by the same agent. This interchangeability is nicely illustrated by the following examples. (The first pair is taken from Alig's *Epistolas* in Old Surselvan, published in 1674; the second, from Bifrun's Puter translation of the New Testament, published in 1560; both are anthologized in Ulrich 1882):

Old Surselvan

(2) Scha manen els   suenter schend   'Q'
     so went they after   saying (gerund)
     'So they went after, saying "Q".'

(3) Cun tut tarmettenan sias sururs tier el, Schent   'Q'
     with that sent   his sisters to him saying (participle)
     'With that, they sent his sisters to him, saying "Q".'

Old Puter

(4) sauiãd (gerund) Iesus che füss gnieu la sia hura ...
     knowing   Jesus that was come the his hour
     'Jesus, knowing that his hour had come ...'

                                                    (John 13: 1)

(5) et subbittamang es stô cun l'g aungel üna grand
     and suddenly   is been with the angel a   great
     quantited dals   celestiels exercits, ludant (participle)
     number   of-the heavenly   host   praising
     Dieu e schent ...
     God and saying
     'And suddenly there appeared with the angel a great number of the
        heavenly host, praising God and saying ... '

                                                    (Luke 2: 13)

We have seen only the participial orthography for complements of verbs of perception (e.g. 'I hear them sing-ing'), as in the following examples, also from Alig:

(6) A   cur ca Jesus vaset ella bargient
     and when that Jesus saw   her crying

(7) scha el anflau els   dormint
     as   he found them sleeping

As a relative-clause form without number agreement, the orthographic participle in {-ont} does not contrast with the gerund in {-ond}, as the following examples would seem to indicate (the first from Alig, the second from Wendenzen's (1701) life of Jesus):

(8)   A   schet   ils   vivont   plaids
       and said   the   living (participle) words
(9)   el   perduna a   scadin puccond   Christiaun
       he   pardons to every   sinning (gerund) Christian

There is scattered evidence throughout Rhaeto-Romance that gender is more faithfully copied than is number. While participles do not seem to agree with their heads or their subjects in number, they do seem to agree in gender, as in the Surmeiran examples:

(10)   igl   mattatsch   cantont
       the   boy   singing
(11)   la   matta   cantonta
       the   girl   singing (f.)

Where agreement is marked, only the participial orthography seems possible.

In Friulian, the present participle is more an adjective than a verbal form; yet it exhibits no agreement. Given the adjectival class to which a participle belongs, we only expect plural agreement, but we encounter phrases like /ku li mans scasant/ 'with dangling (=empty) hands'. Arguably, /scasant/ in examples of this sort is a gerund with underlying form /skasand/, the final consonant being regularly devoiced.

2.1.1.5 *Finite non-personal suffixes*

We may divide those suffixes which co-occur with personal desinences into two classes: in the first class are the now almost totally meaningless (but functionally motivated) augments like the reflexes of the inherited inchoative in -ISC-; in the second are the various and familiar reflexes indicating the verbal categories of tense, aspect, and mood.

2.1.1.6 *The augments*

(a) Inherited -ISC- and its descendants

Throughout Rhaeto-Romance, as in French, Italian, and Italian dialects, reflexes of -ISC- are found with fourth-conjugation verbs: Surselvan, Surmeiran, and Puter have /eʃ/, presumably from *-ESC-, while all other dialects continue /iʃ/. In Romansh alone, the augment occurs on a large number of verbs of the first conjugation as well (see Gartner 1883: 128). In Surselvan, Sutselvan, Surmeiran, and Puter, the form of the augment is invariable, thus [gratuleʃ-əl] '(I) congratulate' from /gratula/ 'to congratulate', and [fineʃ-əl] '(I) finish' from /fini/ 'to finish'. Vallader, the only other Romansh dialect, has created *-ESC- > /eʃ/ exclusively for verbs of the first conjugation, thus [gratuleʃ] '(I) congratulate', but [finiʃ] '(I) finish'. Gartner (1883), citing Carigiet, cites only a minuscule number of verbs of the second or third conjugations which have generalized this augment. (One example is /Smaladir/ 'curse', which occurs with the [eʃ] augment in Sutselvan.)

The paradigmatic distribution of the augment is the same as in French and Italian, at least in the present tense of the indicative: it occurs in complementary distribution with the stressed personal desinences and, consequently, those verbs which appear with the augment regularly eliminate stress alternations (and attendant changes of vowel quality) on the invariably unstressed verb stem.

(Two Romansh dialects have gone beyond this. *Surmeiran* has generalized the /eʃ/ suffix for singular *imperatives*, so that in this dialect, there is no stress shift for /eʃ/ verbs in either the indicative or the imperative: /translat-'eʃ-a/ 'translate (sg.)!' vs. /translat-'e/ 'translate (pl.)!'. *Puter* seems to be unique among the Romansh dialects in generalizing the /eʃ/ augment so that it occurs throughout the *subjunctive* paradigm of those verbs which have it (only in the singular and 3rd plural) in the indicative (Scheitlin 1962: 175). Thus the indicative and the subjunctive first persons for /Spɛr/ 'hope':

	Indicative	*Subjunctive*
1st singular	ʃpər-ɛʃ	ʃpər-ɛʃ-a
1st plural	ʃpər-ɛns	ʃpər-ɛʃ-ans

No other dialects have generalized the augment beyond the present tense of the indicative.)

Whether the fixing of mobile stress, an incidental consequence of the generalization of the augment, can be said to explain its occurrence, as a number of scholars have urged (see Rohlfs 1949: II, 285; Tekavčić 1974), is perhaps questionable, since we are then left to account for the fact that it happened only in Romansh. But in fact, something analogous occurred in Badiot and Fassa Ladin, although using different morphological material for its realization.

(b) Badiot /ɛ/, Fassa /e/ < -I-

Following the palatalization of -CA-, Latin verbs in -ILIARE, -ICARE,

-ECARE, and -IGARE tended to lose the consonant before -ARE, thus creating a set of verbs in */ . . . i + are/ (see Zamboni 1982–3, 1983). Alton and Vittur (1968: 43) and Elwert (1943: 144) suggest that in Ladin this was reinterpreted as / . . . + i + are/, with the commonly occurring /i/ no longer perceived as a part of the verb stem. Unlike -ISC-, the 'augment' -I- co-occurs with the stressed infinitival suffix. However, like -ISC-, it is stressed in the present indicative and, in the present indicative, in complementary distribution with the stressed (first and second plural) personal desinences. All Ladin verbs in / . . . + e/ are therefore exempt from stress-conditioned vocalic alternations of the root vowel. Rightly or wrongly, Elwert proposes this consequence as the functional explanation for the existence and distribution of the augment in Ladin. This augment is often indistinguishable from the type reconstructed as an evolution of -IDIO (see Venetian *-ejo*, Italian *-eggio*, for which a similar, functionally motivated explanation has been proposed – (see Rohlfs 1949: II, 285; 1968: 244–5, Zamboni 1980–1).

2.1.1.7 Tense, aspect, and modal categories

(a) The imperfect indicative

The imperfect past-tense suffix continues Lat. -ABA-, -EBA-, and *-IBA-. On the basis of the neutralizations which have occurred, the dialects fall into three major groups. The most conservative are Ladin and Friulian, which retain a three-way contrast, in contradistinction to all the Romansh dialects, which maintain only two conjugations. Vallader and Puter assimilate the II/III conjugation -EBA- to the first conjugation, while Surselvan assimilates it to the fourth. Surmeiran, which seems to maintain a three-way contrast /av/ ~ /ev/ ~ /iv/, has actually innovated in scrambling the membership of verb classes. All verbs whose final consonant is a palatal glide or liquid (like /piʎ/ 'take') have the imperfect suffix /iv/; those whose final consonant is another palatal consonant (like /laʃ/ 'let'), take /ev/; all other first-conjugation verbs take /av/. Otherwise, the basic contrast is between fourth-conjugation /iv/ and, all other, /ev/.

Source	Surselvan	(Surmeiran)	Puter	Vallader	Fassa	Ampezzan	Friulian
-ABA	av	av	ɛv	ev	ɛ	a	av
-EBA	ev	ev	ɛv	ev	e	e	ev
-IBA	ev	iv		iv	iv	i	i	iv

It is likely that in Romansh, the conflation of conjugations resulted from paradigmatic borrowing (analogical levelling) rather than sound change. In Surselvan, the fourth conjugation borrowed its forms from the second/third; in the central dialects, first conjugation borrowed its forms from the same source, probably over the sixteenth and seventeenth centuries (Grisch 1939: 210).

This suffix is invariably stressed except – remarkably – in Fassa, Erto, and in Ampezzan, where following first and second plural personal desinences are stressed. Before such stressed desinences, the imperfect suffixes /ɛ/ and /e/ lose their stress, and in so doing, become [a]: thus, in Fassa, [can'tɛ + a] '(s/he) was singing' contrasts with [canta + 'ane] '(we) were singing', (see Elwert 1943: 149); while in Ampezzan [kar'de + a] '(s/he) believed' contrasts with [karda + 'on] '(we) believed' (see Appollonio 1930: 57–8).

In Badiot, where the deletion of intervocalic /v/ is followed by vowel assimilation and crasis, no stress shift is to be observed:

*a'ma + a >	/ama + a/	[a'maa]	'3sg. loved'
*ama + 'an >	/ama + an/	[a'maan]	'we loved'

(b) The imperfect subjunctive

The imperfect subjunctive continues Lat. -ASS-, -ESS-, or -ISS-. Again, different patterns of conflation allow us to identify three dialect groups. Friulian and Fassan (like Venetian and Italian) are the most conservative, retaining a three-way distinction, while the Romansh dialects, Badiot, Gardenese, and Fodom, continue only two, which differ from each other in exactly the same way as in the imperfect indicative. Surmeiran is regular, and patterns with the Engadine dialects (Grisch 1939: 201):

Source	Surselvan	Other Romansh	Fassa	Badiot	Friulian
-ASS	as	ɛs	as	ɛs	as
-ESS	ɛs	ɛs	es	ɛs	es
-ISS	ɛs	is	is	is	is

Throughout Rhaeto-Romance (again with the exception of Fassan), the imperfect subjunctive is invariably stressed, and followed by secondary personal desinences. In Fassan, the personal desinences of the 1st and 2nd plural rob the imperfect subjunctive of both stress and vowel quality in exactly the same way that they rob the imperfect indicative (Elwert 1943: 153): thus [can'tas + e] 'I would sing', [cantas + 'ane] 'we would sing' (no reduction of unstressed /a/) contrast with [ve'des + e] 'I would see', [vedas + 'ane] 'we would see' (reduction of unstressed /e/ to [a]).

Variation among the Ladin dialects is shown in the following chart (from Kramer 1976). Not one dialect represents a completely regular continuation of the Latin morphological forms. Stress is on the second syllable except where indicated.

Badiot	*Marebban*	*Fodom*	*Fassan*
cantes	cantas	tʃantase	tʃantase
canteses	cantas	tʃantase	tʃantases
cantes	cantas	tʃantasa	tʃantasa
cantesun	cantasun	tʃantonse	tʃantas'ane
canteses	cantases	tʃantejse	tʃantas'ede
cantes	cantas	tʃantasa	tʃantasa

(c) The future

We are confronted here with a major dialect split between Surselvan and Sutselvan, on the one side, and, on the other, all the other Rhaeto-Romance dialects. Throughout the written history of both the westernmost Romansh dialects, the future has never been a verbal suffix, and has always been expressed, as it is in German (or English), by means of an auxiliary verb: /veɲi/ 'come' or /(vu)lejr/ 'want, will'. This auxiliary verb is followed by some preposition and the infinitive. Throughout the written history of all the Italian Rhaeto-Romance dialects, the future has always been expressed, as it is in Italian (or French), by means of an invariably stressed suffix which consists of the infinitive followed by the personal desinences (which are the forms of the present indicative of the verb 'have'). In the Engadine dialects, as in Surmeiran, both futures have coexisted for over a hundred years, naturally with slight differences in meaning. Very roughly, the periphrastic future corresponds to 'be going to', the synthetic future both to 'will' and 'is probably'. (For a thorough survey of the literature and extensive examples from the spoken language, see Ebneter 1973.) These three 'transitional' dialects also exhibit a hybrid 'double future' in which the auxiliary verb /ɲir/ occurs with the synthetic future suffix:

> *Surmeiran*
> (12) ia niro   a   kantar
>   I   come = will = I to sing
>   'I will sing.'
> *Puter*
> (13) e ɲaro   at   deklarer keko py   tart
>   I come = will = I you explain this more late
>   'I will explain this to you later.'

Vallader

(14) lura ɲirana   baɲ eir da bajvər
      then   come = will = we = we   well   too   of   to = drink
      yna butiʎa vin
      a   bottle wine
      'Then we will certainly also drink a bottle of wine.'

The peculiar meaning of the double future is unclear. Thöni dismisses it as simply a colloquial and sub-standard variant of the synthetic future in Surmeiran (1969: 123–4), which is to be avoided – as it makes the learning of Italian and French more difficult(!). It is, in any case, a relatively new phenomenon, and illustrates a process of *double marking* which is amply attested elsewhere both within Rhaeto-Romance and in other languages. We leave a detailed discussion of this process until we survey the development of subject pronoun clitics in chapter 4.

Another hybrid future, apparently confined to Puter (Ebneter 1973: 36ff.; Scheitlin 1962: 81), consisting of

verb stem + ar + ɛj + personal desinences

has a definite meaning of 'uncertainty', neatly illustrated by Ebneter's minimal-contrast pair below:

(15)   Al   piʎaro (*piʎarɛja)   beɲ   yna   tatsa
       You   take = will   certainly   a   cup-of
       kafe   ku   nus
       coffee with us

The ungrammatical form is excluded in the invitation above, Ebneter points out (Ebneter 1973: 36), because it 'would express the unfriendly hope that the chance visitor to whom it was extended would refuse the invitation'. The morphological origins of the -ɛj- enlargement of the 'suppositive' future are not entirely clear. As the personal desinences of the synthetic future in Rhaeto-Romance derive from the present indicative HABEO etc., so the -ɛj- + *personal desinences* of the suppositive future may derive from the present subjunctive. The present subjunctive stem of 'have' is /aj/ in Surselvan, /ɛj/ in Puter, and /aj/ in Vallader (see Friulian /abj/). It is, unfortunately, not clear how Puter /ɛj/, Surselvan /aj/ nor the cognate Engadine /aj/ could have derived from HABEAM etc.

The question arises which of the two 'basic forms' of the future, if any, represents the home-grown Rhaeto-Romance form. Gartner (1883: 118) argued for the priority of the Surselvan and Sutselvan periphrastic form. Noting that the synthetic future was a recent innovation in the Engadine dialects (sixteenth- and seventeenth-century texts exhibit only the periphrastic future with 'want' or 'come'), he claimed that the synthetic future was not colloquial, even at the time he wrote, in any Romansh dialect. It was colloquial, admittedly, in Ladin and Friulian, but this was presumably under heavy Venetian influence. And even in these dialects, a periphrastic future coexists with the synthetic future. For the Gardena dialect, Gartner (1879: 74) was able to report three common futures: the synthetic future, similar to that of standard Italian, the present-as-future, and a periphrastic form, with the auxiliary /ʒi/ 'go'. Gartner was supported in his conjecture by Vellemann (1924: 528), who claimed a recent origin for the synthetic future at least in Puter. One argument in favour of Gartner's conjecture (and, indirectly, in favour of the unity of Rhaeto-Romance), is possibly the behaviour of Friulian. Although written Friulian uses the synthetic future, Iliescu (1972: 175ff.) maintains that in the language spoken by Friulian expatriates in Roumania, the synthetic future is quite rare, and that a periphrastic future with one of the auxiliaries /ave/ 'have', /viɲi/ 'come' or /vole/ 'want' is common in all the dialects she investigated. (But the influence of Roumanian may have been responsible for at least the choice of auxiliary, if not for the periphrastic construction itself; see Iliescu 1972: 228).

Against Gartner, Ebneter (1973) argued at great length and very convincingly that the infinitival future is just as colloquial as the periphrastic future throughout Romansh – and therefore presumably no more artificial. Where the two coexist, they differ subtly in meaning from each other, as well as from the even more popular present-as-future, which is universal throughout Rhaeto-Romance, Italian, and Romance.

In our opinion, the absence of a synthetic future in Surselvan and Sutselvan is evidence against Rhaeto-Romance unity. Where the synthetic future exists, however bookish it may now seem, it seems to be autochthonous. The evidence for this is that the actual forms of the personal desinences in each dialect seem to have undergone the diachronic phonological changes characteristic of these separate dialects.

In the synthetic future, conflation patterns allow us to distinguish two dialect groups. On the one hand, the Engadine dialects and Ladin retain a two-way contrast in the infinitival portion of the future between I–III /ar/ and IV /ir/; on the other, Friulian has /ar/ throughout. A peculiarity of some varieties of Friulian is that fourth conjugation verbs in -ISC-retain (and destress) this augment in the future, thus [part-is-ar-'aj] 'I will leave' (Iliescu 1972: 175).

(d) The past definite

Deriving from the Latin perfect, the past definite survives now only in

Table 2.3 Past definite in Friulian

	-AVI	**-EVI*	*-IVI*
Singular			
1	aj	ej	ij
2	aːs	eːs	iːs
3	a	e	i
Plural			
1	asin	esin	isin
2	asis	esis	isis
3	ar	er	ir

the Engadine dialects and Friulian (although it was attested in Old Surselvan, Old Vallader, and Old Puter also). It is explicitly dismissed by Gartner (1883: 116) as a (bookish) Italianism, but we do not share this view. At least in Friulian, in the small areas where it survives, it is used in colloquial speech.

Francescato (1966) reported different forms of the past definite in various small villages, but the conjugation reported in the grammars (Marchetti 1952: 152; Gregor 1975: 99, Frau 1984: 80) is the form used in the written koine. In table 2.3 is the (relatively widespread) paradigm found in northwestern varieties (e.g. Clauzetto). This paradigm nicely reflects the Vulgar Latin paradigm reconstructed by Rohlfs (1968: 312) for the weak past definite of the majority of Romance languages (CANTAI, CANTASTI, CANTAUT; CANTAIMUS, CANTASTIS, CANTARUNT). In other Friulian dialects, among them that of Pesariis, the /-ar/ of the 3rd plural is generalized to the 1st plural and 2nd plural as well: thus 1pl. /kantarin/, 2pl. /kantaris/.

Iliescu (1972: 173) notes that her expatriate Roumanian subjects used the perfect exclusively. Haiman has failed to encounter or elicit past definites from expatriate subjects in Winnipeg.

In Old Surselvan, Puter, and Vallader, only the third person forms were common, and reflected a parallel kind of structure, inasmuch as tense and person could not be separated (see table 2.4). There were hints of imminent restructuring using the 3rd singular as the basic form: side by side with {schenan} 'they said', {vasenan} 'they saw', {bungianen} 'they watered', {laschanen} 'they let', we encounter {tarmettenan} 'they sent' where we should have expected *{tarmenan}. Exactly parallel forms and hints of possible restructuring are attested in the old Engadine dialects, illustrated here with Puter forms:

Old Puter

3rd singular	et ~ o	et	it
3rd plural	aun	aun	en

Table 2.4 Past definite in Old Surselvan

	-*AVI*	**-EVI*	*IVI*
Singular			
1	a	e	?
2	?	?	?
3	a ~ at	e ~ et	e ~ it
Plural			
1	?	?	?
2	?	?	?
3	anen	enan	?

(Not too much should be made of the orthographic contrast between the various 3rd plural forms, incidentally: it may be that the orthography {au} already represented the sound [ɛ], as is suggested by the apparently free variation between {cumanzaun} and {cumanzên} 'they began'.) Side by side with the regular 3rd plural forms in {-aun}, however, we encounter a handful of forms like {pigliettan} 'they took' and {s'preschentettan} 'they appeared'. It seems that such forms involved a reinterpretation of the original 3rd singular along the lines suggested by Watkins (1962):

(16) pigli + et   > pigli + et + ∅
      take   3sg. past   take   past 3sg.

The past definite, quite common in Bifrun's New Testament of 1560, has been almost eliminated in favour of the periphrastic perfect in Gritti's translation of 1640. But the form does survive in both Puter and Vallader. From the paradigms in these languages (which are practically identical) we can see that the reinterpretation which was beginning in Surselvan and Puter is accomplished. The invariable (and invariably stressed) suffix -/ɛt/ ~ /it/ has been reinterpreted as a non-personal suffix which marks the literary past tense, and is followed by secondary personal desinences (see Gartner 1883: 117).

(e) The counterfactual conditional

The Romansh dialects, in common with many Italian dialects and other Romance languages, use the imperfect subjunctive with the meaning of the counterfactual conditional (e.g. /ʃi vəɲisəs/ 'if you came': see Elwert 1943: 155; Rohlfs 1969: 141; *AIS*: table 1685, maps 1613, 1627, 1630, 1633, etc.). Some of the Italian dialects are more consistent in using the conditional proper, which is, throughout Roumania, an innovation formally parallel to the future tense. The evolution of the paradigm is in some cases not entirely clear: as shown by Rohlfs (1968: 339–49), this mood more than other verbal forms seems to have undergone innovations under the influence of Italian and French. The common Romance core is given by the infinitive followed by a reduced (indicative imperfect or past definite) form of HABERE 'have'.

This is found in Friulian (Iliescu 1972: 175), as well as in the transitional dialect of Erto, spoken on the western fringes of Friulian (Gartner 1892: 206; Francescato 1966: 268). The compound suffix /ar + es/, like the future /ar/ may co-occur with the /is/ augment in some Friulian varieties: thus /part-is-ar-'es-is/ 'you would leave'. (Formally, the compound counterfactual conditional is exactly parallel to the 'suppositive future' in Puter, which, as we recall, consists of verb stem + infinitival suffix + εj, followed by the personal desinences. Etymologically, and semantically, however, the two forms are distinct.)

In Ampezzan, the counterfactual conditional is a mixed form. In the 1st plural and 2nd plural, it consists of the imperfect subjunctive, while in other persons, it consists of the infinitive (Appollonio 1930: 66). Both suffixes are followed by a reduced set of the personal desinences:

> daj-as-on 'if we gave'
> daj-as-e 'if you all gave'

but

$$\text{d-ar-ae} \quad \text{'if} \quad \left\{ \begin{array}{l} \text{I} \\ \text{3sg.} \\ \text{3pl.} \end{array} \right\} \text{gave'}$$

> d-ar-aes 'if you gave'

(f) The personal desinences

Markers of person and number, as we have already noted, may be either primary or secondary. While there is no logical necessity that the features defined as primary (preservation of conjugational allomorphy, adjacency to the verb stem, and movable stress) should go together, they do appear concomitantly in both Romansh and Friulian for all categories but the present subjunctive (in the Engadine dialects only) and the past definite (in Old Romansh, and modern Friulian: modern Vallader is no exception, in that the personal desinences here are regular secondary ones).

The presence of personal desinences which are separated from the verb stem and neutralize conjugational allomorphy, but nevertheless

Table 2.5 Present indicative personal desinences

	Surselvan		Vallader		Fassa		Friulian (Clauzetto)	
Singular								
1	əl		*null*		e		I	i
							others	*null*
2	as		aʃ(t)		es		I	Vs
							others	s
3	a		a		I	a	I	ə
					others	null ~ e	*others*	*null*
Plural								
1	IV	in	IV	in	IV	joŋ	I	aŋ
	other	ejn	*other*	ajn	*other*	oŋ	*others*	iŋ
2	IV	is	IV	ivat	IV	ide	IV	iːs
	other	ejs	*other*	ajvat	*other*	ɛde	II(I)	iəs
							I	ajs
3	an		an		(= 3sg.)		(= 3sg.)	

exhibit movable stress, is one of the most striking features of the Ladin dialects, and may be adopted as criterial. (Indeed, if we do this, we will recognize the dialect of Erto as Ladin, see Gartner 1892: 206.) Leaving these problematic cases to the side, we arrive at the following classi- fication: primary personal desinences include the present indicative and the imperative; secondary personal desinences include the imperfect indicative, the present subjunctive, the imperfect subjunctive, and the future(s). (Puter has two futures, one set for the regular infinitival future, and another, contrasting minimally, for the suppositive future.)

(g) The present indicative

As we might expect, the present indicative has the richest system of personal desinences. In Dolomitic Ladin (including, once again, Erto and Ampezzan – see Gartner 1892: 205, Appollonio 1930: *passim*) and in some Friulian dialects (in the north-west and along the Venetian dialect border), the 3rd plural is identical with the 3rd singular. All other Rhaeto-Romance languages distinguish three persons in both the singular and the plural. All retain vestiges of conjugational allomorphy in the 2nd plural; all Romansh dialects, a minority of Friulian, and some Ladin dialects do the same in the 1st plural. The Italian Rhaeto- Romance dialects distinguish conjugations in the 3rd singular, and Friulian alone distinguishes conjugations in the 1st singular.

Broadly speaking, the present indicative desinences separate the more conservative Italian Rhaeto-Romance languages from the more innov- ative or degenerate Romansh dialects (see table 2.5).

Most Surmeiran is like Surselvan except in the 1st singular (null), the

1st pural (/aɲ/ ~ /iɲ/) and the 2nd plural (/ets/ ~ /its/). Puter is like Vallader except in the 1st plural (/ɛns/ ~ /ins/) and the 2nd plural (/ɛs/ ~ /is/). In central Friulian, 2sg. I -*es*, 3sg. I -*a*, 1pl. -*iŋ* (invariable), 2pl. II(I) -*eːs*, 3pl. -*iŋ*.

In all the present indicative paradigms, 1st plural and 2nd plural desinences are stressed.

1st singular Throughout most of northern Italy, the 1st singular desinence -*o* was simply dropped, as a consequence of the general diachronic loss of non-stressed final non-low vowels. Ampezzan is alone among the Rhaeto-Romance languages in reconstituting, presumably by borrowing from Venetian, the 1st singular ending -*o*. In Old Paduan, Bergamasque, and Milanese, as in some varieties of Friulian, a new 1st singular, -*e* ~ -*i*, was reconstituted from an earlier schwa (see Rohlfs 1949: II, 287). There is evidence of such a ghost vowel even in those dialects where no vowel appears. The evidence seems to suggest that this reconstitution began in the first conjugation: for example, in Badiot, final consonants are generally devoiced, but not in the 1st singular of first-conjugation verbs. This in turn suggests the following functional explanation for the origin of the vowel.

Benincà and Vanelli (1976) note that the regular phonological change which dropped final non-low vowels would have created the following paradigms for I, II–III, and IV conjugation verbs

First conjugation	Second/third	Fourth
AMO > am	PERDO > pjerd	SENT(I)O > sent
AMAS > ames	PERDIS > pjerds	SENTIS > sents
AMA(T) > ame	PERDI(T) > pjerd	SENTI(T) > sent

Except in the first conjugation, the singular forms were isosyllabic. The striving for paradigmatic coherence (see Haiman 1971) may then have motivated a paragogic vowel in the 1st singular of the first conjugation.

Luedtke (1957: 124) identifies the possibility of Friulian 1st singular null as a dialectal trait separating the language from Venetian. In fact, this feature distinguishes not Friulian, but all northern Italian dialects from Venetian.

Among the more puzzling innovations is the Surselvan 1 sg. -*əl* ending, which is all the more exasperating in having occurred right beneath our noses. Old Surselvan consistently has null until the -*əl* ending begins to make its appearance ca 1700. Ascoli (1883: 461) confidently derived the ending via a reinterpretation of verb stems in final [. . . əl]: [afəl] 'find', originally /afl + o/ 'find + 1sg.' became /af + l/ 'find + 1sg.', and then, presumably under paradigmatic pressure reconstituted itself as /afl + l/ . Not only is the latter part of this process somewhat difficult to understand, the entire reinterpretation depends for its plausibility on the existence of a large number of extremely common stems in [. . .əl]. Still, none of the other conjectured origins for this ending are any more convincing. Gartner's confident approval of Carisch's conjecture that -əl derived from the unmarked object ILLU 'that' makes no sense semantically (Gartner 1883: 110). Another possibility is that -əl represents a hypercorrect 'restoration' of /əl/ from borrowed Italian /-o/ '1sg.', parallel to the etymologically unmotivated /gald-/ < GAUD 'enjoy', or /Stankəl/ < Italian /stanko/ 'tired'. These two are common throughout Rhaeto-Romance; and it is undeniable that Surselvan seems to have pushed 'restoration' of unmotivated [l] further than any of the other Rhaeto-Romance languages. For a survey of the theories, see Ulleland 1965.

2nd singular   The retention of 2sg. -*s*, as we have already seen, is invoked as a characteristic feature of Rhaeto-Romance by almost all comparative Romance scholars. Nevertheless, as Ascoli (1873: 461ff.) and subsequently Battisti pointed out, 2sg. -*s* was found in Venetian until ca 1400. Rohlfs (1949: II, 300) adds that in Old Lombard, as represented in the Valtellina and in Livigno, monosyllabic verb stems retained 2sg. -*s*. Moreover, even today, conservative speakers of Venetian retain this ending in inverted word order, for example *Parlistu?* 'Do you speak?'.

The final /t/ in the 2nd singular of Surmeiran, Puter, and Vallader (which is also typical of the Lombard dialects), is clearly the result of the cliticization of the pronoun /ty/ in inverted word order (Gartner 1883: 111; Grisch 1939: 197). The best evidence for this in the currently spoken dialects is the fact that in Surmeiran /s/ does *not* become [ʃ] before this final /t/, indicating the presence of a morpheme boundary between them. From the written record, the best evidence is the fairly regular absence of the /t/ enlargement in normal word order, contrasted with its presence in inverted word order, in Old Puter. Thus, in Bifrun 1560:

(17) tü   vaes
      you go

                                                          (John 14: 5)

(18) tü   nu   pous
      you not can

                                                          (John 13: 36)

contrast with examples such as

(19) innua vaest tü?
     where goest thou

(John 13: 36)

(By Gritti's time, ca. 1640, the /t/ enlargement is regularly spelled in both normal and inverted word order.)

In the Gorizian dialect of Friulian, we observe a transitional phase of the degeneration of /tu/: in both direct and inverted word order, it appears as an invariable suffix on the verb, but one with the final vowel still preserved. (We will return to the topic of the degeneration of subject pronouns in chapter 4.)

1st plural Conjugational allomorphy of this desinence is general only in Romansh. The Ladin dialects of Gardena and Ampezzo have generalized -/on/, as has Venetian. Friulian koine and Carnic have generalized -/in/, but some Friulian dialects are more conservative. Rizzolatti (1981: 39) notes that Clauzetto has I -*aŋ*, other -*iŋ*, while Concordiese has IV -*iŋ*, other -*eŋ*. The most conservative Friulian dialects, those of Val Meduna and Val Colvera in the western foothills, retain I -*aŋ*, II(I) -*eŋ*, IV -*iŋ*.

In a number of Lombard dialects, including those of Milan, Poschiavo, and Chiavenna, stress in the 1st plural is rhizotonic (Ettmayer 1903: 48–50; Rohlfs 1949: II, 295). The only Rhaeto-Romance dialect which shares this remarkable feature seems to be that dialect of Surmeiran which is spoken in Bravuogn/Bergün. Although the fact itself is thus incidental to a survey of Rhaeto-Romance, the mechanism which produced it is not. The most plausible development, given other developments in both the 2nd singular and the 1st plural is the following. First, the 1st plural was expressed by *HOMO*/*UNUS* + *3sg.* (compare, on the one hand, the use of *on* in colloquial French and other impersonal forms with 1st plural meaning in Tuscan and Friulian; on the other, the use of *we* as the unspecified agent in English). Second, this PRO form appeared postverbally in inverted word order as a clitic. Finally, -VN was reinterpreted as a bound suffix on the verb stem, obligatory in both direct and inverted word order.

The 1st plural ending -*ɛns* ~ *ins* in Puter probably owes the /s/ enlargement to the same mechanism of cliticization: this time, of the pronoun NOS in inverted word order. Consider representative examples in Old Puter such as John 14: 5 (both Bifrun and Gritti):

(20) nus nu savain ... co pudains ...
     we not know   how can=we

Given the regularity of verb-second order in all the Romansh dialects, the subject pronoun in the second clause above must follow the verb. Linder (1987: 80) provides evidence of an *-s* enlargement in inverted word order in Old Vallader and Old Sutselvan as well.

Further evidence in favour of the cliticization hypothesis is offered by currently spoken dialects of Ladin, wherein – for a number of verbs – the /s/ enlargement of the 1st plural ending occurs only in *inverted* word order: thus, in Badiot:

(21) i   ɲuŋ
      we   come

but:

(22) ɲuns- (e)
      come we
      'Let's come.'

(Pizzinini and Plangg 1966: xl)

The same pattern exists in Gardena (see Gartner 1879: 76–7.

The cycle of cliticization is repeated in much of Romansh with the 1st plural subject clitic /a/. In spoken Surselvan, Sutselvan, and Surmeiran, the clitic shows up postverbally only after oxytonic verbs. For example, in Surmeiran: /munˈtaɲ-sa/ 'do we climb' contrasts with /ˈiʃan-s/ 'are we'. Linder (1987: 77–81) shows that this pattern is in conformity with the stress target noted by Haiman (1971), which forbids antepenultimate stress on verbs. But if this is so, then of course the postverbal subject clitic /a/ must be acting as a verbal suffix, not as a separate word. (Compare our discussion of the genesis of the non-null 1st singular personal desinence, motivated by just such a structural pressure for isosyllabicity within the paradigm).

In fact, Linder shows, there is at least one Puter dialect, spoken in Pontresina, where *-sa* has been reinterpreted as a verbal desinence entirely independent of word order (and entirely dependent on the stress pattern of the verb):

(23) a kur-ˈin*sa*   'we run'
      a ˈ ʝ ajn*sa*   'we go'

but

(24) ad ˈɛs-an*s(*a)*   'we are'
      a durm-ˈivan*s(*a)*   'we were sleeping'

2nd plural The Vallader 2pl. *-ajvat/-ivat* is totally isolated in Rhaeto-Romance. It was explained by Gartner (1883: 113) as the outcome of a complex history of changes: reduction of inherited *-ajs* to *-aj*; cliticization of the 2nd plural pronoun *vos* in somewhat reduced form as [va]; and, finally, suffixation of the final /t/, which Gartner identified as the characteristic sign of the secondary 2nd plural desinence. Given the near identity of the Vallader present and imperfect indicative endings in this person, a more direct development (which is rendered more plausible by the absence of any of Gartner's conjectured transitional forms) is that for some reason Vallader borrowed from the imperfect paradigm. A possible explanation for either line of development may be found in the resulting stress patterns in Vallader. While all the Romansh dialects observe the three-syllable rule, which militates against antepenultimate stress in verbs, they differ somewhat in how faithfully they obey this rule in *verb + clitic* combinations. Puter tolerates occasional (and systematic) antepenultimate stress in the 3rd plural while Vallader does not. Given that the 2nd plural clitic subject in Romansh is typically null, forms in final *-ajs ~ -is* deviate from regularity in exhibiting final stress: but forms in *-ajvat ~ -ivat* do not. Consequently, Vallader exhibits absolutely regular penultimate stress in both *verb* and *verb + clitic* structures, and it may be that a striving to attain this regularity motivated the restructuring or borrowing of the 2nd plural primary desinence (see Haiman 1971).

Friulian, like standard Italian, but unlike Venetian, maintains a three-way conjugational distinction in the 2nd plural (Frau 1984: 78). The first conjugation by regular phonological development should have *-aːs* (still attested in old texts and some isolated modern dialects). The now common *-ajs* form is the result of analogical pressure from FACITIS > /fajs/ (see Benincà and Vanelli 1976: 31–9). Carnic and central Friulian offer isolated examples of the inherited *four-way* conjugational contrast in the 2nd plural, for example rhizotonic /pjérdis/ < PERDITIS contrasts with forms in the first, second, and fourth conjugation, all stressed on the desinence.

The Gorizian dialect of Friulian (which has generalized the *-tu* enlargement on 2nd singular forms) also has the 2nd plural atonic pronoun subject *-o* as an invariable suffix on the verb: *o fevel-ez-o* 'you (pl.) talk'.

3rd plural   The formal identity of 3rd singular and 3rd plural is a feature which the Ladin dialects, and some of the Carnic dialects of Friulian, share with Lombard, Venetian, and Romagnol (Rohlfs 1949: II, 299), and cannot therefore be taken as a Ladin characteristic. Thus, Luedtke (1957: 124) identifies a distinct 3rd plural (with final *-n*) as a characteristic trait distinguishing Friulian koine from the immediately adjacent Venetian dialect.

Table 2.6 Rhaeto-Romance positive imperative desinences

	Surselvan		Vallader	Fassa		Ampezzan	Friulian	
Singular	a		a	I	a	a	I	e (a, o)
				other	null		other	null
Plural	IV	i	i	IV	i	idɛ	iːt	
	other	ej	aj	II(I)	e	edɛ	eːt (ejt, iat)	
				I	a	adɛ	ajt	(aːt)

In Ladin and Venetian, 3rd singular and plural are identical for all verbs. In Carnic Friulian, however, a distinction is maintained in athematic verbs (e.g. /a/ 'has' vs. /aŋ/ '(they) have'). This suggests that the formal identity of 3rd singular and plural in Ladin and Venetian is a morpho-syntactic fact, while in Carnic Friulian, it is a consequence of the purely phonological reduction of unstressed syllables of proparoxytones: see Benincà and Vanelli (1976: 39–43).

(h) The imperative

In dealing with the imperative, it should be emphasized that we must distinguish between the positive imperative, which is an inflectional category of the verb, and the negative imperative, which is almost always rendered by some periphrastic infinitival construction. As in the case of the present indicative desinences, we observe the relative conservatism of the Italian dialects, which contrast with the levelling Romansh dialects. All plural imperative desinences are stressed; all singular imperative desinences are unstressed. The Romansh dialects differ from each other only in the non-fourth-conjugation form of the plural: Surselvan /ej/, Surmeiran and Puter /ɛ/, Vallader /aj/.

The hortatory (1pl.) imperative in all Rhaeto-Romance languages but Surselvan, Puter, and Ladin, is identical with the present indicative (in all but a handful of irregular verbs). In Surselvan, it consists of /lejn/ 'we want' followed by the infinitive, as in /lejn ir/ 'let's go!'. In Puter, it is derived from the indicative by the deletion of final /s/ – or the addition of another 1st plural subject clitic /a/: /ʝɛns/ '(we) go', but /ʝɛn (sa)/ 'let's go'. In Badiot Ladin, the hortatory imperative is derived from subject–verb inversion of the indicative/subjunctive 1st plural: /ɲuns(e)/ 'let's come', /faʒunde/ 'let's do it'. The -e suffix is a calque translation of the German 1st plural pronoun, typically reduced in inverted word order. The -de suffix, on the other hand, is probably an analogical extension of the 2nd plural suffix -(e)de to the 1st plural (compare, perhaps, Russian forms like *poidem-te* 'let's go (polite)', whose final -te enlargement is also a borrowing from the 2nd plural).

Friulian, Ampezzan, and Gardena may be conservative in retaining 2pl. /t/, /dɛ/, and /dɛ/, thus resisting a morphologically conditioned alternation that is otherwise generalized in all the Rhaeto-Romance languages (see Iliescu 1972: 172; Badiot and Gardena drop -*dɛ* before a following object clitic: /dun-adɛ/ 'send!', but /duna-mɛ/ 'send me!').

Finally, Old Surselvan offers us forms like {tettlad} 'listen (pl.)!' and {laudad} 'praise (pl.)!' alongside the more common pattern exemplified by {vegni} 'come (pl.)!'.)

The negative imperative, at least in the currently spoken languages, is one category which exhibits a fundamental split between Surselvan on the one side, and all the other Rhaeto-Romance languages on the other. In Surselvan alone, the negative particle *buka* is a separate word which may either precede or follow the imperative (which has the same form as the positive imperative): /buka kanta/ or /kanta buka/ 'don't sing! (sg. or familiar)' vs. /buka kantej/ or /kantej buka/ 'don't sing! (pl. or polite)'. In all the other dialects, the negative particle *no* or *nu* is a proclitic on the following verb.

The Italian dialects are divided into two groups. The dialects which express negation by a postverbal particle (Emilian *brisa*, Piedmontese *nen*) parallel Surselvan in that the positive and the negative form of the imperative verb are identical. Those which express negation by a preverbal proclitic express the negative imperative in some other way.

Dialects differ in the form of the verb in the negative imperative. The possible options are:

(a) root + infinitival suffix;
(b) root + personal desinence;
(c) root + infinitive + personal desinence.

In standard Italian, for example, the negative imperative is expressed by the infinitive in the singular, and by the personal desinential form in the plural:

(25) non cantare   'Don't sing (sg.)!'
      non cantate   'Don't sing (pl.)!'

No Rhaeto-Romance dialect seems to follow exactly this pattern. At one extreme are Surselvan and Ampezzan, which use option (b) in both the singular and the plural:

	Surselvan	*Ampezzan*
Singular	buka kanta	no canta
Plural	buka kantej	no cantadɛ

Almost like Italian are Vallader and Moena, which use option (a) in the singular, but option (c) in the plural:

	Italian	*Vallader*	*Moena*
Singular	non cantar	nu cantar	no cantar
Plural	non cantate	nu cantar-'aj	no cantar-'edɛ

The -*aj* and -*edɛ* suffixes are clearly the same as in the plural imperative, but, as secondary suffixes separated from the verb stem, undergo no allomorphic alternation.

Friulian (like Venetian) employs option (a) throughout. In both singular and plural, the negative imperative (and negative hortatory imperative) construction is

no + 2sg. *Sta*/2pl. *Stajt*/1pl. *Stin* + (*a*) + infinitive

where number is marked on the auxiliary of the imperative verb /Sta/ 'stay, be'.

(26) no Sta ʒi in nisuna banda
      not be go in any   direction
      'Don't go anywhere!'
(27) no Sta rompi-mi i   wesh
      not be break-me the bones
      'Don't break my bones!'

The Friulian option is also available in Ampezzan:

| Singular | no sta a loura | 'Don't work!' |
| Plural | no stajedɛ a loura | 'Don't work!' |

Except in the Engadine dialects, Surmeiran, and Friulian, the polite form of address is invariably 2nd plural, and the polite imperative is the 2nd plural. In Vallader and Puter, where the only polite form of address is the third person (and in Surmeiran and Friulian, where *one* possible polite form of address is third person), the polite imperative is the third-person subjunctive introduced by the complementizer /c(a)/, Friulian /ke/, as in the Vallader

(28) c(a) el am ʃcyza
      that he me excuse = 3sg.subj.
      'Excuse me (to male interlocutor).'

or the Puter

(29) c(a) ela nu   ɟaja   davɛnt
      that she not go = 3sg.subj. away
      'Don't go away (to female interlocutor)'.

or the Friulian

(30) k   e   vɛɲi
     that she come = 3sg.subj.
     'Come (in) (to female interlocutor).'

Polite imperatives of this sort are also attested in Milanese (Rohlfs 1949: II, 405), and other dialects (Rohlfs 1968: 354–5). In standard Italian, the complementizer and the subject pronoun are absent, but the morphology of the verb is identical with that of the subjunctive.

(It should be noted that the 3rd singular indicative and subjunctive are identical for all but the most common irregular verbs in both Vallader and Puter. The only consistent mark of the imperative in the polite form is therefore the complementizer /ca/. The verb of the negative polite imperative is identical with that of the positive polite imperative.)

2.1.1.8 Secondary personal desinences

No personal desinences are secondary in every single Rhaeto-Romance language. Those which are secondary in *some* languages include the imperfect indicative, the subjunctive, the imperfect subjunctive, and the future. All of these, for example, are secondary in Surmeiran and the Engadine dialects; the future desinences are secondary in all dialects in which the synthetic future exists; the imperfects are secondary except in Ladin; the subjunctive is secondary only in Surmeiran and the Engadine dialects.

(a) The imperfect indicative

The imperfect indicative desinences occur exclusively with the imperfect suffix. Except in Ladin, they are secondary in all respects. Note that the absence of movable stress and vowel reduction in post-tonic syllables of proparoxytones entail the identity of the 1st plural and the 3rd plural. In maximally levelled secondary paradigms, 1st singular is identical with 3rd singular, and 2nd singular with 2nd plural as well (see table 2.7).

Ladin 1st plural and 2nd plural desinences are stressed on the first syllable. All other imperfect indicative desinences are unstressed. For example, in Ampezzan, /da'ɟea/ '3sg. was giving', but /daɟa'on/ 'we were giving'.

A peculiar usage of the imperfect, confined apparently to Surselvan (Nay 1965: 132n.) is as a counterfactual imperative (e.g. 'You should have gone'). Thus,

Table 2.7 Imperfect indicative desinences

	Surselvan	Surmeiran	Puter	Vallader	Fassa	Friulian
Singular						
1	əl	a	a	a	e	i
2	as	as	aʃt	aʃt	es	is
3	a	a	a	a	a	ə
Plural						
1	an	an	ans	an	ane	iŋ
2	as	as	as	at	ɛde	is
3	an	an	an	an	a	iŋ

(31) pag- av-as   tes   dejvəts
      pay impf.2sg. your   debts
      (Literally: 'You were paying your debts.')
      (As an imperative: 'You should have paid your debts.')

What is interesting about this use of the imperfect indicative is not that it is counterfactual: the imperfect indicative is used in both the protasis and apodosis of counterfactual conditionals in some dialects of Friulian, and in the protasis of counterfactual conditionals in French. It is the use of the imperfect indicative as a kind of imperative which is unique.

(b) The unmarked subjunctive

The subjunctive desinences occur immediately after the verb root for the expression of indirect speech, and in the complements of verbs expressing fear, desire, belief, or uncertainty. The use of the subjunctive for the expression of indirect speech is widespread in Romansh, probably under German influence. Consider the Surselvan examples in (32) and (33):

(32) El Skriva 'jaw aj   fac   in bi   viadi'
      he writes 'I have (1sg.ind.) made a   good trip'
      (cf. German: *Er schreibt, 'Ich habe eine schöne Reise
      gemacht.'*)
(33) El Skriva ke   El aɟ-i   fac   in bi   viadi
      he writes that he have (3sg.subj.) made a   good trip
      (cf. German: *Er schreibt, er habe eine schöne Reise gemacht.*)

Surselvan has completely regularized and generalized the use of the subjunctive for the expression of indirect speech. Alone of all the Rhaeto-Romance languages, it allows the unmarked subjunctive desinences to occur with the imperfect indicative (/av/ ∼ /ev/) and the

Table 2.8 The unmarked subjunctive as a primary desinence

	Surselvan		Erto		Ampezzan	Friulian	
Singular							
1	i		e		e	i	
2	jəs		es		es	is	
3	i		e		e	i	
Plural							
1	IV	iən	ona		one	iŋ	
	other	ejən					
2	IV	iəs	IV	ida	ede	IV	i:s
	other	ejəs	*other*	ejda		II(I)	e:s
						I	ajs
3		iən	e		e	iɔ	

imperfect subjunctive (/as/ ~ /es/) suffixes, to indicate reported imperfects and reported counterfactuals. The subjunctive in this dialect may be said to function as a kind of evidential marker, unique in Rhaeto-Romance, and possibly in Romance generally:

(34) jaw avev-a
    I   had (impf.ind.1sg.)
    'I had'

(35) jaw avev-i
    I   had (subj.1sg.)
    'I am said to have had.'

(36) jaw lɛs
    I   would-want (impf.subj.1sg.)
    'I would like'

(37) jaw lɛs   -i
    I   would-want (subj.1sg.)
    'It is said that I would like.'

Within Rhaeto-Romance, the subjunctive desinences are secondary only in Surmeiran and in the Engadine dialects. However, a similar pattern occurs in Lombard and Piedmontese (Rohlfs 1949: II, 346). Elsewhere they are primary, and in this they are closer to the inherited Latin present subjunctive. See tables 2.8 and 2.9.

Plural forms happen to be absent in the Ladin dialect of Fassa described by Elwert. Elsewhere in Ladin, as in Surselvan and Friulian, the 1st plural and 2nd plural forms are stressed on their first syllable, and exhibit conjugational allomorphy.

In all Rhaeto-Romance languages but Ladin, personal desinences can only be primary if they occur immediately after the verb stem. If a suffix

Table 2.9 The unmarked subjunctive desinences as secondary

	Surmeiran	Puter	Vallader
Singular			
1	a	a	a
2	as	aʃt	aʃt
3	a	a	a
Plural			
1	an	ans	an
2	as	as	at
3	an	an	an

intervenes between the verb stem and the desinence, the desinence must be secondary. The behaviour of the unmarked subjunctive desinence in Surselvan attests to the productivity of this general constraint. In fact, tables 2.8 and 2.9 reproduce the forms of the unmarked subjunctive only where it immediately follows the verb stem. Where they follow one of the imperfect suffixes, the unmarked subjunctive desinences lose both stress and conjugational allomorphy in the 1st plural ([jən]) and the 2nd plural ([jəs]):

(38) ke   nus kant- 'ejən
     that   we   sing   (subj.1pl.)

(39) ke   nus kant- 'av-   jən
     that   we   sing   (impf.)   (subj.1pl.)

(40) ke   nus kant- 'as-   jən
     that   we   sing   (impf.subj.) (subj.1pl.)

Here is at least one case where the secondary desinences can (still?) be derived from the corresponding primary desinences by synchronically productive reduction rules.

In Friulian, the levelled subjunctive (*-i, -is, -i*) is an innovation. The old texts show forms reflecting regular phonological developments of the Latin subjunctive (Benincà 1989: 577).

	Latin	Friulian
I conjugation	-EM	*null*
	-ES	-s
	-ET	*null*
Other conjugation	-AM	-a
	-AS	-as
	-AT	-a

This is still found in Collina, Clauzetto, and Paularo dialects.

Table 2.10 Imperfect subjunctive desinences

	Surselvan	Puter	Vallader	Fassa	Friulian
Singular					
1	*null*	*null*	*null*	e	*null*
2	əs	aʃt	aʃt	es	is
3	*null*	*null*	*null*	a	*null*
Plural					
1	ən	ans	an	ane	iŋ
2	əs	as	at	ɛde	is
3	ən	an	an	a	iŋ

(c) The imperfect subjunctive desinences

In all the Rhaeto-Romance languages, the imperfect subjunctive desinences follow the imperfect subjunctive suffix /as/ ∼ /es/ ∼ /is/. In Vallader, they are used for the past definite as well (and thus follow the suffix /ɛt/ ∼ /it/). It is only in Ladin that these desinences – identical, in this dialect, with those of the imperfect indicative – exhibit any of the features of primary desinences, namely their stress in the 1st plural and 2nd plural. Elsewhere, they are very reduced and exhibit considerable syncretism: in all dialects but Ladin the first and third persons are identical, in both the singular and the plural; in Surselvan and Friulian, the second person singular is also identical with the second person plural. See table 2.10. (Surmeiran is like Surselvan. The differences are even smaller than they appear among the Romansh dialects, when one bears in mind that unstressed /a/ is almost identical with /ə/).

(d) The future desinences

The synthetic future is absent in Surselvan and Sutselvan (nor was it attested from the older stages of the Engadine dialects). Where it appears, the desinences are regularly stressed throughout the paradigm, the only secondary desinences in Rhaeto-Romance which exhibit this feature. Note that in Vallader, stress is the only feature which distinguishes the future personal desinences from those of the imperfect or the subjunctive (see table 2.11).

Puter, which is alone in having a special suppositive future suffix (/ar + ɛɪ/), is also alone in having a minimally different set of future desinences which occur only with this compound suffix (see table 2.12).

Table 2.11 Rhaeto-Romance synthetic future desinences

	Surmeiran	Puter	Vallader	Fassa	Badiot	Friulian
Singular						
1	ɔ	o	a	e	a	aj
2	ɔsas	aʃ(t)	aʃt	ɛs	as	as
3	ɔ	o	a	a	a	a
Plural						
1	ɔn	ons	an	oŋ	uŋ	iŋ
2	ɔsas	os	at	ɛde	ɛjs	ejs
3	ɔn	on	an	a	a	aŋ

Table 2.12 Puter suppositive future desinences

	Singular	Plural
1.	a	ans
2	aʃ(t)	as
3	a	an

Source: Ebneter (1973: 36, 41)

2.1.2 Verbal categories expressed by auxiliary verbs

The major auxiliary + verb constructions in any of the Rhaeto-Romance languages are the future, the passive, and the perfect.

2.1.2.1 The analytic future

Futures in inherited VENIRE AD + infinitive (less frequently DE + IRE or VELLE + infinitive) are found throughout Rhaeto-Romance, as they are in French, Italian, Spanish, and Roumanian (see Ebneter 1973: 244). There is therefore no need, Ebneter argues (216–17), to trace the prevalence of this construction in Romansh to Germanic influence. On the contrary, the comparative rarity of the synthetic future in the Engadine dialects (ibid. 35 *et passim*), and even in Friulian (Iliescu 1972: 175, 178), and the tendency, throughout Rhaeto-Romance, to use in its stead the present tense with future reference, allow one to draw no conclusions about the relative authenticity of either the analytic or the synthetic future within Rhaeto-Romance. In fact, if common usage were the criterion, we could even infer that Rhaeto-Romance inherited no future construction at all.

There is inconsistency, even within a single dialect, concerning the presence and the nature of a possible preposition between the auxiliary and the infinitive. Ebneter (1973: 238) finds /a/ in Surselvan and Sutselvan, /da/ in the Engadine dialects, and both /a/ and /da/ in Surmeiran: but this distribution is confined to the single expression 'It is going to rain'. Another pattern is reported for 'There is going to be a snowstorm' (ibid. 239). In Friulian the future-tense auxiliary is the verb /ve/ 'have':

(41) viŋ   di lavora   insjeme
    have = 1pl. of to = work   together
    'We will work together.'

(42) aj   di vjodi   lu
    have = 1sg. of to = see him
    'I will see him.'

A possible substitute is /ole/ 'want':

(43) voj   parti
    want = 1sg. to = leave
    'I will leave.'

The meaning of HABERE + preposition + infinitive is very near that of English 'have to'. The use of VOLERE + infinitive is very limited, and Iliescu, as we have already seen, suspects Roumanian influence may lie behind the /voj/ auxiliary in the dialects of Friulian that she investigated. This conclusion, perhaps, is too cautious, given the (admittedly not very frequent) occurrence of the same auxiliary in Old Surselvan, Old Sutselvan, and Old Puter:

Old Surselvan (L. Gabriel's Bible translation of 1648)
(44) a   chei ca   vus vangits a dumandar en
    and whatever ye come to ask   in
    mieu num, quei vi jou a far
    my   name that will I to do

                           (John 14: 13)

Old Sutselvan (D. Bonifaci's Catechism of 1601)
(45) Io vus vij mussar la temma digl   Segner
    I you will show the fear   of = the Lord

                           (Psalm 34)

Old Puter (*Histoargia dalg Patriarch Joseph* of 1534)
(46) a   nun achiatand impedimaint, voelg cun
    and not finding obstacles   will (I) with
    raspoasta turner
    answer   return

2.1.2.2 The passive

The passive consists of an auxiliary verb, followed by the predicate perfect participle, inflected to agree with its subject in number and gender.

The passive in the Romansh dialects employs the verb 'come' as the auxiliary in non-compound tenses:

Surselvan
(47) jaw vɛɲəl   klam-aws
     I   I=come call (prf.part.m.sg.)
     'I am called.'

Vallader
(48) ɛ vɛɲ   klam-a
     I I=come call (prf.m.sg.)
     'I am called'

In the Engadine dialects, the passive auxiliary may also be 'be' in compound tenses, when this auxiliary is itself a perfect participle (Arquint 1964: 99):

(49) ɛ sun ɲy   / Stat   klam-a
     I am come (prf.m.sg.) / be (prf.m.sg.) call (prf.m.sg.)
     'I have been called.'

In Ladin, the auxiliary 'be' is used when the action is viewed as completed, and the focus is on the resulting state; 'come' is used when the action is in progress (Elwert 1943: 158; Pizzinini and Plangg 1966: xlviii; Alton and Vittur 1968: 48). That is, just as in Engadine Romansh, the auxiliary 'be' is used in compound tenses in which the perfective auxiliary is present.

In Friulian also, as in the Engadine dialects (and Venetian, and standard Italian), the choice of passive auxiliary is determined by whether the auxiliary is itself in the perfect-participial form. In the simple passive, the auxiliary is 'come', (or, subject to semantic constraints, 'go'), while in compound forms, it is 'be' (Iliescu 1982: 203; Benincà and Vanelli 1985: 178–94).

2.1.2.3 The perfect

As in other Romance languages, the perfect auxiliary is either 'have' or 'be'. The sub-class of intransitive verbs which take 'be' is familiar to all students of languages like French, Italian, and German, including (in Vallader): run, grow, fall, become, enter, flee, arrive, go, climb, die, be born, leave, pass, and stay (Arquint 1964: 21). The verb 'be' itself takes the 'be' auxiliary in all Rhaeto-Romance except Friulian, which allows both 'have' and 'be'.

Like popular and regional French, and conservative northern Italian dialects, Friulian has a complete paradigm of doubly marked perfects with two perfective auxiliaries, of which the second appears in the perfect participial form:

(50) o aj   vuːt   fat
     I have have + p.p. do + p.p.
     'I have done' (literally, 'I have had done')

Flöss (1990) notes that this 'passé surcomposé' is encountered in Ladin as well. For a general survey, see Schlieben-Lange (1971). It seems that this doubly marked form (which coexists with the singly marked perfect and with the simple past) is employed to mark a tense which is past with respect to a given reference point other than the time of speaking. Its usage is most widespread after the inflected auxiliary 'have'.

The Romance languages have split in their choice of a perfect auxiliary for reflexive verbs: Italian and French have generalized 'be', while Roumanian and Spanish have generalized 'have'. The same split has been replicated in Rhaeto-Romance.

The Engadine dialects and Ladin – what we might call central Rhaeto-Romance – have generalized 'have' (Arquint 1964: 44–5; Scheitlin 1962: 45; Elwert 1943: 151; Appollonio 1930: 16). The situation in Surselvan is more complex, in that both auxiliaries are in fact attested, subject to poorly understood constraints.

The standard pedagogical grammar of Surselvan (Nay 1965: 42) insists on 'be' in all cases. On the other hand, Gartner (1910: 96) found only 'have'. Other descriptive grammarians have encountered both (da Rieti 1904: 220; Arquint 1964; *DRG* 5: 704). A possible explanation for the attested variation is attempted in an illuminating article by Stimm (1976).

Stimm begins by noting that in Surselvan, as in German, the choice of perfect auxiliary for intransitive verbs in general correlates with semantic properties. The same intransitive verb may occur in the perfect with either auxiliary, depending on whether the action described is viewed as completed (in this case 'be' is appropriate), or merely terminated (in which case the auxiliary of choice is 'have'). He adduces (among others) the minimal contrast pair:

(51) ɛl ej morts Sko kwej k   ɛl *ej* viv- iws
     he is died as that comp. he is live (prf.m.sg.)
     'He died as he lived.' (completed action, ergo 'be' auxiliary)

(52) pli   bawl *vɛsəs*   ti   viv-iw
      more soon have = impf.subj. = 2sg. you live (prf.n.sg.)
      in   əntir ɔn
      a   whole year
      'Earlier, you could have lived a whole year (on 400 francs).' (not
      completed action, *ergo* 'have' auxiliary)

Stimm then argues that reflexive verbs are like other intransitive verbs,
and that we encounter the 'be' auxiliary with completed actions for
reflexives, just as we do for other intransitive verbs in the perfect:

(53) la   malawra *ej* sə-rətrac-a   ən las muntɔɲas
      the storm   is self withdrawn (f.sg.) in the mountains
      'The storm has retreated into the mountains.' (completed action,
      ergo 'be' auxiliary)

(54) El *a*   sə- mudərʝ- aw   ʎ əntir di pərsuls
      he has self exerted (n.sg.) the whole day alone
      'He has exerted himself all day alone.' (not completed action,
      ergo 'have' auxiliary)

Preference for the 'be' *reflexive* auxiliary in marking completed action is
reminiscent of a similar preference for the 'be' *passive* auxiliary in
compound or perfect tenses (where completion is marked morphologically):

	Unmarked action	*Completed action*
Passive	come	be
Reflexive	have	be

In Friulian, as in Venetian etc., both auxiliaries are found in apparent
free variation for reflexives (Benincà and Vanelli 1985: 178–84),
although there is a tendency to favour 'be' in the first and second
persons, and 'have' in the third. Note that the past participle agrees with
the subject only when the auxiliary is 'be':

(55) a. je   si   *a*   mituːt   a   vai
          she self has put (m.sg.)   to cry = inf.
      b. je   si   e   mitude   a   vai
          she self is put (f.sg.)   to cry = inf.
          'She began to cry.'

(56) a. a   si   an   fat   batia
          they self have made (m.sg.) baptize (inf.)
      b. a   si   son fats   batia
          they self are made (m.pl.) baptize (inf.)
          'They had themselves baptized.'

When the reflexive is an indirect object, however, only the 'have' auxiliary is possible:

(57) si   *a*   limat   i   diɳtʃ
      self   has   sharpened   the   teeth
      'S/he sharpened his/her teeth.'

It should be noted that this is one area of morpho-syntax where foreign influence cannot be said to play a major role. If the choice of auxiliary were determined by the neighbouring prestige language, we might expect that Surselvan, like German, would have generalized the 'have' auxiliary for the perfect, while Friulian, like Italian, would have generalized 'be'.

In fact, there is some evidence within Rhaeto-Romance that the status of reflexives is indeterminate: this evidence relates to the agreement of the perfect participle, irrespective of choice of auxiliary in the perfect. Generally speaking, the perfect participle agrees with its subject for gender and number only when linked by one of the copula verbs: be, become, seem. Thus, the Surselvan pattern noted by da Rieti, among others, is parallel to that of the Friulian examples immediately above:

(58) a. ɛl *ej* sə- ʃmarviʎaw- s
      he is self amazed   (m.sg)
    b. ɛl *a* sə- ʃmarviʎaw-
      he hasself amazed   (n.sg: unmarked)
      'He was amazed.'

Surmeiran and Ladin, which use 'have' alone, are also regular in consistently lacking agreement (Thöni 1969: 78; Elwert 1943: 151; Appollonio 1930: 16), as illustrated in the following examples:

Surmeiran
(59) ɛla s o lava-
      she self has washed (m.sg.: unmarked)
Fassa
(60) la vaca   se   a   ʃkorna-
      the cow (f.sg.) self has broken = horn (m.sg.: unmarked)
      'The cow has broken her horn.'
Ampezzan
(61) ra s a stabili-   in America
      she self has settled (m.sg.: unmarked) in America
      'She settled in America.'

In the Engadine dialects, however, the reflexive auxiliary in the perfect is consistently 'have' – as it regularly is for all transitive verbs. Nevertheless, the participle consistently agrees with its subject – as it regularly does for intransitive verbs with the auxiliary 'be'. The structural ambiguity of the reflexive is graphically displayed in the following Vallader and Puter examples:

> *Vallader*
> (62) ɛla   s-   a   lava-   da
>   she self has washed (f.sg.)
>   'She has washed.'

> *Puter*
> (63) la ɟunfra s-   ɔ   kɔmprɛ- da   yn cape
>   the girl   self has bought (f.sg.) a   hat
>   'The girl has bought herself a hat.'

(Example (63) makes clear that agreement occurs with both direct and indirect objects in Puter.)

One could argue that what is at issue here is actually the status of the reflexive morpheme: whether it carries abstract features of number and gender (yes in Vallader, no in Ladin), and whether it functions as the object argument of a transitive verb at all (again, yes in Vallader, no in Ladin). On either view, this variation reflects the syntactically ambiguous status of reflexives between transitive and intransitive verbs. The syntactic ambiguity, in turn, reflects the semantic ambiguity of the reflexive: see Haiman (1985) and Kemmer (1988).

2.1.3 The order of auxiliaries

The auxiliary complex is strikingly similar to that of English. The order of auxiliaries, where they co-occur, is future–perfect–passive. And, as in English, the synthetically expressed categories of tense and mood discussed in the previous sections, may occur only on the first word of the *(auxiliary) + verb* complex. The structure in its maximal efforescence is exemplified in Surselvan in (64):

> (64) jaw vəɲ- ɛs   ad ɛsər vəɲ- iw   -s   klam- aw   -s
>   I   come would to be   come (p.p.) (m.sg.) call (p.p.) (m.sg.)
>   FUTURE   PERFECT PASSIVE   MAIN VERB
>   'I would have been called.'

2.1.4 Summary

With the exception of the 2nd singular personal desinence in -*s* (which distinguishes Rhaeto-Romance only from standard Italian, and not from Venetian, or Gallo-Romance or even Ibero-Romance) and the periphrastic expression of the future tense, most of the verbal morphological features we have discussed serve to identify dialects within Rhaeto-Romance rather than to demarcate major boundaries between Rhaeto-Romance and other Romance languages. Matters are much more interesting and complicated when we turn to the nominal morphology.

2.2 NOMINAL CATEGORIES

The term 'nominal' is used in the broadest sense, to identify those parts of speech which are inflected for number and gender as well as (to a much more limited extent) case. Nominals, then, include not only nouns and pronouns, demonstratives, and numerals, but also adjectives, including such derived adjectives as the perfect participle. Here, there are many features which are peculiar to some or all Rhaeto-Romance dialects, among them the following:

(a) the nearly pan-Rhaeto-Romance retention of the -*s* plural for at least some paradigms;
(b) the retention of an inherited dative case for both pronouns and definite articles (now only in Surmeiran; formerly also in the other Romansh and northern Italian dialects);
(c) the retention (and transformation) of an inherited contrast between - (U)S and -U(M) in both nouns and adjectives. The inherited contrast, of course, was in both gender (masculine vs. neuter) and case (nominative vs. accusative, for masculines).

Traces of this opposition survive in the lexicon throughout Rhaeto-Romance (some nouns are clearly derived from inherited Latin nominatives, others from inherited nouns in the oblique case; in addition, remnants of a bicasual declension are encountered in the rules of plural formation for various Italian Rhaeto-Romance and non-Rhaeto-Romance dialects), but the opposition survives as a systematic and productive feature of the language only in Surselvan, where -UM forms of adjectives are both neuter and *attributive* masculine, while -US forms are exclusively *predicative* masculine.

All of these features have been claimed, by some people at some time, as defining features of Rhaeto-Romance. If we were to adopt the position that such a group were absolutely real, we should have to say that Romansh was more conservative than the Italian dialects in still maintaining (b) and (c) in historical times; while within Romansh, Surselvan and Surmeiran were more conservative in still maintaining (b) and/or (c) to the present day. Just as they failed to participate in some of the more striking phonological innovations which allegedly characterize Rhaeto-Romance, so too, the Italian Rhaeto-Romance dialects seem to have avoided participating in two of the morphological retentions which – again allegedly – characterize this hypothetical group. Here, as so often, it seems that what we really mean when we speak of 'Rhaeto-Romance', is simply 'Romansh'.

2.2.1 Nouns

Nouns in Latin were marked for gender (masculine, feminine, and neuter) and case. By the time of our earliest Romansh texts, the distinction between masculine and neuter nouns was almost entirely lost. Some old authors seem to make an effort to distinguish between masculine and neuter possessive pronominal adjectives: Bifrun's Bible translation of 1560, for example, sporadically distinguishes between *mes Bab* 'my father' (<MEUS) and *mieu plaid* 'my word', *mieu Thierp* 'my body' (<MEUM), but this was almost certainly a self-conscious Latinism. Later texts, in all the Romansh dialects, have what seems to be free variation between 'masculine' and 'neuter' attributive forms of possessive pronominal adjectives, before codifying one of these as the correct form for masculines.

In reducing the inherited three-gender system of Latin to one of only two, Rhaeto-Romance is similar to standard French and Italian. However, Romance dialects may differ in how the inherited neuter nouns were reclassified.

Luedtke (1962: 113) tried to establish isoglosses on the basis of the reclassification of the originally neuter nouns 'salt', 'honey', and 'gall'. In Lombard Italian generally, they became feminine, while in standard Italian and elsewhere, they became masculine. Luedtke claims that in Romansh, these nouns are generally masculine, while in the Italian Rhaeto-Romance dialects and in the Romansh dialect of Müstair, they are feminine. In fact, it seems that a number of the Italian Rhaeto-Romance dialects also have masculine forms for these nouns. Thus, Ampezzan *el sa* 'salt' patterns with Surselvan *il sal*, for example. While the Müstair dialect is unique within Romansh, the situation among the Italian dialects is probably less regular than Luedtke proposed.

Frau (1984: 64) notes that different recategorizations of the original neuters AERE 'air', LUMEN 'light', and MEL 'honey' establish an isogloss between standard Italian and Friulian:

	Friulian	Italian
AERE	ajar (m.)	aria (f.)

LUMEN	lum (f.)	lume (m.)
MEL	mi:l (f.)	miele (m.)

Again, this is an unacceptable oversimplification, if it is meant to suggest an isogloss between Rhaeto-Romance and non-Rhaeto-Romance varieties. In learned Italian, *aere* 'air' is masculine, as it is in Friulian. *Aria* has a different history and cannot be considered a simple instance of recategorization. And, while the reflexes of LUMEN and MEL are masculine in standard Italian, they are feminine in Venetian and other non-Rhaeto-Romance northern Italian dialects (see *REW* 5469).

Almost all common nouns in Rhaeto-Romance represent reflexes of an inherited oblique, probably accusative, case. Thus, for example, Old Surselvan /ciərf/ 'crow' continued Lat. CORVUM, rather than CORVUS, given that only -UM could cause umlaut of inherited */ɔ/ to [iə] (see Prader-Schucany 1970: 61). Similarly, the stress contrast between ['paʃtər] 'Alpine shepherd' and [pəʃ'tur] 'lowlands shepherd' continues an inherited contrast between PASTOR (nom.) and PASTOREM (acc.) (see Schmidt 1951/2: 42; cf. Ladin [pɛʃter], also from PASTOR – see Elwert 1943: 112). Finally, although the evidence for this is much more dubious, words like [cavaʎ] 'horse (m.)' , especially when contrasted with [cavala] 'mare' and [cavals] 'horses' in Surselvan, suggest a derivation from CABALLUM, whose final -UM is then held to account for the palatalization of the final liquid. Attestation of the inherited oblique case is almost always indirect and fragmentary in the singular, being limited to the umlauting and palatalizing traces of -UM, or the differing stress patterns resulting from *nominative* ROOT + *null* vs. *oblique* ROOT + *EM*.

On the other hand, attestation of an inherited nominative case may sometimes be direct: the nominative ending in /s/ survives as part of the modern form. In one Surselvan form, the name of the Deity, final /s/ survives as a (frozen) case suffix. There is a formulaic contrast between nominative /diws/ (as in [diws sejɟi ludaws] 'God be praised'), and oblique /diw/ (as in all other expressions).

Probably not too much should be made of this example, since it is easy to dismiss it as a learned Church Latinism. (In older texts, proper names regularly were declined according to Latin declensional patterns.) However, it is impossible to dismiss other nominatives in /s/ in this way. Among these are Surselvan doublets like *dis/di* 'daylight/day' (the nominative form also being used in compounds for days of the week in Surselvan, although not elsewhere: compare Surselvan [ʎiəndiʃdi-s] with Vallader [lyndəʃdi] 'Monday' – see Schmidt 1951/2: 42), and, throughout Romansh, agent nouns in inherited *-one + s*, whose final /s/ has now been reinterpreted as part of the nominal root. FILONES becomes [filunts] 'spinner', whose feminine is [filuntsa] (see Prader-Schucany 1970: 116).

The name of the indefinite agent PRO, when it is derived from Latin UNUS, remains [ins] in both Surselvan and Surmeiran, surviving in the other Romansh dialects only as [yn]. On the other hand, in Ladin, the indefinite subject pronoun is rendered by /aŋ/. If it derives from HOMO, then this is another nominative survival, albeit one which is shared by the great majority of Romance languages.

Some Friulian nominative survivals are /ete/ < AETAS 'age' (but see the discussion in *REW* 251), and /folk/ < FULGUR 'lightning'; less characteristic is /suːr/ < SOROR 'sister', while /fradi/, considered a nominative survival < FRATER 'brother', is, like /mari/ 'mother', almost certainly derived from an inflected form *FRATR- (> *fradri) > *fradi*. (The doublet /frari/ 'friar' derives from the same source by another cluster simplification.)

2.2.1.1 Plural marking on nouns

The best and most general evidence that it is usually the (accusative) oblique case that has been maintained from the inherited paradigm is the fact that the nominal plural marker is generally -*s* (< -AS, -OS, -ES, -US) rather than (as in Italian and Venetian) -*i* (< I) or -*e* (< AE). This is a frequently cited characteristic of Rhaeto-Romance.

The retention of plural -*s* for nouns is absolutely regular in Romansh. The inherited pattern in the Italian Rhaeto-Romance dialects, on the other hand, was that feminine nouns had -*s* plurals, while most masculine nouns were split into two classes, essentially forming their plural through the adjunction of either -*s* or -*i*. As pointed out by Elwert (1943) and subsequent scholars (see Benincà and Vanelli 1978 for additional bibliography) this must be viewed as a sign that vestiges of the two-case declensional system survived in this area up until the Middle Ages. Roughly speaking, when final vowels dropped, masculine nouns of the second declension maintained the -*i* (nominative) plural if they ended in a coronal consonant which contrasted with a palatalized coronal (*n/ɲ; t/c; l/ʎ*). This clear distinction between Swiss and Italian Rhaeto-Romance is probably the major morphological isogloss between the two groups.

The inherited split in plural marking morphology has been modified by the Ladin and Friulian dialects in different ways. In the Ladin dialect of Moena (Heilmann 1955: *passim*), masculine nouns in final /r/ form plurals in -*es*, while masculine nouns in final /t/, /n/, and /nt/ form their plurals by a palatalization of this consonant (cluster). Some monosyllables in this latter group (like /an/ 'year') also mark plurality by umlauting the stem vowel to /ɛ/. Both changes, of course, consonantal palatalization and vocalic umlaut, indicate a final (synchronically underlying) -*i*, now lost.

In the Gardena dialect (Gartner 1879: 84–5), masculine nouns in a final nasal (like /lan/ 'tree' < LIGNU, and /uəm/ 'man') take the plural suffix -*əs*. Masculine nouns in final /l/, /nt/, and /k/ form their plurals by changing this final consonant (cluster) to /j/, /ntʃ/, and /c/. Again, a final -*i* nominative plural suffix is indicated.

In the Badiot dialect (Pizzinini and Plangg: xxxviii; Alton and Vittur 1968: 17), masculine nouns ending in a vowel or /m/ form their plurals by the addition of a suffix -*s*. Masculine nouns in final /t/, /k/, and /n/ palatalize this consonant to /tʃ/ and /ɲ/:

gjat	∼ gjatʃ	'cat'
fyk	∼ fytʃ	'fire'
an	∼ aɲ	'year'
mys	∼ myʃ	'mouse'

A handful of Badiot nouns are doubly marked for plurality: these are masculine nouns in final /a/, whose plurals in /ɛʃ/ suggest an original plural compound suffix *-*s* + *i*:

profeta	∼ profetɛʃ	'prophet'
papa	∼ papɛʃ	'Pope'

In Ampezzan (Appollonio 1930: 19), masculine nouns ending in a vowel add -*s* in the plural. Nouns in /l/ change this to /j/. A number of other common nouns (among them /ɟato/ 'cat', /paesan/ 'farmer', /fo/ 'fire', /luo/ 'place') form their plurals in an irregular fashion by adding -*e*: /ɟate/, /paesane/, /foge/, /luoge/. These forms are probably borrowed from Venetian, as their final vowels attest.

A very detailed and insightful description is given for Fassa by Elwert (1943: 112–31), who notes that the -*s* plural occurs regularly with first-declension nouns in inherited -*a*, for example /lɛŋga ∼ lɛŋges/ 'tongue ∼ tongues', /poeta ∼ poetes/ 'poet ∼ poets'. Given the fate of all final vowels other than /a/, all other Latinate nouns in Ladin now end in a consonant. Some, but not all, Latin second-declension nouns ending in a coronal form their plurals, as noted, with *-*i*:

Singular	*Plural*	
nes	neʃ	'nose'
ɔs	ɔʃ	'bone'
cavel	cavej	'hair'

Singular	Plural	
aŋ	eɲ	'year'
agut	agutʃ	'nail'
vis	viʃ	'forehead'

Other masculine nouns add -*s* to form the plural. The following nouns exemplify the addition of an epenthetic vowel between the nominal stem and the plural consonant -*s* (there is no difference between masculine and feminine nouns in this respect):

Singular	Plural	
krowʃ	krowʒes	'cross'
sam	sames	'swarm'
kjef	kjeves	'key'

It is easy to see that the palatal plural represents an inherited plural in -*i*, which happened to survive only in those cases where it could leave a phonological imprint. (For the theoretical implications of this kind of change, see Schane 1971.)

(Originally third-declension nouns, not surprisingly, form their plurals in -*s*: /caŋs/ < CANES 'dogs', /pɛnts/ < PONTES 'bridges'. On the other hand, since there is no trace of this inherited distinction in the modern language, such forms are synchronically arbitrary, and there are instances of plurals which seem equally arbitrary from both a synchronic and a diachronic perspective: /leʃ/ < LOCI 'places' is regular, but /ʒeges/ < IOCI 'games' and /fjokes/ ⟨ FLOCCI 'flakes' are not.)

In Friulian, all originally second-declension masculine nouns except a partly variable list in final /-l/ (see Iliescu 1972: 132–7; Marchetti 1952: 122), final /-s/ (Frau 1984: 69), final /St/, and final /nt/ (Gregor 1975: 84) form their plurals in /s/: before this final /s/, the final consonant of the stem is often simplified or deleted.

Regular -*s* plurals are:

/kunin/	~ /kunins/	'rabbit'
/fradi/	~ /fradis/	'brother'
/frut/	~ /fruts/ ([fru(t)s])	'son'
/klap/	~ /klaps/ ([kla(p)s])	'rock'
/bratʃ/	~ /bratʃ-s/ ([brats])	'arm'
/potʃ/	~ /potʃ-s/ ([pots])	'well'

Regular -*i* plurals are:

/animal/	~ /animali/ ([animaj])	'animal'
/utʃel/	~ /utʃeli/ ([utʃej])	'bird'
/marcel/	~ /marceli/ ([marcej])	'hammer'

(with present-day final /j/ deriving from {lj}, still attested in sixteenth-century texts),

/foreSt/	~ /foreSti/ ([foreSc])	'foreign(er)'
/dint/	~ /dinti/ ([diɲc])	'tooth'
/peːs/	~ /peːsi/ ([peːʃ])	'weight'
/pajs/	~ /pajsi/ ([pajʃ])	'village'
/dut/	~ /duti/ ([duc])	'every, all'

Feminine *a*-stem nouns without exception add -*s* to form the plural; nouns in -*a* generally show surface modification of the vowel, raising it to /e/ or /i/ (see Benincà and Vanelli 1978: 268ff.). The most widespread feminine plural suffix is -*is*.

Feminine -*i* stems (old third- and fourth-declension nouns) also usually form their plurals in -*s*, irrespective of their phonological shape (Rizzolatti 1981: 41): /suːrs/ 'sisters', /vɔlps/ 'foxes', /mans/ 'hands', /kla(f)s/ 'keys', and /vals/ 'valleys'.

A handful of Friulian masculine nouns are doubly marked for plurality. Thus /aɲs/ < *an* + *i* + *s* 'years'.

2.2.1.2 *Collective plurals*

In the modern Rhaeto-Romance dialects, most collective plurals are lexical derivations like 'foliage' and 'shrubbery' (thus, for example, Puter /la pɛna/ 'feather', but /il pɛnam/ 'plumage'; Friulian /il rover/ 'oak tree', but /il rovereːt/ 'oak grove'), but there are traces in Romansh of a more regular collective suffix -*a*. There are a few dozen pairs like /krap/ 'rock (m.)' vs. /krapa/ 'rocks (f.)', /iʎ mɛjl/ 'the apple' vs. /la mɛjla/ 'apples' (Surmeiran; see Thöni 1969: 61), /il boSc/ 'tree' vs. /la boSca/ 'trees' (Puter; see Scheitlin 1962: 64) /il dajnt/ 'finger' vs. /la dajnta/ 'fingers' (Vallader; see Arquint 1964: 101) which hint at an inherited neuter plural collective. In Old Surselvan, this was more (possibly entirely) productive, as in example (65):

(65) salida- da   sei- as vus, soingi- a   schanugli- a
     saluted f.sg. be 2 2 pl. holy f.sg.   knee   f.sg.
     'Hail to you, o holy knees'.

where what looks like the feminine singular ending is clearly both syntactically and semantically plural (see Ascoli 1883: 439).

This use of the -*a* collective links Romansh with Italian, but distinguishes it apparently from the Italian dialects of Rhaeto-Romance (see Gregor 1982: 58n.).

2.2.1.3 Summary

The inflectional category of number is the only one that is regularly maintained in common nouns in Rhaeto-Romance without some reduction from the system in Latin. There are traces of a neuter gender, but basically, only the masculine and the feminine survive. Finally, the formation of the plural suggests the loss of the inherited case distinction: either the accusative plural in -*s* has been generally adopted, as in Romansh, or the nominative -*i* and accusative -*s* plurals are lexically conditioned allomorphs, as in the Italian dialects. Only in a handful of artificial archaisms or lexical doublets in Surselvan do we now encounter traces of an inherited case contrast within a single paradigm.

Both gender and case are better maintained in some of the other nominal categories, among them the pronouns and the adjectives.

2.2.2 Inflected pronouns

Inflected pronouns include demonstrative pronouns (among them, the definite articles) and personal pronouns.

2.2.2.1 Demonstrative pronouns

(a) Definite articles

The common inherited paradigm for 'the' throughout Rhaeto-Romance is one of four contrasting forms, wherein all distinctions of case have been neutralized. Surselvan may stand here for our exemplar:

	Singular	*Plural*
Masculine	il	ils
Feminine	la	las

All oblique cases are marked by prepositions.

A recurrent pattern throughout the demonstrative paradigms is a difference between the Romansh and the Italian dialects in the formation of the plural. While Romansh consistently forms the plural by means of the -*s* suffix, the Italian dialects use -*s* in the feminine, and -*i* in the masculine. Thus the masculine plural definite article in both Ladin and Friulian is /i/ (Old Friulian /ju/ – Marchetti 1952: 112; Francescato 1966: 388–9 – deriving from **/ʎu/ corresponds to a singular /lu/), while the feminine plural is a regular reflex of /la(s)/ (Friulian koine /lis/, other Friulian /les/, /las/, /los/).

A further peculiarity of many Italian Rhaeto-Romance dialects is that the feminine plural suffix -*s* is frequently absent. In some cases, this means that feminine plural and feminine singular demonstrative pronouns are identical: for example, the definite article in Ampezzan has f.sg = f.pl. /ra/. In other cases the feminine singular differs from the feminine plural only through the quality of its vowel: for example, in Friulian, f.sg. /la/ is distinct from f.pl. /li/. The loss of the /s/ plural marker has been grammaticized in different ways in the Italian Rhaeto-Romance dialects. A full discussion is postponed to chapter 4, where it will be linked with other questions of agreement.

In some, but not all dialects of modern Surmeiran, there is a case distinction between the unmarked forms above and a common-gender dative form sg. /li/ (< ILLI), pl. /lis/ (< ILLIS). Note the following examples from the dialect of Bergün (Lutta 1923: 326):

(66) muser iʎ tɛərm li feʎ
　　 show the boundary to=the son

(67) fer dzo la plɛtsa liz ardɛfəlts
　　 make down the skin to=the potatoes
　　 'to peel the potatoes'

The same form is used as the dative of the personal pronoun of the third person. In this use, it was still attested in Old Surselvan and Old Puter in the fifteenth and sixteenth centuries. The transition from {lgi} to the modern /ad ɛl/ was almost certainly mediated by the doubly marked construction {a + lgi}, which is also attested in texts from all the major Romansh dialects (see Schmidt 1951/2: 69). There are therefore no great difficulties in reconstructing an inherited dative case deriving from ILLI(S) in Romansh. Nothing similar has ever been attested for definite articles in the Italian Rhaeto-Romance dialects.

(b) The stressed demonstratives

All the Rhaeto-Romance languages have reflexes of ECCU ISTE (/kwɛSt/) and ECCU ILLE (/k(w)ɛl/). In addition, some have a third series of demonstratives derived from ECCE ILLE (/tʃɛl/) (see Prader-Schucany 1970: 151), and Surselvan and Surmeiran have a fourth series derived from ILLE IPSE (see Nay 1965: 134; Thöni 1969: 119; Prader-Schucany 1970: 155). The latter form /ʎets/ 'the same' or 'that' is specifically anaphoric, and is used to refer to entities which have just been (meta-)named, as in the Surselvan dialogue:

(68) – tji a rut il kar?
　　　 who has broken the wagon?

>   – ljets   saj   jaw bUk
>   that   know I   not

Similar is Surmeiran /ʎɛts/ (see Thöni 1969: 122).

   Surselvan and Sutselvan distinguish three genders for ECCU ILLE (Surselvan /kwɛl ~ kwɛla ~ kwej/ ; Sutselvan /kwɪl ~ kwɪla/ ~ kwɪʎ/ 'that'). Surmeiran distinguishes three genders in reflexes of ECCU ILLE (/cɛl ~ cɛla ~ cɛʎ/ 'this'), ECCU ILLE (/tʃɛl ~ tʃɛla ~ tʃɛʎ/ 'that'), and possibly ILLE IPSE (/lets ~ letsa ~ ʎets/) (see Thöni 1969: 119, 122). The bimorphemic origins of this demonstrative are still reflected in the Surmeiran plurals /iʎs ɛts/ (m.) /las ɛtsas/ (f.). Surselvan and Surmeiran are alone in having a series of emphatic pronouns composed of the personal pronouns followed by (reduplicated) reflexes of (ME/TE/SE) + IPSE: thus Surselvan /jaw mets/ 'I myself', etc. There is apparently free variation within Surselvan between 1pl. /nussets-s/ [nussets] ~ /nussets-i/ (see Nay 1965: 134; Prader-Schucany 1970: 157). In Surmeiran, the emphatic pronouns mark gender in the third person: /sets/ 'himself', but /setsa/ 'herself'. Remarkably, Surselvan and Surmeiran also mark case inasmuch as the nominative consists of the unreduplicated form: /mets/ 'I myself', but /mamets/ 'me myself'. The nominative and oblique forms are identical in the 1st plural (/nusets/) and the 2nd plural (/vusets/) (see Thöni 1969: 88).

   Once again, we must note a split between the Romansh and the Italian dialects in the formation of the plural. While the Romansh dialects have the *-s* plural consistently, Ladin and Friulian have *-s* or ∅ in the feminine, but *-i* in the masculine: thus Badiot (Pizzinini and Plangg 1966: xxxix) and Ampezzan (Appollonio 1930: 30):

	Badiot		Ampezzan		Friulian	
	this	*that*	*this*	*that*	*this*	*that*
m.sg.	kɛʃ	kɛl	kesto	kel	kɛSt	kel
m.pl.	kiʃ	ki	kiste	ke	kɛSc	kej
f.sg.	kɛʃta	kɛla	kesta	kera	kɛSte	ke
f.pl.	kɛʃtes	kɛles	kesta	kera	kɛStis	kees

In English, there is a syntactic distinction between demonstratives and the definite article, inasmuch as the latter, which has been effectively reduced to the status of a stressless bound morpheme, cannot function as the surface head of a noun phrase:

	Modifier	*Head*
Demonstrative	that boy	that
Definite	the boy	*the

In the Romansh dialects, and in some Ladin (as also, for example, in

Table 2.13 Rhaeto-Romance interrogatives

Surselvan	Vallader	Fassa	Gardena	Friulian	Gloss	Source
ci	ci	ki	ki	tʃi ~ kuj	'who'	QUI(S)
cej	ce	ke	cɛ	tʃe	'what'	QUID
nua	inɟo				'where'	INDE UBI
		ola	ula			UBI ILLAC
				dula		(IN)DE UBI ILLAC
kura	kura				'when'	QUA HORA
		kaŋ	kaŋ	kwand		QUANDO
pərcej	pərce	pərke		pertʃe	'why'	PER QUID
ko	ko	ko	ko	koɲ	'how'	QUOMODO
				~ tʃemuːt		QUIDMODUM

Spanish) this distinction does not hold, and the definite article may function as the head of a nominal expression when it is itself modified by a relative clause or prepositional phrase.

Surselvan
(69) ils də flɛm
 the of Flem
 'the people (m.) of Flem'

Vallader
(70) ils da gwarda
 the of Guarda
 'the people (m.) of Guarda'

This distributional fact supports classification of the definite article as a form of demonstrative.

A related fact in several Ladin dialects, including Badiot and Gardena, is that reflexes of ILLE and ILLA not only function as definite articles but as the full lexical noun phrases 'man/male' and 'woman/female'.

2.2.2.2 The interrogative pronouns

All Romansh dialects derive 'where' from INDE UBI. Ladin and Friulian derive 'where' from a further composition with ILLAC: Ladin from UBI ILLAC, Friulian from (IN)DE UBI ILLAC. There is a split between Romansh and the Italian Rhaeto-Romance dialects for 'when', Romansh deriving from QUA HORA, the Italian dialects, from QUANDO. See table 2.13

In the modern languages, interrogative pronouns are uninflected for number, gender, or case. Old Surselvan may have retained a case distinction for the pronoun 'who', but it was already in the process of being replaced by the time of the earliest texts:

(71) da cui   filgia   eis ti?
     of who(dat.) daughter   are you
(72) da chi   filg eis ilg matt?
     of who(nom.) son is   the boy

(The examples are from the seventeenth-century text *Barlaam and Josaphat*, annotated by Ascoli (1883: 450)).

Old Friulian generalized QUIS > /tʃi/, while modern Friulian has almost entirely generalized CUI > /kuj/. Old Italian generalized CUI > /kuj/ for all cases: today its use is limited to oblique cases only.

Indefinite pronouns are usually compounded forms of the interrogative pronouns. In Surselvan, the indefinite series consists of /ɛntsa/ + pronoun, where the compounding element derives ultimately from UNUS NON SAPIT. There are partial parallels in various Ladin dialects: Badiot /inssatʃi/ 'someone', Livinallongo /tsakɛj/ 'something', Gardena /tsɛkɛ/ 'something' (Prader-Schucany 1970: 142–4). In Vallader, /incyn/ 'someone' is probably formed on the model of /mincyn/ 'everyone', which derives from OMNE UNQUAM (ibid. 147). Common Rhaeto-Romance /alk/ (Romansh /alc/, Badiot /val(k)/), Fassa /valk/, Ampezzan /algo/, Friulian /alk/ 'something' derives from ALIQUID.

2.2.2.3 The relative pronouns and the complementizer

In all Rhaeto-Romance languages but those of the Engadine, the 'relative pronoun' is invariable and indistinguishable from the complementizer: Surmeiran /ca/, Surselvan, Fassa /ke/, Gardena /kɛ/, Friulian /ku/ ~ /ke/. Throughout northern Italian, however, a contrast between nominative and accusative relative pronouns is common (Rohlfs 1949: II, 233). Few Rhaeto-Romance dialects conform with this tendency to distinguish between the two. Vallader and Puter seem to retain a case distinction between a nominative /ci/ and an accusative /ca/ (Arquint 1964: 61; Scheitlin 1980: 171), but this is in fact originally a contrast between the interrogative pronoun /ci/ and the complementizer /ca/. (The Marebban Ladin nominative /ko/ vs. accusative /ke/ reported by Pizzinini and Plangg (1966: xxxix) should be compared with Friulian /ku/ ~ /ke/.)

Not surprisingly, there is considerable ambiguity, manifested at the syntactic level, in the status of relative pronouns. Some Romansh dialects have an unambiguously distinct set of relative pronouns which are required when the relative pronoun is the object of a preposition: thus Surmeiran /iʎ kal/ 'which (m.sg.)', corresponding exactly to

French *lequel*. The impossibility of *preposition* + *ci*, of course, reinforces the suspicion that the latter is not a true pronoun at all.

Even in those dialects where the relative pronoun is morphologically identical with the complementizer, there is some syntactic evidence, to be assessed in chapter 4, that the two are grammatically distinct: in subject position, the relative pronoun is a true pronoun, while in other positions, it is a complementizer.

The subordinate conjunctions 'when', 'where', and their like, consist generally of the interrogative pronoun followed by the complementizer, as is usual in northern Italian dialects. Vallader and Badiot are regular in this. In most of the other Rhaeto-Romance languages, as in standard Italian, the subordinate conjunctions 'because' and 'as' are identical with the interrogative pronouns 'why' and 'how'.

2.2.2.4 *The personal pronouns*

All the Rhaeto-Romance languages today but Surselvan have two sets of pronouns: a full, stressed, or disjunctive set which pattern syntactically with common nouns (these are all that survive in Surselvan), and an atonic or clitic set. This distinction is relatively recent: Old Surselvan had atonic pronouns, and their replacement over the last several hundred years by the stressed forms is generally considered the outcome of German influence (see Ascoli 1883: 453–4; Stimm 1973). (It should be noted, however, that the loss of atonic pronouns may be internally motivated also. Tagliavini (1926: 69) noted that atonic pronouns were scarcely used in the Comelico dialects. Their loss cannot be ascribed to German influence. Nor can the loss of atonic object pronouns in the transition between Old and Middle English, which resulted in the generalization of SVO order.) Of course, the predominance of atonic pronouns in the Engadine dialects, Ladin, and Friulian could just as readily be ascribed to northern Italian influence, and the question of which was the 'original' Rhaeto-Romance structure is completely open.

The universally shared inflectional categories of Rhaeto-Romance personal pronouns are the three persons in both singular and plural, and the two animate genders in the third person. Many dialects have a 3rd singular 'expletive' or dummy pronoun (usually the masculine, in a few cases, the feminine, or, as in the Romansh dialects, a special neuter form). There is considerable variation in the case systems, both in the cases that are maintained, and in the places where they are retained.

The pronoun of polite address (V) is third person in the Engadine dialects. It is 2nd plural in Surselvan, and in Ladin (Elwert 1943: 133). In Surmeiran, V is usually 2nd plural, but the third person is used for clergy. In Friulian, as in northern Italian generally, 2pl. /vo/ is used (or used to be) for polite address to friends and relatives, and contrasts with the exclusively *plural* (doubly marked) 2pl. /voaltris/ 'you others'. The third person is used with superiors and strangers (Marchetti 1952: 136). That is, in those dialects where both 2nd plural and third person are possible forms of V, the latter connotes greater respect than does the former.

(a) Object pronouns

In all Rhaeto-Romance languages but Surmeiran and the Engadine dialects, object pronouns distinguish a dative and accusative case in at least some persons. The Engadine dialects still had the oblique/direct distinction in the sixteenth century (but no nominative/accusative distinction in the third person).

The Italian dialects and the eastern Romansh dialects retain a partitive pronoun from INDE corresponding to French *en*, Italian *ne*, Venetian (*ghe*)*ne*: Surmeiran /and/, Puter /(a)nd/, Ladin /n(e)/, Friulian /ndi/. In many Ladin and Friulian varieties, this pronoun is limited in its distribution to those forms of the verb 'be' which begin with a vowel. In the Engadine dialects, the form survives mainly as an enlargement of postvocalic vowel-initial forms of 'have' and 'be': thus Puter {eau d'he} 'I have', but {eau nun he} 'I have not'; Vallader {i'd eira} 'it was', but {i nun eira} 'it was not'.

Surselvan

Table 2.14 Surselvan oblique personal pronouns

	Stressed		Atonic (Old Surselvan only)	
	Dative	*Accusative*	*Dative*	*Accusative*
Singular				
1	a mi	me	mi	mi
2	a ti	te	tgi	tei ~ ta
3m.	ad ɛl	ɛl		
	aʎi		lgi	ilg
f.	ad ɛla	ɛla		
Plural				
1	a nus	nus	nus	nus
2	a vus	vus	vus	vus
3	ad ɛls	ɛls	–	–

Except in the 1st singular and 2nd singular, the stressed pronouns are identical not only in the dative and the accusative, but in the nominative as well. (Note that the accusative form is used as the object of the preposition /de/ for the expression of the genitive case.)

Clearly, the morphological differences between tonic and atonic object pronouns are trivial. Given the uncertainty of phonetically interpreting Old Surselvan orthography, the only reliable way to identify atonic pronouns is from their word order. Stressed object pronouns follow the finite verb, while atonic object pronouns precede it, and may undergo 'clitic climbing', appearing with the inflected verb which governs the infinitive with which they are in construction. Contrast the following examples, both from the New Testament translation of L. Gabriel 1648 (examples of both kinds of pronouns could be multiplied until the eighteenth century, by which time tonic pronouns increasingly predominate):

(73) un da vus *mi* ven ad antardir
      one of you me will to betray
      'One of you will betray me.'

(John 13: 21)

(74) Philippe, chi c' ha vieu *mei*, ha vieu ilg Bab
      Philip who that has seen me has seen the Father

(John 14: 9)

Surmeiran

Table 2.15 Surmeiran oblique personal pronouns

	Stressed	Atonic (now literary only)
Singular		
1	me	am
2	te	at
3m.	ɛl	iʎ
f.	ɛla	la
Plural		
1	nus	ans
2	vus	ats
3m.	ɛls	iʎs
f.	ɛlas	las

It should be noted that the stressed pronouns fail not only to distinguish dative from accusative, but also nominative from oblique. Except in the 1st singular, the stressed forms above are identical with the nominative forms.

Puter

Table 2.16 Puter oblique personal pronouns

	Stressed	Atonic Accusative	(Dative)
Singular			
1	me	am	
2	te	at	
3m.	ɛl	al	(il)
f.	ɛla	la	
Plural			
1	nus	ans	
2	vus	as	
3m.	ɛls	als	(ils)
f.	ɛlas	las	

Again, the stressed pronouns are almost entirely analytic, and mark case only in the 1st singular and 2nd singular.

Old Puter had a set of stressed dative common-gender third-person pronouns which were doubly marked:

(75) Iesus   arespundet   *agli*
      Jesus   answered   him

(John 1: 36 in Bifrun 1560)

Vallader

Table 2.17 Vallader oblique personal pronouns

	Stressed	Atonic
Singular		
1	maj	(ə)m
2	taj	(ə)t
3m.	ɛl	til
f.	ɛla	tila
Plural		
1	nus ~ no	(ə)ns
2	vus ~ vo	(ə)s
3m.	ɛls	tils
f.	ɛlas	tilas

Old Vallader forms of the atonic pronouns were indistinguishable from subject pronouns in the third person: 3sg. *il* ~ *al*, 3pl. *ils* ~ *als*. The following examples, from the Bible translation of Vulpius and Dorta of 1679, are representative:

(76) meis maun vain *als* sterminar
     my hand comes them exterminate
     'My hand shall destroy them.'

(Exodus 15: 9)

(77) e'l   mar *ils* ha cuvernads
     and the sea them has covered (m.pl.)
     'and the sea covered them.'

(Exodus 15: 10)

The modern forms are an innovation whose origin is unclear.

Fassa

Table 2.18 Fassa oblique personal pronouns

	Stressed		Atonic	
	Dative	Accusative	Dative	Accusative
Singular				
1	a mi	me	me	me
2	a ti	te	te	te
3m.	ɛl	ɛl	ʝe ~ j	el ~ lo ~ l
f.	ɛla	ɛla	ʝe ~ j	la ~ l
Plural				
1	nos	nos	ne	ne
2	vo	vo	ve	ve
3m.	itʃ	itʃ	ʝe ~ j	i
f.	ɛles	ɛles	ʝe ~ j	les

Like Fassan, Gardenese distinguishes between dative and accusative tonic pronouns in the first and second persons of the singular.

Typical of Gardenese, Marebban, and Badiot is an atonic 3sg. and 3pl. /ti/ (only feminine in Badiot and Marebban) whose origin is unclear (see Kramer 1977: 59).

The Gardena and Badiot dialects have an indefinite subject pronoun [uŋ] ~ [an(g)], derived from UNUS and, possibly, HOMO.

Ampezzan

Table 2.19 Ampezzan oblique personal pronouns

	Stressed		Atonic
Singular			
1	a mi	me	me
2	a ti	te	te
3m.		el	l(o)
f.		era	r
Plural			
1		nos	me (*sic*)
2		vos	ve
3m.		lore	i
f.		eres	i

Friulian

Table 2.20 Friulian oblique personal pronouns

	Stressed		Atonic	
	Dative	Accusative	Dative	Accusative
Singular				
1	a mi	me	mi	mi
2	a ti	te	ti	ti
3m.	a luj	luj	i	lu
f.	a je	je	i	la
Plural				
1	a noaltris	no(altris)	nus	nus (∼ ni)
2	a voaltris	vo(altris)	us	us (∼ vi)
3m.	a lor	lor	ur	ju
f.	a lor	lor	ur	lis

(b) Subject pronouns

Stressed subject pronouns are distinct from non-subject pronouns in the
1st singular and (except in Surmeiran) in the 2nd singular. Case marking
is much richer in the atonic (synthetic) forms which carry on the
inherited system much more faithfully than the recent stressed analytic
forms. Note that only the Romansh forms have a distinctive neuter 3rd
singular expletive pronoun (and that this form occurs only in the
nominative).

Surselvan

Table 2.21 Subject pronouns in Surselvan

	Stressed	*Atonic (where distinct from stressed)*
Singular		
1	jaw	
2	ti	*null*
3m.	ɛl	
f.	ɛla	
n.	iʎ ~ ej	i
p.	ins	
Plural		
1	nus	
2	vus	*null*
3m.	ɛls	
f.	ɛlas	
c.	ej	

The singular '3p.' form in table 2.21 is the indefinite subject pronoun PRO, manifested in German as *man*, in French as *on*, in Gardenese and Badiot as *aŋ*. It takes singular agreement in direct word order, but (what looks like) plural agreement in inverted word order:

(78) ins   Sto
     PRO   must
(79) Sto- n ins?
     must   PRO?

In fact, the /n/ is a hiatus breaking consonant which is absent after consonant-final stems. Thus /dat ins/ 'Does PRO give?' demonstrates that in the modern language /n/ is not exactly the 3rd plural ending. Nevertheless, it is almost certain that etymologically, that is what it was. The plural '3c' form in table 2.21 is a common-gender pronoun, not a neuter plural. Nor is it an indefinite subject pronoun. The neuter singular occurs in two phonetically conditioned forms (/iʎ/ before vowels, /ej/ before consonants), and is the only Surselvan pronoun which has a true atonic form. This latter occurs exclusively in inverted word order:

(80) ilj   ej   bi
     it   is   fine
     'It's nice weather.'
(81) ej- s-   i   bi?
     is   (hiatus)   it   nice
     'Is it nice weather?'

The distribution of the second-person 'atonic' subject pronoun *null* is exactly the same, but it is unclear whether zero represents phonetic reduction or syntactic deletion attested in Swiss German and other Germanic languages. Assuming that phonetic reduction is exceptionless, but that rules of syntactic deletion are more facultative, the existence of variation between pairs like /ejs (ti) iws/ 'Did you go?' would seem to indicate that second-person postverbal null in Surselvan (as in the other Romansh dialects) is deleted by a syntactic rule analogous to the one which allowed 'Hast killed the Jabberwock?'

The same deletion of the postverbal 2nd singular form is found in Badiot and Gardenese (see Benincà 1985). The feature sharply distinguishes these dialects from Friulian, Fassan, and other northern Italian dialects, where the 2nd singular subject pronoun is the only one that is never deleted.

Surmeiran

Table 2.22 Subject pronouns in Surmeiran

	Stressed	Atonic
Singular		
1	iə	a
2	te	(∅)
3m.	ɛl	l
f.	ɛla	la
n.	iʎ ~ ʎ	i(ʎ)
p.	ins	
Plural		
1	nus	a
2	vus	(∅)
3m.	ɛls	iʎ
f.	ɛlas	iʎ

The singular '3p.' form in table 2.22, as in Surselvan, renders the unspecified agent PRO:

(82) ins   dovra adɛɲa artɛcəl ɛ   furma fɛminina
      PRO uses   always article and form feminine
      'The article and feminine form is always used.'

Puter

Table 2.23 Subject pronouns in Puter

	Stressed	*Atonic*
Singular		
1	ε(w)	i
2	ty	*null*
3m.	εl	
f.	εla	
n.	a(d)	e ~ a ~ o
Plural		
1	nus	a
2	vus	*null*
3m.	εls	e
f.	εlas	e

The 3rd singular neuter pronoun in Old Puter was derived from ILLUD, like the Surselvan form /iʎ/ of today. Note the examples from Bifrun 1560:

(83) eilg es ieu oura üna crida da Caesare Augusto
     it is gone out a decree from Caesar Augustus
     'There went out a decree from Caesar Augustus.'

(Luke 2: 1)

(84) perche elg es huoz naschieu a vus l'g salueder
     because it is today born to you the saviour
     'Because unto you is born this day a saviour.'

(Luke 2: 11)

The likelihood of modern /a(d)/ (see table 2.23) deriving from ID is thus somewhat diminished. Its origin is unclear.

Vallader

Table 2.24 Subject pronouns in Vallader

	Stressed	*Atonic*
Singular		
1	ε(w)	a
2	ty	*null*
3m.	εl	l
f.	εla	la
n.	i(d)	(a)
Plural		
1	no	a
2	vo	*null*
3m.	εls	a
f.	εlas	a
c.	i	a

Note that in Vallader, as in Surselvan and Surmeiran, the common gender 3rd plural is morphologically identical with the 3rd singular neuter form (see table 2.24). (This is a case of homonymy, rather than motivated polysemy, however. The neuter singular form derives from ILLUD, the common-gender plural from ILLI. Nevertheless, the similarity with analogous polysemy in the Friulian dialects and Lombard varieties is striking.)

It may be noted in passing that the distinction between a common gender and a masculine 3rd plural form in Surselvan, Surmeiran, and Vallader marks an idiosyncratic transformation of the inherited case distinction between nominative ILLI and accusative ILLOS: the former became the common-gender pronoun, and the latter the masculine pronoun of the third-person plural.

Ladin

Table 2.25 Subject pronouns in Fassa and Ampezzan Ladin

	Fassa		*Ampezzan*	
	Stressed	*Atonic*	*Stressed*	*Atonic*
Singular				
1	ʝe	e	jo	–
2	tu	te	tu	te ~ to
3m.	ɛl	ɛl	el	(e)l
f.	ɛla	la	era	r
Plural				
1	no	*null*	nos	–
2	vo(etres)	*null*	vos	o
3m.	idz	i	lore	i
f.	eles	les	eres	(e)s

In Marebban, Badiot, and Gardenese, atonic subject pronouns occur only in postverbal position. The Badiot paradigm below is representative.

Badiot

Table 2.26 Subject pronouns in Upper Badiot

	Stressed	*Atonic*
Singular		
1	jø	i
2	tø	(te)
3m.	ɛl	(e)l
f.	ɛla	(ɛ)la
Plural		
1	nos	ze
2	os	ze
3m.	ɛj	aj
f.	ɛles	eles

Friulian Koine

Table 2.27 Subject pronouns in Friulian koine

	Stressed	*Atonic*	
Singular			
1	jo	i ∼ o	(*S. Carnic null*)
2	tu	tu	(*W. Friulian* te)
3m.	luj	al	(*W. Friulian* al ∼ a)
f.	je	e	(*S. Carnic, W. Friulian* a)
Plural			
1	no(altris)	i ∼ o	(*S. Carnic, W. Friulian null*)
2	vo(altris)	i ∼ o	(*S. Carnic, W. Friulian null*)
3m.	lor	a	(*S. Carnic* aj)
f.	lor	a	(*S. Carnic* as)

Some varieties of western Friulian (see table 2.27) have a double series of atonic subject pronouns (see Benincà 1986) : 1/2. *-i*, 3 *-a*. These follow and reinforce the regular atonic pronouns and never occur in postverbal position. Double marking of this sort is endemic in northern Italian dialects (see Spiess 1956).

The comparative syntax of the clitic pronouns in Rhaeto-Romance, as in the other Romance languages, is one of the most interesting topics in Rhaeto-Romance grammar. The morphological parallelism among the various Rhaeto-Romance dialects suggests a close relationship among them, regardless of how profoundly their syntax may differ (see Vanelli 1984a,b; Benincà 1986).

The coexistence of stressed and atonic pronouns is a characteristic feature of all northern Italian dialects above a Spezia–Rimini isogloss. We will return to this topic in our discussion of the comparative syntax of subject pronouns in chapter 4.

2.2.2.5 Atonic reflexive pronouns

Reflexive pronouns are like subject and object pronouns in that they occur both as stressed and atonic forms. The stressed or emphatic reflexive pronouns in Surselvan and Surmeiran have already been dealt with in our discussion of demonstratives, but it is worth mentioning them again here. In addition to their emphatic function as appositives in the nominative case, and as objects of prepositions in the oblique case, emphatic pronouns may act as objects of verbs when they are under contrastive stress. The point is illustrated by sentences like the Old Surselvan (Wendenzen 1701, anthologized in Ulrich 1882):

(85) auters ha   el gidau,   *sesets*   po   el buca gidar
     others has he helped himself can he not   help

The status of stressed reflexives as arguments of the verb is as uncontroversial as that of full noun phrases. The interesting questions concerning reflexive pronouns and transitivity relate only to the reduced incorporated forms: the atonic reflexive pronouns.

The indeterminate status of reflexives between transitive and intransitive verbs is graphically illustrated by the syntax of reflexive pronouns. If reflexive verbs were transitives, we should expect to group reflexive pronouns with object pronouns. The extent to which it is impossible to do this reflects the extent to which reflexive verbs pattern with intransitives.

Generally speaking, reflexive pronouns differ from object pronouns in being more reduced, both morphologically and syntactically. Reduction manifests itself morphologically, by syncretism: a reduction in the number of categories that are overtly expressed in the reflexive paradigm. Reduction is manifested in two ways syntactically: by greater rigidity in word order, and by the loss of agreement with reflexive objects. Both are to be expected as the reflexive pronoun loses argument status and becomes more and more like an affix with a fixed position on the verb.

In view of the fact that Surselvan has in general eliminated atonic object pronouns in favour of the stressed analytic forms, and has only one true atonic subject pronoun, it appears paradoxical that reflexive pronouns in this language are more reduced than they are in any other Rhaeto-Romance language. There is only a single reflexive morpheme /sə/ for all persons and numbers. The position of this invariable morpheme is also fixed: irrespective of mood or the presence of auxiliaries on the main verb, the reflexive morpheme always appears as (the only) prefix on the main verb. Thus:

(86) jaw sun *sə-* ləgr- aw-   s
     I   am self rejoice (p.p.) (m.sg.)
     'I (male) rejoiced.'
(87) *sə-* ləgr- ej
     self rejoice (imp.pl.)
     'Rejoice, you all!'

The reduction of the paradigm is apparently a comparatively recent demolition in Surselvan. In texts of the eighteenth century, we still find reflexives with a full paradigm. However, the position of the reflexive pronoun as an invariable prefix on the verb was already established in

Old Surselvan. In Old Sutselvan, we find the same morphological richness, but a somewhat different syntactic pattern. Reflexive objects, like other object pronouns, always precede the verb whose objects they are, but may, like other clitics, undergo clitic climbing, as in example (91).

Surselvan

(88) *ta*   partraigchie vid' ilg gy d' ilg Sabbath
     yourself bethink   of   the day of the Sabbath
                    (Bible of L. Gabriel, 1648: Ten Commandments)

(89) a *sa*   tschinta' anturn
     and himself girded   about
                     (Bible of L. Gabriel, 1648: John 13:4)

(90) quou *mi*   volve' jou
     when myself turned I
                    (Bible of 1718; Ecclesiastes 2: 12)

Sutselvan

(91) avaunt quellas na *te*   dees   inclinar
     before these not yourself must (you) bow
          (Bonifaci's Bible, 1601: Ten Commandments)

In all the other Rhaeto-Romance languages, the reflexive object either shows some person/number distinctions and/or manifests some syntactic behaviour which reflects the status of a nominal argument.

This is least so in Surmeiran, where an absolutely invariable reflexive /sa/ does occur, but is stigmatized (Thöni 1969: 53). The preferred reflexive paradigm is:

	Singular	Plural
1	ma	ans
2	ta	ats
3	sa	sa

The reflexive auxiliary in the perfect is /aveir/ 'have', as for all transitive verbs. But there are two crucial syntactic differences between the reflexive object and all other object pronouns. First, unlike other object pronouns, the reflexive pronoun does not have argument status in that it does not cause the participle to agree with it in number and gender:

(92) nus vaɲ la da- *da*
     we have her given (f.sg.)
     'We have given it to her.'

(93) nus vaɲ ans do   –
     we have us given (unmarked: m.sg.)
     'We have given it to ourselves.'

(Note that in Surmeiran, agreement of the past participle with a dative object is possible.)

Second, object pronouns in general precede the verb in the indicative, but follow it in the imperative (as they do in French, for example). Reflexive pronouns exhibit such mobility in the 2nd singular imperative, but not in the 2nd plural:

	Object pronoun	*Reflexive pronoun*
Imperative singular	laʃ-m	laʃa-t
	'let me'	'let yourself'
plural	laʃe-m	ats laʃe
	'let me'	'let yourselves'

For purposes of comparison, here are the corresponding forms of the second-person indicative:

Indicative singular	am laʃas	at laʃas
	'let me'	'let yourself'
plural	am laʃajs	ats laʃajs
	'let me'	'let yourselves'

Modern Surmeiran tends to prefer the analytic form of the reflexive pronoun: thus *laʃa me* 'let me' and *laʃe vus* 'let yourselves' (see Thöni 1969: 130).

In the Engadine dialects, reflexive pronouns are treated in almost every way like other objects. The reflexive pronouns in Puter are almost exactly the same as in Surmeiran:

	Singular	*Plural*
1	am	ans
2	at	as
3	as	as

The perfect auxiliary with reflexive verbs is /avɛr/ 'have'. Reflexive objects pattern with other object pronouns in causing gender and number agreement:

(94) ils mats s- ɛm lavo- s
the boys themselves have washed (m.pl.)

in being sensitive to the mood of the verb (reflexive objects, like other objects, follow the (positive familiar) imperative verb whose objects they are):

(95) SdaSda- t
wake(imp.) yourself
'Wake up!'

and in undergoing clitic climbing. From the examples below, where the blank marks the origin of the reflexive clitic, it would seem that agreement of the perfect participle must follow clitic climbing:

(96) l   armɛda   s   ɔ   Stuvi- da   [____rɔtrɛr]
     the army (f.) self has must (f.sg.) to = retreat
     'The army had to retreat.'
(97) nus ans   avɛns Stuviw- s   [____kuntantɛr da pɔc]
     we ourselves have must   (m.pl.) to = content of little
     'We have had to content ourselves with little.'

Although the past participle agrees with both direct and indirect preceding pronominal objects in general, there may be a difference between the two after clitic climbing. Contrasting with examples (96) and (97) above are examples like (98), where a climbed dative reflexive does not cause agreement:

(98) nus ans   avɛns vuliw -   [____ rɛndɔr il vjedi
     we ourselves have wanted (m.sg.)   render the trip
     ply lijɛr pusibɔl]
     more easy possible
     'We wanted to make the trip as easy for ourselves as possible.'

In all significant respects, reflexive pronouns in Vallader, both in their morphology and in their syntax, are indistinguishable from the pronouns in Puter.

In Ladin, atonic reflexives are identical with objects except in the third person and the 1st plural, where the reflexive is /se/ (Elwert 1943: 135). Like atonic objects, the reflexive pronouns are subject to movement depending on the mood of the verb whose objects they are, preceding the verb in all moods but the positive imperative. Ladin reflexive pronouns exhibit the following peculiarities:

(a) the reflexive direct object clitic does not cause agreement of the following perfect participle;
(b) irrespective of its function, the reflexive clitic, where it co-occurs with a third person direct or indirect object, precedes it (agreeing in this respect with Friulian and other northern Italian dialects, as opposed to standard Italian).

In Friulian, there is some variation concerning the reflexive paradigm. Most Friulian varieties have *si* in the third person only. Iliescu (1972: 151) reports on the possibility of invariable *si* (except in the 1st singular, where the only proper reflexive is /mi/), but maintains that the reflexive may be identical with the object pronouns in all persons and numbers but the third (where, of course, the reflexive must be /si/). Thus, the possibility of both (99) and (100):

(99) ruʃi-   *ti*
     scratch yourself
(100) cimo *si*   klamis- tu
      how   yourself call   you
      'What is your name?'

Like atonic object pronouns, reflexive clitics precede the verbal complex except in the positive imperative and the infinitive. In Friulian, as in Ladin, the reflexive object may co-occur with, and precede, the accusative object pronoun. For illustration of this last point, which distinguishes the Italian dialects from those Romansh dialects which allow clitic doubling at all, consider examples (101)–(103):

Surmeiran
(101) i   *la* s- o   pɛrs- a
      PRO her self has lost   (f.sg.)
      'PRO has lost it; it has been lost'

(Bergün; Rohlfs 1975: 55)

Fassan
(102) *se* *la* mɛnar a   casa
      self her take   to house
      'to take her home for himself'
Friulian
(103) *si* *ju*   sint
      self them hears
      'PRO hears them; they are heard'

(In the Surmeiran and Friulian examples, the reflexive clitic is interpreted as an impersonal subject, which, following Perlmutter (1971), we designate as PRO. For the syntax of this 'second si' in Friulian, see Benincà and Vanelli (1985).)

We will return to a fuller discussion of the syntax of reflexive object (and impersonal subject) clitics in chapter 4.

2.2.3 Adjectives

The term 'adjectives', used here in the broadest possible sense, includes four classes of modifiers:

(a) true adjectives like 'big' and 'small';
(b) perfect participles;

Table 2.28 Case and number on adjectives in Old Surselvan

	True adjectives	Perfect participles	Possessive pronominal adjectives
Nom.sg.	sauns	ludaws	mes
Acc.sg.	saun	ludaw	miw
Nom.pl.	sauni	ludaj	mej
Acc.pl.	sauns	ludaws	mes
	'healthy'	'praised'	'my'

(c) possessive pronominal adjectives;
(d) numerals and indefinite articles

In our survey of the morphology of adjectives, so defined, we encounter, for the first time, a morpho-syntactic feature which sets Rhaeto-Romance off from every other Romance language. On closer examination, however, it appears that this feature cannot be used to define Rhaeto-Romance, since it occurs only in Surselvan. Pushing back as far as the written record allows, we may detect traces of the same feature in Sutselvan, Surmeiran, and Vallader. But this is as wide a distribution as we can find for the retention (and transformation) of the inherited -US/-UM distinction.

In Old Surselvan, adjectives were still inflected for case in both the masculine singular and plural. (In the feminine, the oblique or accusative case had been generalized in all Rhaeto-Romance languages. The neuter had disappeared in all Rhaeto-Romance languages but Surselvan. In this language, as in Latin, -UM was ambiguously masculine singular accusative, or neuter singular.)

Formulaically, the oppositions in masculine adjectives were as set out in table 2.28. In this idealized system (which was already in decay by the time of the earliest seventeenth-century texts), nominative singular and accusative plural are identical, as in Old French. In accordance with Kuryłowicz's fourth law of analogy (1949), the relatively peripheral case distinction was sacrificed in favour of maintaining the number distinction. This had already taken place for *nouns* some time after the twelfth century (Ettmayer 1919), but took place only much later for adjectives. Both the past productivity, and the current decay, of the inherited system, are graphically displayed in the single sentence from Alig's (Surselvan) *Epistolas* of 1674:

(104) vus   esses schubr- *i*   aber bucca tuts . . .
      you   are   clean   (m.pl.nom.)   but   not   all (m.pl.acc.)

(105) vus   esses bucca tuts   schuber- *s*
      you   are   not   all (m.pl.acc.)   clean   (m.pl.acc.)

The productivity we may infer from the appearance of the plural -*s*/-*i*
Latin endings on the German borrowing *schuber* (< *sauber* 'clean'). The
decay is evident from the apparently free variation between -*s* and -*i*
plurals in the same line.

The case system is best attested as a case/gender system in the
paradigm of possessive pronominal adjectives in Old Sutselvan and Old
Puter. In the Catechism of Bonifaci and the Bible of Bifrun, there is still
an orthographic distinction between {me(a)s} (usually masculine singular nominative) and {m(i)eu} (usually masculine singular accusative or
neuter singular) 'my', and so on. Examples (106) and (107) are
instructive:

Old Sutselvan (Bonifaci 1601)
(106) (I am the Lord)   *teas*   Deis
                  your   God
(107) (thou anointest)   igl   *meu*   cheu
                  the   my   head

but compare:

(108) incunter   igl   *teas*   prossem
     against   the   thy   neighbour

Old Puter (Bifrun 1560)
(109) (that thou not strike)   *tieu*   pe   in   la   pedra
                       your   foot   in   the   rocks
                                        (Matthew 4: 6)
(110) (if thy hand or)   *tes*   pe   es   a   ti   inskiadel
                  your   foot   is   to   you   offence
                                  (Matthew 18: 8)

but compare, from the same verse:

(111) che   schi   *tieu*   maun   u (thy foot offend thee)
      that   if   your   hand   or

with apparent free variation between {tes} and {tieu}.

All the modern Rhaeto-Romance languages have completely eliminated the case distinction in the plural number. But they have done so in
different ways. Surselvan has generalized the (accusative) -*s* for true
adjectives and possessive pronominal adjectives, but the nominative -*i*
for perfect participles: /bun-s/ 'good (m.pl.)', /me-s/ 'My (m.pl.)', but
/luda-i/ 'praised (m.pl.)'. Surmeiran, Puter, and Vallader, have
generalized the accusative for all plural adjectives. Ladin (both Badiot
and Fassa dialects) has generalized the nominative for (almost) all

masculine plural adjectives, but the accusative for feminines (Elwert 1943: 131; Pizzinini and Plangg 1966: xxxix; Kramer 1976: 29–54). Thus Badiot /debl/ 'weak' has plurals *debli* (m.pl.) and *debles* (f.pl.), /bon/ 'good' has plurals *boɲ* (m.pl.) and *bones* (f.pl.), /nɔʃ/ 'our' has *nyʃ*(m.pl.) and *nɔʃtes* (f.pl.), while /dut/ 'all' has *dyc* (m.pl.) and *dytes* (f.pl.). (On the other hand, note /ladiŋ/ 'ladin', whose masculine plural is /ladiŋs/). Fassan /ʒown/ 'young' has plurals /ʒojɲ/ (m.pl.) and /ʒownes/ (f.pl.), the regular pattern. (But /dur/ 'hard' and /pjeŋ/ 'full' have the -*s* plural in both genders.) Friulian forms the plural of adjectives in the same way as the plural of nouns. Only adjectives in final /l/ regularly form the masculine plural by conversion of this final segment to /j/. A handful of others, like *bon* 'good' and *tut* 'all', form their masculine plurals by palatalization of the final segment. There is a tendency for double marking of plurality to occur: thus *boɲ* and *boɲs* (< *boɲs) are both possible for 'good (m.pl.)'. In fact, even triple marking is possible, as in /bojɲʃ/ (< *boni* + *s* + *i*) (see Benincà and Vanelli 1978; Rizzolatti 1981: 42–3). But perfect participles always form their masculine plurals with -*s*.

The case system has also been entirely lost in the singular for all the modern Rhaeto-Romance languages but Surselvan. Surmeiran has generalized the accusative for true adjectives and perfect participles. But the nominative is apparently in free variation with the accusative for possessive pronominal adjectives: /bun/ 'good', /kanto/ 'sung', but /miə-s/ ~ /mi-ə/ 'my'. The contrast is illustrated by /iʎ miəs bab/ 'my father' vs. /iʎ miə riSplej/ 'my pencil'. There may once have been a time when this was a gender distinction between masculine and neuter: if so, it is not consistent any longer. Puter has generalized the accusative for all singular adjectives: /bun/ 'good', /canto/ 'sung', and /miw/ 'my'. Vallader has generalized the accusative (now *null*) for all adjectives and perfect participles, and the nominative (-*s*) for possessive pronominal adjectives: /bun/ 'good', /canta/ 'sung', but /me-s/ 'my'. The Italian languages have generalized the accusative for all adjectives in the singular. In other words, there is no trace of any case distinction in the singular in any of the Italian Rhaeto-Romance dialects. Surselvan alone retains the inherited -US/-UM distinction, to mark both gender and case.

As a gender marker, -UM carries a very low functional load. No common nouns in the language are neuter; neuter -UM is used as the unmarked gender for predicate adjectives which agree with no noun phrase, or with one of the pronouns /iʎ/ 'it', /kwej/ 'that', or /ʎets/ 'that':

(112)   il   ej   bun-   *s*
        he   is   good   (m.sg.)

(113) iʎ ej biən -
     it is good (n.sg.)

As a case marker, -UM now marks *attributive*, rather than *accusative* masculine singular inflection, while -US now marks *predicative*, rather than *nominative* singular inflection (see Roberge 1989):

Attributive
(114) in biən- ____ ɷm
     a good (m.sg. attr.) man
(115) miw- ____ kudiʃ
     my (m.sg.attr.) book
(116) in kudiʃ əmblidaw- ____
     a book forgotten (m.sg. attr.)

Predicative
(117) il ɷm ej bun- *s*
     the man is good (m.sg. pred.)
(118) il kudiʃ ej me - *s*
     the book is my (m.sg. pred.)
(119) il kudiʃ ej əmblidaw- *s*
     the book is forgotten (m.sg. pred.)

It is of some typological interest that as a consequence of this transformation, Surselvan is now one of the tiny handful of languages (Hungarian is another) in which the attributive adjectives are less richly inflected for agreement than are the predicate adjectives: predicate adjectives mark three genders, while attributive adjectives mark only two.

The stages whereby this reinterpretation and transformation occurred are essentially unknown, but perhaps can be plausibly reconstructed as follows. In the absence of *accusative* + *infinitive* constructions in Surselvan, the predicative adjective (unlike the attributive adjective) could appear *only* in the nominative case. As often happens in semantic change, the *par excellence* meaning of a form – that meaning which only the form in question may have – is reinterpreted as its new basic meaning (see Greenberg 1966). Thus, the original restriction of the predicative position (that it could tolerate only the nominative form of the adjective) might have led to a *par excellence* meaning of the nominative: only this case could mark predicative adjectives. And this could lead eventually to the new meaning of the nominative as the marker of the predicative masculine singular. (In the absence of actual historical attestation, this remains purely speculative: we do not know how -US/-UM became reinterpreted.)

Table 2.29 Gender and number on adjectives in Surselvan

	Singular			*Plural*	
(a) True adjectives (e.g. /grond/ 'big')					
Masculine	grond-s			grond-s	
Neuter	grond				
Feminine	grond-a			grond-as	
(b) Perfect participles (e.g. /ludaw/ 'praised')					
Masculine	ludaw-s			luda-i	
Neuter	ludaw				
Feminine	luda-da			luda-das	
(c) Possessive pronominal adjectives					
	Masculine	Feminine	Neuter	Masculine	Feminine
Singular					
1	mes	mia	miw	mes	mias
2	tes	tia	tiw	tes	tias
3	ses	sia	siw	ses	sias
Plural					
1	nɔs	nɔsa	niəs	nɔs	nɔsas
2	vɔs	vɔsa	viəs	vɔs	vɔsas
3	lur	lur	lur	lur	lur

Representative paradigms for regular adjectives in the major dialects are given below. A distinction must be made between possessive pronominal adjectives (= prenominal attributive forms), and possessive pronouns (= postnominal attributive and predicative adjective forms). A striking feature of the Italian dialects is the near-identity of the singular and plural forms throughout much of the paradigm for the possessive pronominal (attributive) adjectives.

2.2.3.1 Surselvan

Note, once again, that 'neuter' in this language actually has two meanings: 'neuter' and 'masculine attributive'. The label 'masculine' is limited in the singular to masculine predicative forms. Note also that in the paradigm in table 2.29 for possessive pronominal adjectives, the suffix -*s* marks both the masculine singular attributive (< US) and the masculine plural (< OS).

The attributive/predicative distinction in Surselvan is doubly marked for a number of stems where final -UM conditioned either vowel umlaut or palatalization of the final consonant. Thus /il ɔm ej bun-s/ 'The man is good', but /in biən ɔm/ 'a good man'. In Sutselvan, although the predicate -*s* is gone, the difference between -US and -UM remains in contrasts like /in biən kunti/ 'a good knife' vs. /il kunti ej bun/ 'The knife is good' (see Tekavčić 1974: 363n).

In Surselvan, predicate adjectives are morphologically distinct from attributive adjectives in the masculine singular. Possessive pronouns are identical with predicate forms of the possessive pronominal adjectives:

(120) kwej ej miw- _____
      that is mine (n.sg.)

(121) la   kavala ej mi-   *a*
      the mare   is mine (f.sg.)

(122) il   kavaʎ ej miw- *s*
      the horse is mine (m.sg.)

This suggests that the predicative form of the possessive pronominal adjective is simply a predicative adjective. On the other hand, the possessive pronoun looks like this:

	Singular	*Plural*
Masculine	il miw	ils mes
Feminine	la mia	las mias

The masculine singular form is identical with the neuter, or identical with the masculine singular attributive form of the possessive pronominal adjective. This suggests that the possessive pronoun derives from a more abstract noun phrase with a pronominal head.

In Surmeiran, the possessive pronoun is identical with the possessive pronominal adjective. The identity extends to the free variation between reflexes of -UM and -US forms in the masculine or neuter singular:

(123) kɛʎ ɛ miəs/miə
      that is mine (non-f.sg.)

Thöni's claim (1969: 71) that the reflex of -US is confined to predicative adjectives (as in Surselvan) is belied by some of his own examples (pp. 18–19).

2.2.3.2 Vallader

As in Surselvan, the masculine singular and masculine plural are identical for possessive pronominal adjectives in Vallader (see table 2.30) – the only trace, in this dialect, of the inherited double function of the -*s* suffix. (In Puter, which is otherwise identical with Vallader in adjective declension, this trace also has been wiped out: the masculine singular forms of the possessive pronominal adjective derive from ancient -UM forms, and the masculine plural forms are derived from the singular by the addition of -*s*: m.sg. /miw/, m.pl. /miw-s/.)

In Vallader, the possessive pronoun in all gender/number combin-

Table 2.30 Gender and number on adjectives in Vallader

	Singular		Plural	
(a) True adjectives (e.g. /grejv/ 'heavy')				
Masculine	grejv		grejv-s	
Feminine	grejv-a		grejv-as	
(b) Perfect participles (e.g. /ʃmaladi/ 'accursed')				
Masculine	ʃmaladi		ʃmaladi-ts	
Feminine	ʃmaladi-da		ʃmaladi-das	
(c) Possessive pronominal adjectives				
	Masculine	Feminine	Masculine	Feminine
Singular				
1	mes	mia	mes	mias
2	tes	tia	tes	tias
3	ses	sia	ses	sias
Plural				
1	nɔs	nɔsa	nɔs	nɔsas
2	vɔs	vɔsa	vɔs	vɔsas
3	lur	lur	lur	lur

ations but the masculine singular is identical with the possessive pronominal adjective. In the masculine singular, however, we find a set of forms which are derived from old neuter forms in -UM; that is, we find cognates of the Surselvan *attributive* forms:

	Singular	Plural
Masculine	il miw	ils mes
Feminine	la mia	las mias

The predicative form of the possessive pronominal adjective is still identical with the possessive pronoun:

(124) mes (attr.) kunti
       my (m.sg.) knife
(125) il kunti ajs miw
       the knife is mine (pred.)
(126) il miw ajs. . .
       the my is (poss.pron.)
       'Mine is . . .'

Vallader has thus apparently retained and transformed the inherited -US/-UM distinction for possessive pronominal adjectives alone. Moreover, it has done the exact opposite to what Surselvan has, in that the -US reflex is attributive, while the -UM reflex is predicative.

The identity of the possessive pronoun and the predicative form of the possessive pronominal adjective in Vallader, as in Surselvan, argues in

Table 2.31 Gender and number on adjectives in (Fassa) Ladin

	Singular	Plural	
(a) True adjectives (e.g. /lɛrg/ 'broad', /pjen/'full')			
Masculine	lɛrg [lɛrk]	lɛrtʃ (< *lɛrg + i)	
	pjeŋ	pjeŋs (< *pjen + s)	
Feminine	lɛrʒa	lɛrʒes	
	pjena	pjenes	
(b) Perfect participles (e.g. /tira/ 'pulled')			
Masculine	tira	tirats	
Feminine	tirɛda	tirɛdas	

(c) Possessive (attributive) adjectives

	Masculine	Feminine	Masculine	Feminine
Singular				
1	mi	mia	mi	mia
2	tɔ	tia	ti	tia
3	sɔ	sia	si	sia
Plural				
1	nɔʃ	nɔʃa	neʃ	nɔʃa
2	vɔʃ	vɔʃa	veʃ	vɔʃa
3	sɔ	sia	si	sia

(d) Possessive pronouns (and predicate adjectives)

	Masculine	Feminine	Masculine	Feminine
Singular				
1	mie	mia	mie	mies
2	tie	tia	tie	ties
3	so	sia	si	sies
Plural				
1	noʃ	noʃa	neʃ	noʃes
2	voʃ	voʃa	veʃ	voʃes
3	so	sia	si	sies

favour of identifying the two categories as one. In Surselvan, however, it
is possible to derive the possessive pronoun from an abstract structure
with an attributive possessive pronominal adjective:

[Article + possessive pronominal adjective + [∅]]

In Vallader, where the possessive pronoun differs from the attributive
form of the possessive pronominal adjective, this derivation is morphologically impossible.

2.2.3.3 Ladin

In Badiot Ladin, the attributive and predicative possessive pronominal
adjectives are identical except in the following instances (Pizzinini and
Plangg 1966: xxxix):

Table 2.32 Possessive pronominal adjectives in Gardenese

	Singular	*Plural*
1	mi	noːʃ
2	ti	voːʃ
3	si	si

Table 2.33 Possessive pronouns in Gardenese

	Singular		*Plural*	
	Masculine	*Feminine*	*Masculine*	*Feminine*
Singular				
1	mie	mia	miej	mies
2	tie	tia	tiej	ties
3	sie	sia	siej	sies
Plural				
1	noʃt	noʃta	noʃc	noʃtes
2	voʃt	voʃta	voʃc	voʃtes
3	sie	sia	siej	sies

	Attributive	*Predicative*
1pl.m.sg.	noʃ	noʃt
2pl.m.sg.	oʃ	oʃt
f.pl.	*stem*+(e)s	*stem* + es

The last contrast is illustrated by

(127) *mi(e)s* cazes
        my   houses
(128) las cazes   ε   *mies* (*mis)
        the houses are mine

Gardenese has a more coherent system of possessives, possibly because
it has been less exposed to Italian influence. The (attributive) possessive
pronominal adjectives have no number or gender inflection whatsoever
(see table 2.32). Compare the fully inflected (predicative and postnominal) adjectives in table 2.33, which are also the possessive
pronouns.

In Ampezzan, possessive pronominal adjectives do not inflect for
gender or number of the possessum except in the 1st plural and 2nd
plural (where number is marked only in the masculine forms). Possessive
pronouns mark both gender and number in a regular fashion (see table
2.34).

The identity of feminine singular and feminine plural in the possessive
pronominal adjective exemplified in table 2.31, as noted already, is a

Table 2.34 Ampezzan possessive pronouns

	Masculine Singular	Feminine Singular	Masculine Plural	Feminine Plural
Singular				
1	mɛ	mɛa	miei	mees
2	tɔ	toa	tuoi	toes
3	sɔ	soa	suoi	soes
Plural				
1	nɔʃ	nostra	nostre	nostres
2	vɔʃ	vostra	vostre	vostres
3	sɔ	soa	suoi	soes

Table 2.35 Gender and number marking on adjectives in Friulian

	Singular		Plural	
(a) True adjectives (e.g. /maduːr/ 'ripe')				
Masculine	maduːr		maduːrs	
Feminine	madurA		madurAs	
(b) Perfect participles (e.g. /tornaːt/ 'returned')				
Masculine	tornaːt		tornaːt-s ([tornas])	
Feminine	tornadA		tornadAs	
(c) Possessive pronominal adjectives				
	Masculine	Feminine	Masculine	Feminine
Singular				
1	ɲo	me	miej	meːs
	mjo			
2	co	to	toj	toːs
	to			
3	sjo	so	soj	soːs
	so			
Plural				
1	neStri	neStrA	neStrAs	
2	vweStri	vweStrA	veStrAs	
3	sjo	so	soj	soːs
	so			

Note: The phonetic value of /A/ is /a, e, o/ in the singular, /e, i, o/ in the plural, depending on dialect.

striking feature of the morphology of many Ladin dialects. We return in chapter 4 to the question whether this apparent syncretism is a morphological or a deeper syntactic fact.

2.2.3.4 Friulian

In Friulian, the possessive pronoun consists simply of the definite article followed by the possessive pronominal adjective.

There is a tendency in all Rhaeto-Romance languages to allow the definite article to appear with possessive pronominal adjectives, possibly under Italian influence. For example, in Friulian, Iliescu (1972: 172) attests /il ɲo omp/ 'my husband' side by side with /mjo fi/ 'my son'. In general, the article is not used with kinship names.

A possible generalization for distinguishing possessive pronominal forms is that *where the predicative adjective differs from the attributive, it is the longer form.* This is, of course, compatible with the productive contrast in Surselvan between (attributive) -UM and (predicative) -US reflexes (or, for that matter with the English contrast between attributive 'my, your, her, their' and predicative 'mine, yours, hers, theirs'). The linguistic significance of the distinction is questionable.

2.2.4 Numerals and the indefinite article

The morphological similarity, and the syntactic identity, of the indefinite article and the numeral 'one' are well known. Badiot and Gardena, and possibly other Ladin dialects, are unique in syntactically distinguishing the numeral, and the indefinite article which is a phonologically degenerate form of it. In these dialects, the numeral and the indefinite article may co-occur, the numeral being 'doubly marked': once by the indefinite article, and again by the stressed form from which it is derived.

Badiot
(129) Da   *øna na* skwadra (esoŋ   pasa   a   trɛj)
      from *one*   team   are = we passed to three
      'From *one* team, we grew to three.'
Gardena
(130) (l' ɛrt kuntsɛtuala), *una na* rama   dl   ɛrt visiva
      the art conceptual   *one*   branch of = the art visual
      'conceptual art, *one* branch of visual art'

The mechanism of grammaticalization (phonological reduction followed by double marking, or reinforcement) whereby this pattern occurred is familiar: for example, this is how stressed and atonic subject pronouns have come to co-occur throughout the northern Italian dialects, including the Italian dialects of Rhaeto-Romance. But we know of no other examples of this process creating a syntactic distinction between numerals and the indefinite article.

In both Badiot and Gardena, the indefinite article is formed by elision of the initial vowel of the numeral. We have failed to encounter, and been unable to elicit, double marking of the masculine numeral, possibly because the combination (Badiot ?[on n], Gardena ?[uŋ n(g)]) is difficult to pronounce.

The numeral 'two' is uninflected in most of Romansh. In the Müstair dialect of Romansh, and throughout the Italian Rhaeto-Romance dialects, however, it is inflected for gender: the masculine /doj/ contrasts with the feminine /dus/ ~ /dos/. (Compare Venetian /du/ (m.) and /do/ (f.).)

No other numerals are inflected for gender or case in Rhaeto-Romance.

3 Lexicon

Phonological and morphological criteria fail to establish Rhaeto-Romance unity. In spite of occasional claims to the contrary, lexical criteria also fail: nor is this surprising, given the notorious instability of the lexicon. What we expect, in fact, is what we find: like all other Romance languages, the Rhaeto-Romance languages share a great deal of Latin vocabulary. In sharing a Gallic substratum and influences of the Germanic populations with the Central Romance dialects, they share a great deal more specifically with the other Italian dialects north of La Spezia–Rimini. Moreover, since each of them is overshadowed by one or more prestige languages, all of them have borrowed extensively from these prestige languages: in recent times, Romansh has borrowed primarily from German, and the Italian dialects have borrowed from Trentino, Venetian, or standard Italian. Of course, Swiss Romansh and some Ladin dialects (particularly Gardenese and Badiot) are still under heavy German influence.

Theodor Gartner tried to establish a common Rhaeto-Romance lexicon, a topic which Ascoli had completely disregarded. Since then, the attention of scholars has focused mainly on three items which have been regularly offered as evidence of Rhaeto-Romance unity (see most recently Rohlfs 1986: 507): (1) the morpho-lexical innovation SOL-IC-ULU (~ SOLUCULU) for SOLE 'sun', shared by all varieties (found also in French *soleil*, with the same meaning, and in standard Italian, but with a different meaning); (2) a Celticism = DRAGIU 'sieve'; and (3), an early Germanicism (Gothic?) + SKEITHONE 'large wooden spoon, ladle'. The significance of these words as evidence of Rhaeto-Romance unity has been much discussed under several headings. G. Pellegrini, one of the scholars most involved in discussions regarding the Rhaeto-Romance lexicon, has repeatedly shown that the areas where these and other allegedly distinctive lexical items occur extend beyond the Rhaeto-Romance area, and that many words which are now considered typical of Rhaeto-Romance may also be found (or have been found) in Bellunese, northern Venetian, or simply in standard Italian. Zamboni (1984) traced continuations of SKEITHONE (via a later Germanic variant SKAITONE > SKATTONE) outside the Rhaeto-Romance area, in central Italian. What is even more important is the fact that within Rhaeto-Romance, the western region has derivations from SKA(I)TONE ([scaduŋ], [ʃaduŋ]), while the rest of Rhaeto-Romance and adjacent dialects continue SKEITHONE (e.g. Frl. *sedon*, Eng. *zdun*). This suggests independent origins from different German dialects, not Rhaeto-Romance unity.

Due to the continuing contacts these territories had with German populations (as did the rest of northern Italy) from the Middle Ages up to the present, we find a very complicated lexical stratification of the various Germanic layers, which is sometimes impossible to define very clearly (see Frau 1989: 594).

The earliest Germanic stratum dates back (for all Rhaeto-Romance, and much of the Roman Empire) to well before the collapse of Rome in AD 476. In the most careful study of Germanic penetration, Gamillscheg (1935: 273) distinguishes three main layers or stages of Germanic lexical borrowing:

(a) third-century in Raetia and Noricum only;
(b) fifth-century Gothic borrowings;
(c) sixth–eighth century Longobard borrowings.

Frankish contact was too short to allow us to identify clear cases of Frankish borrowing. Words of Frankish origin probably entered the Rhaeto-Romance languages later through Old French.

In a survey of 1,552 words in Friulian, Iliescu (1972: 205) found that 51 per cent were Latin, 25 per cent were borrowings from standard Italian or Venetian, 13 per cent were Friulian innovations, 5.5 per cent were of obscure origin, 4 per cent were older (Gothic, Frankish, or Lombard) Germanic borrowings (e.g. among the Gothic borrowings, *bant* 'side, direction', *buta* 'throw', *sklɛt* 'clear, frank', *sedón* 'spoon', *bruːt* 'daughter-in-law', *bisuɲe* < ?Goth. **bisunnia* 'need', *blank* < *blank* 'white'; *barbe* < Long. *barbas* 'father's brother', *bleón* 'sheet' < Long. **blajô* 'rag'), and 1 per cent were either more or less recent German borrowings (e.g. *beːs* 'money' < Renaissance (and modern) Swiss *baetze* 'coins, change', via Venetian, *pawr* 'farmer' < *Bauer*, *kramar* < *kramer* 'pedlar', *tsiruk* 'back' < *zurück* (this, throughout Ladin as well as Friulian), *Smiːr* 'axle grease' < *Schmiere*, *russak* < *Rucksack*, *stankol* 'coal' < *Steinkohle*), *ʃlosər* 'locksmith' < *Schlosser*).

Hardly any of the lexical stock, whether original or borrowed, link

Friulian exclusively with either Ladin or Romansh (Iliescu: 225). Rizzolatti (1981: 47) cites exactly one pair of cognate forms (Frl. *dorta:l*, Livinallongo *rodhela* 'layer of new-mown hay' < *derotulare*) which is confined to Friulian and Ladin alone. In the same vein, when surveying the lexicon of Ladin dialects, Pellegrini (1987a: 294) notes that:

> The Ladin lexical base of Rhaeto-Romance, especially of its purported central Dolomitic and its Friulan components, is essentially identical with that of the Northern or Cisalpine Italian dialects. Common peculiarities, i.e. unique features shared by the three putative Rhaeto-Romance zones, which would set them off *en bloc* from their immediate southern neighbours, are singularly absent.

Not surprisingly, given the political history of Brixen/Bressanone over the last six hundred years, the number of recent German borrowings in Ladin dialects is high. Gardenese and Badiot share *tseruk* 'back', *minouŋa* 'opinion', and *tiər* 'animal'.

Gardenese has transparent German borrowings like *luʒoŋa* 'solution', *tsajta* 'newspaper', *ſtrawfoŋa* 'punishment', *ſtrom* 'electricity', *ſkjatse* 'esteem' (< *(ab)schatzen*), *gɛn* 'gladly' (< *gern*), *pite* 'offer' (< *(an)bieten*), *ſtlet* 'bad', *pawr* 'farmer', *ſlosər* 'locksmith', *ʒnel* 'quick', *mɛsaj* 'must', and *ſterk* 'strong, loud', as well as calque translations like *l da* 'there is', and a series of verb + particle constructions on the model of the German separable prefix + verb constructions: *fɛ prɔ* 'close' on the model of *zu-machen*, *dɛ prɔ* 'concede' on the model of *zu-geben*, *udi: ite* 'admit', on the model of *ein-sehen,* and many others. Notice that verb + particle constructions are lexical rather than syntactic borrowings, the order and behaviours of the two components of the compound word being radically different in the different languages. The Ladin syntactic model is clearly Romance.

Badiot has *gonot* 'often' (< **ge-nötig*), and transparent *alt* 'old', *ſkone* 'spare', *ſtøa* 'dining room' (< Stube) (but see *REW* 3108), and *jagri* 'hunter'. Fassan has several layers of Germanic borrowings, like *ſkjet* 'bad' < OHG *sleht*, *bjɛra* 'beer' < MHG *bier*, *ſmawts* 'butter' from early Modern German *smalz*, and much more recent Tyrolian German borrowings like *ſlosər* 'locksmith', *pek* 'baker', *tiſlər* 'carpenter' of nineteenth-century vintage brought back by Gastarbeiter painters and masons (Elwert 1943: 238–47). (The closely related Moena dialect also has *Snɔps* 'brandy' (< Schnapps).)

The number of German borrowings in Romansh is even higher: so high that enumeration of individual examples seems likely to be misleading. A better appreciation of the extent of German influence can be gained from noting the existence of calque constructions like the *verb*

+ *particle* combinations /ʃkrivər sy/ (< *auf-schreiben* 'write up'), or /rer owra/ (< *aus-lachen* 'laugh at') which are even more common in the Engadine dialects than they are in Ladin. (They are foreign to French and far less productive in northern Italian dialects and in Italian than they are in Rhaeto-Romance.) In addition, some idea of the peculiar German flavour of Romansh comes through in older and less self-consciously purist texts such as Luci Gabriel's Bible translation of 1648, where we read in Psalm XLVI:

(1) quel velg anamig
     Ristiaus ei fick
     Cun *lists* a cun *guauld*
     'That old enemy
     is very well *equipped* (*ausgerüstet*)
     with *cunning* (*List*) and *force* (*Gewalt*).'

or in Willy's 1755 *Historias Biblias*:

(2) Mo ses frars purtavan un sgrischeivel *Has* ancunter el, a pudevan
     buc plidar cun el un *frindli* Plaid.
     'But his brothers had a terrible *hatred* for him, and could not say a
     friendly word to him.'

Nevertheless, it is Romansh, in particular the Surselvan and Sutselvan dialects of Romansh, which have the highest proportion of 'uniquely Rhaeto-Romance' conservative lexical features inherited from Latin. As we shall soon observe, this leads to misleading claims about 'Rhaeto-Romance' when Romansh is treated as a typical dialect of this conjectured group.

Discounting natural reservations about the value of a shared vocabulary as an index of genetic affiliation, there are three possible kinds of evidence which could support a claim of common origin: first, common retention of Latin etyma that have been lost in other Romance languages; second, common borrowing of foreign words that were not borrowed in other Romance languages; third, and most important, is the common morphological or semantic development of an inherited lexical form. (It should go without saying, of course, that common retention of an inherited vocabulary is a much more convincing sign of ethnic unity than common borrowing of vocabulary from some other language. For example, the German words *Schlosser* and *Bäcker*, specifically identified as recent borrowings in Friulian (Iliescu 1972) are found throughout Rhaeto-Romance as we have already seen (see Kuen 1968: 52–3). Common borrowing, in other words, occurred long after any conceivable Rhaeto-Romance unity must have ceased to exist.)

None of these signs of commmon Rhaeto-Romance unity, however, is much in evidence. It is an eloquent testimony to the fragmentation of 'Rhaeto-Romance' that in a partisan restudy of the Rhaeto-Romance lexicon based on the great dialect atlas of Jaberg and Jud (1928–40), Redfern (1971: 88–9) was able to find only *sixteen* items like *AIS* no.93 ⟨caf⟩ 'head' < CAPUT and *AIS* no.982 ⟨cədon⟩ 'spoon' < Goth. *skeithone* that were attested throughout 'Rhaeto-Romance'. Both of these, as it happens, are also attested outside Rhaeto-Romance, while the second (as we have noted) effectively *splits Rhaeto-Romance* into two areas. (We will follow Redfern in using '⟨ ⟩' to indicate a 'common lexical type' whose phonetic realization may differ considerably from one dialect to another.)

In fact, there are many more than sixteen such forms which are found throughout Rhaeto-Romance – and beyond. To make the strongest possible case for Rhaeto-Romance unity, we should indicate some of them. Hubschmid (1956) provides several pre-Indo-European roots that were continued throughout Rhaeto-Romance and far and wide beyond it: notable among these are two Alpine words. First, the word for 'mountain goat' < **kamoːrkjo-*: Eng. /tʃamuɛʃtʃ/, Fassa /tʃamortʃ/ , Friulian /camóts/, but also attested in Late Latin, in Old High German, Italian (both standard and dialects), Portuguese, Spanish, and French. Second, the word for 'cliff' or 'rock face' < **krippa*: Romansh /krap/, Fassa /krepa/, Badiot /krap/, Gardena /krɛp/, but this word also has reflexes throughout central Italian, southern French, and Old Provençal.

Wartburg (1956: 29) provides a handful of Celtic items which are common to Rhaeto-Romance and French, among them the words for 'sieve' (Fr. *tamis*, Puter /tamyʃ/, Frl. /tameːs/; see also Venetian /tamizo/) and 'to card, tease (hemp, flax, wool)' (Fr. *serancer*, Puter /tʃanəʃar/).

Moreover, Gamillscheg (1935: 273–304) provides many other examples of Germanic words that were borrowed throughout Rhaeto-Romance, and in Italian and French as well, probably via medieval Latin. Among these are the words for 'rob' < OHG *raubon*, 'daughter-in-law' < OHG *bruthiz* 'Roman wife of German soldier' (Gamillscheg 1935: 291), 'hostel' < Goth. **haribairg*, and 'rich' < Goth. *reiks*.

Finally, there are Romance developments which are peculiar to Rhaeto-Romance and French, such as the use of reflexes of SOLICULU (not SOL) for 'sun' (see, however, Pellegrini 1987a: 294n., who notes reflexes of *SOLUCULU in Old Bellunese and Cadorine), and the use of the reflexes of FRATER (not FRATELLU) and SOROR (not SORELLA), for 'brother' and 'sister' (see Kuen 1968: 56–7).

Of Redfern's sixteen 'pan-Rhaeto-Romance' words, however, only two words were said to be exclusive to the Rhaeto-Romance dialects. Of these two words, one, ⟨taliar⟩ 'plate', is a variant of the very common Italian type *tagliere*. The other ⟨strom⟩ 'straw' is a regular outcome of Latin STRAMEN, which is also continued in Italian, Italian dialects, and other Romance languages.

For all its methodological faults, Redfern's study is of interest, because it constitutes an attempt to achieve the impossible: establish the unity and independence of Rhaeto-Romance on the basis of a shared vocabulary. Even if one were to accept his results, however, they do not favour his thesis.

Exclusively Rhaeto-Romance (but not found everywhere in Rhaeto-Romance) may be UNUS NON SAPIT QUI for 'someone', COCCINU for 'red', BELLU for 'only', VOLIENDO for 'gladly', MUTU for 'child', and *DE AVORSUS for 'behind' (for this last, see Kuen 1968: 51). The total number of these, so far from providing evidence for Rhaeto-Romance unity, scarcely exceeds what could be attributed to chance.

Recently, a selection of twelve well-studied lexical 'types' in Rhaeto-Romance dialects has been presented in Pfister (1986). The author shows that some types, or peculiar semantic evolutions, are attested in areas that do not correspond to Rhaeto-Romance, but often unite a *part* of Rhaeto-Romance with other areas of the Alps or northern Italy, such as Alpine Lombard, Piedmontese, northern Venetian, etc. We present a few of his examples:

ABUNDE shifted its meaning from 'abundantly' to 'enough' in Friulian and Swiss Rhaeto-Romance, as in Tessin, the Tellina Valley, and in dialectal Portuguese (see Benincà-Ferraboschi 1973: 123).
ALTIGORIUM/ALDIGORIUM 'aftermath, second haying' is widespread within Rhaeto-Romance (and beyond), but is opposed within Friulian by the equally ancient *ryézi* < RESECARE.
ALIQUID 'something' unites Rhaeto-Romance with Old Lombard, Spanish, etc. (see Rohlfs 1949: II, 253; *REW* 345).
ALICUBI 'somewhere' unites the Italian Rhaeto-Romance dialects with Western Lombard, but excludes Swiss Romansh.
ARMENTUM 'herd' has shifted its meaning to a 'single animal (usually bovine)' only in central Ladin and northern Lombard.
QUADRIGA 'plough' going from Swiss Rhaeto-Romance through central Ladin and Bellunese to a very small area of Carnic Friulian, is also attested in Lombard as 'large plow drawn by four oxen' (see Pellegrini and Marcato 1988: 13–16, for detailed discussion and bibliography).

There are perhaps two dozen words which are exclusively western Rhaeto-Romance, that is, found (with exactly their peculiar meanings) only in Romansh. A number of these are Latin survivals attested in no other Romance language: note *AIS* no.321 ⟨sarkladur⟩ 'June' < SARCULARE + ATORE; *AIS* no.322 ⟨fanadur⟩ 'July' < FENU + ATORE; *AIS* no.363 Surselvan /awra/ 'weather' < AURA; *AIS* no.763 ⟨kudiʃ⟩ 'book' < CODICE; and *AIS* no.1575 ⟨alv⟩ 'white' < ALBU, *AIS* no.444. (But note Frl. /stradalbe/ 'Milky Way', literally 'white way'.)

Almost as many, however, are shared by Romansh with French (and sometimes Spanish), to the exclusion of all other Rhaeto-Romance dialects and Italian: among these are *AIS* no.284 ⟨dus⟩ 'two' (m.) (< DUOS: other Rhaeto-Romance dialects, including the Romansh dialect of Müstair, have a reflex of *DUI); *AIS* no.19 Surselvan /awk/ 'uncle' < AVUNCULU; *AIS* no.351 ⟨ʃto⟩ 'must' < Old Fr. *estovoir*, ultimately < EST OPUS (see *REW* 6079), *AIS* no.788 ⟨sɛnts⟩ 'bell' < SIGNUS (with survival of the nominative -US; compare Old Fr. *sein*, modern French *toc-sin*), *sonda* 'Saturday' < SAMBATA DIE (see *REW* 7479), ⟨klucǝr⟩ 'belfry' < CLOCCARIU, Surselvan /tʃinkwejsmas/ 'Pentecost' < QUINQUESIMAS (compare Old Picard *chinquesme*) (for the last three, see Jud 1919: 176–7).

A small number of Germanic borrowings are shared by Ladin and Friulian, to the apparent exclusion of Romansh. Among them is OHG *suf*, Lombard *supfa* 'broth', with reflexes in Fassa /ʒufa/ 'broth' and Frl. /zuf/ 'polenta and pumpkin soup'.

Gamillscheg (1935: 304) gives two Germanic borrowings which are also restricted to (Engadine) Romansh and (Gardena) Ladin: OHG *gadum* 'room' and **piwat* 'clothing'.

All in all, then, the lexical evidence for Rhaeto-Romance unity is minimal. More than is the case for other areas of grammar, the lexicon has been abused by proponents of Rhaeto-Romance unity. Time and again, a 'case' has been made for the conservatism of Rhaeto-Romance on the basis of one single dialect, usually Surselvan. Typically, an author will note, say, that ALBU is retained as the word for 'white' in Surselvan, while all other Romance languages have borrowed Frankish *blank* (see *AIS* no.1575). This is undeniably an interesting archaism – but of Surselvan alone! All the other so-called 'Rhaeto-Romance' dialects, just like Spanish, French, and Italian, have borrowed *blank*: thus even the Engadine dialects have /blɛnc/, while Ladin and Friulian have /blank/ (Gamillscheg 1935: 279).

Rather than pursuing the elusive goal of Rhaeto-Romance unity, we should look for lexical 'signatures' of the various dialects/languages within Rhaeto-Romance. Even these do more to distinguish the Rhaeto-Romance languages from each other than from the dialects which surround them.

3.1 FRIULIAN

The Friulian lexicon is particularly well studied: it has one of the best dictionaries of a Romance dialect, Pirona 1935, and an atlas especially devoted to the lexicon, the *ASLEF* directed by G.B. Pellegrini. A series of dissertations of Padua University and of articles, in particular by Pellegrini, analyse the data from a historical–etymological point of view. Edited by various scholars, the first two volumes (up to the letter E) of an etymological dictionary (*DESF*) have appeared. Pellegrini and Zamboni (1982) explore in detail the names of Friulian flora. An article by G. Frau (1989) on the Friulian lexicon appears in the third volume of *LRL*.

Friulian is set off from the other Rhaeto-Romance dialects by some Latin inherited forms which have undergone a peculiar semantic development. Among these are /frut/ 'child, boy' < FRUCTU, /prindi/ 'Monday' < PRIMU DIE, /tʃercá/ 'to taste' < CIRCARE. The word ⟨víe⟩ < VIA 'way' is also used characteristically as a suffix /vie/ '-ly'. It can be added redundantly to adverb phrases: /sot man/ and /sot man vie/ 'underhanded'. Or it can be added to adjectives to form adverb phrases: /a la mate vie/ 'crazily' (literally, 'to the crazy way'). Or it can be added to bare noun stems: /a frutvie/ 'childishly', /a matvie/ 'foolishly'.

Additional Friulian peculiarities unmatched outside this dialect area include /glendon/ 'louse egg' < *lendone*, /spa:li/ 'string' < *spagulu*, and (West Friulian only) /vjerte/ 'spring' < *aperta* (Rizzolatti 1981: 46–7). To this list we should add /mandi/ 'ciao', used by some speakers for both greetings and goodbyes, by others for the latter only, from (*m-arco*)*mandi* (< *m'arecomandi*) 'I commit myself'.

All Rhaeto-Romance dialects, like standard Italian, have an augmentative suffix ⟨-ɔN⟩, but in Friulian, this derivational suffix can occur not only on nominal roots, but also on verbs and adjectives: /fevel-on-a:/ 'to talk a lot', and /grand-on/ 'very large' have no congeners in other Rhaeto-Romance, although nouns occur with this suffix. (Compare Vallader /om-un/ 'big man', Surselvan /vadl-un/ 'big calf'.)

Veneto-Friulian isoglosses include: /kja:f/ 'head' (Ven. *testa*, but some Venetian varieties have /káo/), /kjalá/ 'watch' (Ven. *vardár*), /fevelá/ 'speak' (Ven. *parlare*), /kumó/ 'now' (Ven. *adesso*), /(v)we/ 'today' < HODIE (Ven. *ancuo* < HANC HODIE). These isoglosses, however, do not separate Friulian from all other Romance dialects.

As well as common retentions and semantic innovations, common borrowings may identify a dialect. Among the peculiarities of Friulian, we may identify:

(a) Celtic borrowings: ⟨broili⟩ 'orchard' < BROGILOS; ⟨grave⟩ 'gravel'

< GRAVA, ⟨glázinje⟩ 'blueberry, bilberry' < + GLASINA, ⟨cjarpint⟩ 'cart axle' < CARPENTUM, ⟨dratʃ⟩ 'sieve' < DRAGIU;

(b) several layers of Germanisms: among the Gothisms are ⟨bruːt⟩ already discussed; among the Longobard forms are ⟨bleóns⟩ 'sheets', already discussed and ⟨beártʃ⟩ 'piece of ground near a house' < BIGARDIUM; the Germanic borrowing *bisunnia 'it is necessary' is often treated as a 'signature' of Friulian (see *AIS* no.351), albeit one which separates it only from Romansh, and not from Ladin, French or Italian: but there are other ways of expressing necessity in Friulian which are shared by other Rhaeto-Romance dialects. Among them are /skunjí/ (compare Gardena /koɲe/) < CONVENIT, /dové/ (cognates throughout Italian and French, as well as Gardena) < DEBERE, and the periphrastic construction /avé di/ + *infinitive*), which is shared by many Italian dialects.

(c) Friulian is also unique in having a handful of Slavic (mainly Slovenian) borrowings, among them ⟨brítule⟩ 'pocketknife' < Slov. *britva* 'razor', ⟨pustóte⟩ 'untilled land' < Slov. *pustota*, and other names of fruits and animals (see Pellegrini 1975; Frau 1989).

As Frau and others have pointed out, although Friulian is homogeneous in many respects, there is an interesting split in the region and two distinct sub-regions can be identified. The division corresponds to the two dioceses of Aquileia (eastern) and Concordia (western). Eastern Friulian are ⟨altiúl⟩ 'second haying', ⟨wargine⟩ 'plough' < ORGANUM, and ⟨la⟩ 'go' < AMBULARE (see Fr. *aller*); western Friulian are ⟨rjézi⟩ 'second haying' < RESECARE, ⟨varsór⟩ 'plough' < VERSORIUM and ⟨zi⟩ 'go' < IRE (compare Italian *gire*).

3.2 ROMANSH

Romansh conservative peculiarities are widespread. All Rhaeto-Romance, from Surselvan and Vallader to Friulian, have a collective masculine derivational suffix -*om* ~ -*am* ~ -*um* (< -AMEN, -UMEN): Val. /la muəsca/ 'housefly', but /il muəsc-om/ 'flies', Surs. /la feʎa/ 'leaf', but /il feʎ-am/ 'foliage', Frl. /rifut/ 'rubbish', but /rifud-um/ 'pile of rubbish'. In Vallader, the suffix (like other collective suffixes) has a pejorative meaning as well: /la femna/ 'woman', but /il femn-om/ 'nasty woman'. For a comparison with Italian dialects, see Rohlfs (1969: 407–8).

Both Surselvan and Vallader have the Italian pejorative suffix -*atʃ*: Val. /la duəna/ 'lady' but /la duən-atʃ-a/ 'nasty woman', Surs. /la val/ 'valley', but /la val-atʃ-a/ 'wild valley', /il ɟuvən/ 'boy', but /il ɟuvn-atʃ/ 'churl'. Surselvan alone has another pejorative suffix -*ankəl*: /il pur/

'peasant, farmer', but /il pur-ankəl/ 'Schuldenbauerlein'. Surselvan is alone in having the augmentative *-əneri*: /il um/ 'the man', but /il um-əneri/ 'the giant'.

Surselvan and the Engadine dialects have lexicalized the -US/-UM distinction in adjectives ending in -OSU. -OSUS (Surs. -ʌs, Eng. -uəs) denotes a habitual quality, while -OSUM (Surs. -us, Eng. -us) denotes an occasional one: thus, according to Prader-Schucany (1970: 117), Puter /inviʎus/ contrasts with /inviʎuəs/. Both mean 'envious', but only the latter means 'envious by nature'.

Romansh dialects have lexicalized -ONE + S (in *filone-s* 'spinner', and *texone-s* 'weaver') as a derivational agentive suffix (see Prader-Schucany 1970: 116), thus Val. /il filunts/ 'the spinner (m.)', and /la filunts-a/ 'the spinner (f.)'.

Romansh dialects retain HEBDOMA 'week': thus Surs. /jamna/, Surm. /ɛmda/, Eng. /ɛjvna/, while all other Rhaeto-Romance, like French and Italian, have a compound of the numeral 'seven'.

Similarly confined to Romansh are reflexes of MILLIARDU 'many' (Surs., Surm. /blɛr/, Eng. /blɛr/ ~ /bjɛr/), TITULARE 'listen', QUIESCERE 'be silent', INCIPERE 'begin', and NIMIS 'too much', as well as the already noted words for 'June', 'July', 'time, weather', 'book', and 'white'.

Even within Romansh, however, there are considerable divergences which tend to make mutual intelligibility difficult, and increase reliance on the use of German as a *lingua franca*.

Engadine dialects alone retain /inkler/ 'understand' < INTELLIGERE. Surselvan alone retains /vɛs/ 'unwilling' < VIX 'scarcely', and /kuzeʃər/ 'accustom' < CONSUESCERE.

For hundreds of other common words, every village has its own etymon. For example, 'liver' is a reflex of DURU throughout much of the Surselvan, Sutselvan, and Surmeiran area, but it is /fioː/ in Puter, /nirɔm/ in Vallader, and /brasɛ/ in Bivio (Wartburg 1956: 39).

A structural description of the Romansh lexicon is given in Liver (1989).

3.3 LADIN

Distinctively Ladin words are: Bad. /(de)sɛɲ/, Liv. /desɛn/ 'now' < DE SIGNU; Bad. /adym/, Gard. /adum/, Amp. /aduna/ 'together' < AD UNUM ~ AD UNAM. (The same Latin source yields 'always' in the Romansh dialects); Bad. /daɲɛra/, Gard. /danora/ 'always' < DE OMNI HORA; and the expression for 'thanks' Liv. /diotəlpaje/, Gard. /diətəlpaja/, Bad. ?/dilan/.

More commonly cited is the German borrowing /mɛsaj/ 'must' (see the Appendix), to which we may add /an/ ([an], [aŋ], [ən], əŋ]) 'PRO', 'unspecified agent', presumably from HOMO 'man'. The latter (not found in the Gardena dialect) is very close to Gard. /un/, Eng. /yn/, Surm. and Suts. /in/, Surs. /ins/ (all indisputably from UNU). It may be that the development of the PRO form in Ladin was affected by contamination from the 3rd plural *verbal* ending *-*ən*, now lost in all Ladin dialects (see chapter 2). Semantically, this is plausible: the 3rd plural is used for unspecified agent in many languages, and it is notable that the PRO form /ins/ in Surselvan takes 3rd plural agreement at least in inverted word order. (Moreover, Linder observes (1987: 89) that the Sutselvan 3rd plural verbal desinence in inverted word order is not -/an/ or -/ən/ but -/in/, and speculates that this ending derives not from any inherited verbal desinence, but from UNU.)

Creation of a new PRO form from a verbal desinence is also plausible from a strictly mechanical point of view. The Lombard dialects of Bergell and Mesolcina (as noted by both Elwert and Rohlfs) have permitted the copying of 3rd plural -*ən* from verb to subject noun phrase, where it serves as the only mark of the plural (see Rohlfs 1949: II, 62). Thus, the plural verbal desinence -*ən* migrated to the head noun or to the article of the subject noun phrase in the examples below:

| (Mesolcina) | la gambe-n | 'the legs' |
| (Bergell) | la-n rosa | 'the roses' |

It is at least conceivable that this copying from the verb to the subject noun phrase was a contributing factor which permitted the verb eventually to lose the 3rd plural ending. (Compare also Old Italian *eglino* 'they', which seems to have consisted of *egli* '3 p.masc.' + -*ino* '3 pl. verbal desinence'.)

In the case of Ladin /an/ PRO', an intermediate stage in the development of *an* ‡ verb may have been offered in inverted word order. A structure like . . . *verb* + *an* . . . (for example, /mɛs aŋ/ 'must one') would be ambiguous between the original *verb* + *3rd plural* and the novel structure *verb* ‡ PRO.

4 Syntax

The standard handbooks list exactly one syntactic feature which 'defines' Rhaeto-Romance as a language distinct from Italian and French: this is the use of the inherited pluperfect subjunctive in both the protasis and the apodosis of counterfactual conditionals (Prader-Schucany 1970: 185). (In the discussion to follow, sentence examples will be cited in the various standard orthographies when they are taken from written sources. Examples in phonetic or phonemic transcription from spoken sources will be indicated by the usual square brackets or obliques.) For example:

Surselvan
(1) Jeu *mass*, sche jeu *savess*.
     I   go   if   I   can
     'I would go, if I could.'

Puter
(2) Scha nu *füss* la   mamma, schi   *füss* que   ün
     if   not be the mom   then-it be   there a
     dischuorden complet.
     disorder   complete
     'If it were not for mom, there would be complete disorder.'

Gardena
(3) /ʃ ɛl tʃiel *fosa* ʃta tler, *fos-* i zaŋ mort tlo/
     if the sky be   been clear be   I now dead here
     'If the sky had been clear, I would be dead here now.'

On the other hand, the tendency to make counterfactual protasis and apodosis morphologically symmetrical is widespread even in non-standard French (Harris 1986), as well as in many other languages (Haiman 1985): so even if all the Rhaeto-Romance dialects shared this feature, it would constitute weak evidence for genetic unity, at best.

    In fact, however, the use of the pluperfect subjunctive is by no means common to all Rhaeto-Romance. In Friulian, the 'Italian' pattern is found, with past perfect subjunctive in the protasis, and past conditional in the apodosis:

(4) a. /se jo ves fevelaːt tu mi vares kapiːt/
         'If I had spoken, you would have understood me.'

This is not necessarily the outcome of standard Italian influence: the pattern is attested in other regional varieties of Italian, and has been since the Middle Ages (Rohlfs 1969: 142–4). In some varieties of Friulian, the imperfect indicative is used in both protasis and apodosis:

b. / se tu   *eris*   viɲuːt ki, jo i *podevi* vjodi- ti/
    if you were   come here I I could   see   you
    'If you had come here, I could have seen you.'

It is probable that there is no 'Rhaeto-Romance syntax': the syntactic rules which are shared by all Rhaeto-Romance dialects are also shared by other Romance languages. Alternatively, structures which are peculiar to some Rhaeto-Romance dialect distinguish this dialect not only from other Romance languages, but also from other Rhaeto-Romance dialects. Those dialect-particular features which call for special commentary are:

(a) word order in the simple sentence and in particular verb-second (V/2) order;
(b) the distribution of subject and dummy subject pronouns: all Rhaeto-Romance languages seem to resemble French, German, and English (and differ from standard Italian) in requiring these to occur;
(c) the syntactic status of these subject pronoun morphemes: in modern Surselvan, these are clearly noun phrases, as they are in modern English or German, while in the Italian dialects, they are agreement-marking affixes, as they are in the Gallo-Italian dialects of northern Italy, and as they arguably are in non-standard French;
(d) ways in which different dialects are 'lazy' in marking agreement, and in particular their propensity to relax *plural* agreement requirements when the target (a verb) occurs before the controller (its subject).

While these topics clearly do not provide a comprehensive survey of the syntax of any single Rhaeto-Romance dialect, they do allow us to deal with systematic aspects of Rhaeto-Romance syntax which distinguish Rhaeto-Romance from other Romance, and separate the various Rhaeto-Romance dialects from each other.

4.1 WORD ORDER

In standard German, the classic V/2 language, the finite verb in principal clauses of declarative sentences is the second major constituent immediately dominated by the S-node. A number of 'deformations of normal SVO order' comply with this V/2 pattern (as, of course, does SVO order itself). Accordingly, the V/2 constraint can be decomposed into a number of features:

(a) when a constituent other than the subject begins the sentence, 'subject–verb inversion' creates a word order X V S . . . , which avoids *V/3;

(b) where the logical subject is left to the end of the sentence in 'presentative order' (Hetzron 1975), a sentence-initial topic constituent creates a word order T V . . . S, which avoids *V/1;

(c) in the absence of a 'T(opic)' constituent, insertion of a 'dummy subject' (if the subject is postposed or the sentence has no genuine subject) creates an order D V . . . (S), which also avoids *V/1.

Another feature contributing to the maintenance of verb-second order is that V/2 languages are 'Type A' languages (Perlmutter 1971; Haiman 1974):

(d) the presence of a personal pronoun subject (even though person and number of the subject are generally marked on the verb) creates word order P V . . ., and also avoids *V/1.

Roughly speaking, Romansh and Badiot and Gardenese dialects of Ladin are equally committed to (a), the avoidance of V/3, and to (b) and (c), the avoidance of V/1. (The remaining dialects tolerate V/3, V/4, etc. Moreover, some Ladin dialects, like Fassan, actually *require* V/1 in presentative sentences.) On the other hand, all Rhaeto-Romance dialects, together with the northern Italian dialects, are committed to (d): whether this constitutes an avoidance of V/1 depends on how subject pronouns are analysed.

In no Rhaeto-Romance dialect does the verb come at the end of a subordinate clause: rather, the V/2 order of SVO clauses is only minimally perturbed. The nature of the perturbation, however, depends on our analysis of the relative pronoun. If this is a true pronoun, then SVO remains SVO where the relative pronoun is the subject noun phrase, and SVX becomes XSV, or V/3, where the relative pronoun is the object (or any other non-subject) noun phrase. On the other hand, if the 'relative pronoun' is actually an extra sentential complementizer, then the relative clause is affected only by the zeroing of the noun phrase which is co-referential with the head. SVO then becomes ＿＿＿VO, or

V/1, when the subject is co-referential with the head, and SVX remains
SV ___ when the object is.

The morphological diagnostics for pronounhood in Rhaeto-
Romance are mutually contradictory in the case of relative pronouns. In
his study of Engadine dialects, Linder (1987: 4) observes that both
subject and object nouns are apparently *replaced* by the relative
pronouns /ci/ (nom.) and /ca/ (acc.). In so far as the relative pronouns
mark case, they seem to be noun phrases and relative clauses like the
Vallader in example (5):

(5)   la   spassegiada [cha   nus   avain   fat]
      the   walk   that   we   have   made
      'the walk we took'

manifest V/3 order. (Note, however, that the relative pronoun fails to
cause the past participle [fat] to agree with it.) On the other hand, there is
no morphological evidence that invariable /ke/ in Surselvan is a
pronoun, and structures like (6):

(6)   in grond flum [che [fa   viadi tras   biaras tiaras]]
      a big   river that makes trip   through many   lands
      'a big river that crosses many lands'

seem to manifest V/1 order, resulting from zeroing of the subject.

In Friulian, it seems that the relative pronoun (like all subject NPs) *co-
occurs with* subject pronoun markers (as in the examples of (7), but (like
all object NPs) *replaces* object pronoun markers (as in those of (8)).

(7)   a.   chel omp [che   no   l   diseve nancje 'Bondi']
           that man that   not he said   even   'hello'
           'that man who didn't even say 'hello''
           (*che* co-occurs with subject pronoun *l*)
      b.   /al e kwalkeduɲ k   al ti   spete/
           he is someone   that he you awaits
           'There is someone waiting for you.'
           (*k* co-occurs with the subject pronoun *al*)
      c.   /al ere l   unik om k   al e viɲuːt/
           he was the only man that he is come
           'He was the only man who came.'
           (*k* co-occurs with the subject pronoun *al*)
(8)   a.   /teŋ se   ke   tu   as   dibizuɲ/
           hold what that you have need
           'Keep what you need.'
           (*ke* replaces any object noun phrase)

b. che libris che tu mi disevis
   the books that you me told
   'the books you were telling me about'

c. /al ere i   mjor om k   i aj   kuɲusuːt/
   he was the best man that I have known
   'he was the best man I have ever known.'
   (*k* totally replaces any object noun phrase.)

Since the pronoun subject markers generally do co-occur with lexical subject noun phrases in Friulian, sentences like (7) are compatible with the analysis of the relative pronoun as a subject noun phrase and a relativization strategy whereby the relative pronoun replaces the lexical noun phrase in the relative clause. Given that predicate adjectives agree with the relative pronoun subject in number and gender, as they do with noun-phrase subjects, a consistent analysis of subject *che* is that of a noun phrase. Depending on the analysis of subject pronoun markers, the word order in sentences (7) is either V/3 (if the markers are noun phrases), or V/2 (if they are affixes on the verb). Since the markers do co-occur with subject noun phrases, they are probably best analysed as affixes, and the word order of the relative clauses in (7) is V/2. (Subject pronoun markers are omittable under different circumstances in Ladin and Friulian dialects: the conditions under which they disappear do not affect the basic pattern illustrated by the sentences of (7).)

The sentences of (8) are different. The relative pronoun seems to replace all object noun phrases and pronoun clitics: in that case, the word order in the relative clauses of (8) is also V/2.

On the other hand, there is evidence that 'object relative pronouns' are not really pronouns or noun phrases at all: unlike subject relative pronouns, they cannot cause agreement. This suggests that they are complementizers. This would suggest a totally different relativization strategy in relative clauses like those of (8), whereby the noun phrase co-referential with the head noun phrase was zeroed. In this case, the word order in relative clauses like those of (8) would be V/1.

One class of subordinate clauses is verb-initial in Rhaeto-Romance, as throughout the Italian dialects: this is the set of gerundive clauses, whose subject generally fails to appear, or appears following the verb. The function of gerundive clauses is to mark concomitant action by the same subject as the subject of the main clause. So fixed is the pattern of verb-initial order in such clauses, indeed, that even where they function, as they occasionally do, like the Latin ablative absolute, to mark backgrounded activities or situations, they manifest verb-initial order, as in the following Surselvan example:

(9)　vegniend l'　autra damaun il　pader guardian
　　　coming　the other　morning the father guardian
　　　en la　combretta, fuva il　cavrer　morts
　　　in the room　　　was the goatherd dead
　　　'When the father came into the room the next day,
　　　the goatherd was dead.'

The whole question of word order within a clause is naturally complicated by the ambiguous status of two classes of morphemes:

(a) reduced or clitic pronouns which exist in every Rhaeto-Romance language except modern written Surselvan;
(b) relative pronouns.

We have touched on both of these already. The relationship between word order and the 'subject pronouns' will be the subject of two of the following sections, while the ambiguous status of the 'relative pronouns' will be further discussed in the treatment of agreement in section 4.4.

First, however, a brief discussion of the avoidance of V/3 in Romansh, Gardenese, and Badiot is in order.

4.1.1 The avoidance of *V/3

Here, we will focus on only one aspect of V/2 order: XVS order, or the apparent inversion of subject and verb when some constituent X other than the subject occurs sentence-initially.

There is total agreement on the avoidance of V/3 among all Romansh dialects. Thus Surselvan:

(10) a.　Ed　aschia *fa*　　*el* il　patg cul　　　nausch
　　　　　　　　　　　 V　　 S
　　　　and so　　makes he the pact with-the devil
　　　　'And so, he makes the pact with the devil.'
　　b.　Cun in viadi en gondola sur il　Canale Grande *ei*
　　　　　　　　　　　　　　　　　　　　　　　　　　　V
　　　　with a　trip　in gondola on the Canal　Grand　is
　　　　Papa Gion Paul II arrivaus dumengia vargada a　Vaneschia.
　　　　S
　　　　Pope John Paul II arrived　Sunday　past　　at Venice
　　　　'With a gondola trip on the Grand Canal, Pope John Paul II arrived last Sunday in Venice.'

Similar are the Engadine dialects, illustrated by sentences (11) in Puter and (12) in Vallader:

(11) a. Eir in Grischun *vains nus* industrias chi   prodüan
                    V   S
      even in Grisons have we industries that produce
      auncha memma bger tössi per l' ajer
      also   too   much poison for the air
      'Even in Grisons, we have industries that produce too much
      poison in the air.'

    b. Minch' an   *urtescha bgera sulvaschina giuvna* suot
                 V   S
      every year dies   many wild-animal young beneath
      ils curtels da las maschinas da sger.
      the blades of the machines of to-mow
      'Every year many young wild animals perish beneath the
      blades of mowing machines.'

(12) a. A la surditta   temma dal dialect
      to the above-mentioned fear   of dialect
      ringraziain nus ün bod   incredibel impovrimaint
      V   S
      thank   we an almost incredible impoverishment
      da vocabulari.
      of vocabulary
      'To the above-mentioned fear of dialect we owe an almost
      incredible impoverishment of vocabulary.'

    b. Per furtüna *s' han las chosas* fermamaing müdadas
                   V   S
      by fortune self have the things greatly   changed
      'Fortunately, things have changed greatly.'

On the other hand, Ladin dialects are not entirely alike. Linder (1987: 94–5) observes that subject–verb inversion occurs in questions throughout Ladin: but subject–verb inversion following sentence-initial *X* occurs only in the more northern Gardena and Badiot dialects, not in the more southern Fassa, Livinallongo, or (we may add) Ampezzan dialects. The geographical distribution of this feature clearly suggests the importance of German influence: the closer to Bressanone/Brixen, the greater the influence of German; the closer to Trento, the less the influence of German. The dialect split is illustrated by the following examples from Gardena (from Gartner's texts) and Badiot (from textual examples in *La Usc di Ladins*), on the one hand, and Fassa (from Elwert), and the Livinallongo dialect (again, based on examples from *La Usc di Ladins*) on the other:

Gardena:

(13) a. [ilo   *a*   *l*   ʃkumɛntʃa a   mɛne na   ʃtleta vita]
             V   S

    there has he begun   to lead a   bad   life
    'There he began to lead a dissolute life.'

b. [pɛr la   carɛʃtia ke   foa, *mɛsove l*   *sɛ*]
                        V   S

    by   the famine that was musted he self
    [kuntɛnte de maja kuŋ k la beʃtiɛs]
    to-content of to-eat with   the animals
    'Because of the famine, he had to content himself with eating
    with the animals.'

c. [tɛ kal paviʃ   *foɛ* l   n ajla]
              V   S

    in that country was she a   woman
    'In that country there was a woman.'

d. [pɛrmo da samartin   *mats uŋ*   l   aucɛs]
                      V   S

    not-before St Martin's kills PRO the geese
    'Geese aren't killed before St Martin's day.'

e. [da   tlo inant n   *uə* *i* plu mɛ   dɛʒmɛnca]
                     V   S

    from now on   not will I more myself forget
    'From now on, I won't forget.'

Badiot:

(14) a. [inshø *e* *l*   *alkol*   ruve   a fa   pɛrt da nɔʃta]
               V S

    thus   is the alcohol arrived to make part of our
    [alimɛntatsiun]
    diet
    'Thus alcohol has become a part of our diet.'

b. dl 1909 *s*   *a*   *la*   *familia P*. trasferi a W.
             V   S

    in   1909 self has the family P. moved to W.
    'In 1909, the P. family moved to W.'

c. [plø tɛrt *uns-* *e* ince pudy   ʒi   a udɛj]
                V   S

    more late have we also been-able to-go to see
    [la ʃtamparia]
    the press
    'Later, we were also able to go see the printing press.'

Fassa:

(15) a. [intorn les tʃiŋk de sera,   *el   patroŋ el se*]
                                       S   V
about   five   of evening the master he self
[*tol*   na kandola ɔ na kopa de ɛga   sɛnta]
takes a   bucket   or a   cup of water holy
'At about five in the afternoon, the master takes a bucket
or a cup of holy water.'

b. [dapø da sera, *la vacɛs ʒu n ʃtala i se pɛrla*]
                   S   V
'Afterwards, in the evening, the cattle down in the stable talk
among themselves.'

c. [indomaŋ, *el   patroŋ l   era* mɔrt]
              S   V
next-day   the master he was dead
'The next day, the master was dead.'

d. [kala valɛnta *sia mɛre*   no la   la   *podea* veder]
                  S   V
that worthy her mother not she her could see
'The worthy one her mother couldn't stand to look at.'

Livinallongo/Fodom

(16) a. davo vot   agn   de viera *la rusa la   se   retira*
                                   S   V
after eight years of war   Russia she self retires
dal   Afghanistan
from   A.
'After eight years of war, Russia is withdrawing from
Afghanistan.'

b. Nte le Filippine   mpruma *l   a*   mpare la
                               S   V
in   the Philippines first   he has learned the
linga   visaja
language V.
'It was in the Philippines that he first learned Visayan.'

Thus, the Romansh dialects consistently avoid V/3 order, while among
the Ladin dialects, there is a split: Badiot and Gardena (the dialects more
consistently exposed to German influence) avoid V/3 order, while Fassa,
Livinallongo, and Ampezzan (more consistently exposed to Italian)
allow the finite verb to appear third, fourth, or even later in the sentence.

Finally, in Friulian, there is no evidence of subject–verb inversion
after sentence-initial *X*:

(17) a. Une sabide   matine   *il Pari   Eterno al puarte*
                                   S   V
one Saturday morning the Father Eternal he brings
a ciase un biel ciavret
home   a   fine kid
'One Saturday morning, the Eternal Father brings home a
fine kid.'

   b. Dongje di chel omp, *Linde e   viveve* par so   cont.
                                   S   V
along of that man Linda she lived on her account
'In the company of that man, Linda lived her own life.'

   c. Ta prima comedia che vin   imparàt *tu   tu   vevis*
                                                    S   V
in first   comedy that have learned you you had
la   part di Allegro
the part of Allegro
'In the first comedy we learned, you had the role of Allegro.'

   d. Da pîs   di un cocolâr, *Zuanut al vedé* une cocule
                                              S   V
at foot of a   walnut Johnny he saw a   walnut
'At the foot of a walnut tree, Johnny saw a walnut.'

The distribution of subject–verb inversion within Rhaeto-Romance
strongly supports the hypothesis that XVS word order (whether in itself
an inherited feature, as argued in Benincà (1985) and Vanelli (1984b), or
a later development, as suggested in Kuen (1957), Haiman (1974), and
Helty (1975)) is a result of German influence.

We turn now to the more complicated problem of the causal
relationship between V/2 word order and the presence of unstressed
pronoun subjects.

4.1.2 V/2 and pronoun subjects

The idea that V/2 motivates the presence of personal pronoun subjects in
the Germanic languages, French, and Romansh, is quite old. It dates
back at least to Wackernagel's theory that the finite verb in Indo-
European was originally atonic and could therefore be subject to the
syntactic rule which put unstressed clitics into sentence-second position.

Thurneysen (1892) may have been the first to point out that in
medieval French, pronoun subjects were more or less obligatory if their
absence would lead to *V/1 order. In inverted word order, however
(TVX in declaratives, (T)VX in interrogatives), where the V/2 constraint

was either satisfied by another sentence-initial constituent or inoperative, subject pronouns were generally *omitted*. Darmesteter (1897: section 390) and Foulet (1930: 313) speak of this as 'a fundamental point of Old French syntax'.

Eggenberger (1961: 143–4) makes exactly the same point with reference to Old High German: 'the unstressed subject pronoun is generally only present when not driven from preverbal [i.e. sentence-initial] position by some competing constituent'. More recently, Haiman (1974) claimed that both dummy pronoun subjects and personal pronoun subjects, whose presence defined Perlmutter's 'Type A' languages were motivated in Germanic *only* by the V/2 constraint.

Clearly, if only V/2 motivates the presence of personal pronoun subjects, then these subjects (from a syntactic point of view) are noun phrases dominated by S, and not verbal prefixes. The reason for this conclusion is that a structure

##prefix + verb

in itself cannot satisfy the verb-second constraint.

Section 4.2 will demonstrate that all Rhaeto-Romance dialects, like many northern Italian dialects have dummy-pronoun subjects and obligatory pronoun subjects as German, French, and English do. Wherever there is a transparent correlation between the presence of these pronouns and the V/2 order requirement, it will be pointed out. Section 4.2.1 will discuss the form and distribution of indefinite agent pronouns. Section 4.2.2 will detail the syntactic criteria which force us to analyse both Ladin and Friulian subject pronouns as bound affixes on the verb rather than as sentence-initial noun phrases dominated by S. Finally, section 4.2.3 will sketch what seems a plausible series of developments whereby personal-pronoun subjects degenerated from nominal arguments to agreement markers in the Italian dialects of Rhaeto-Romance, and in Gallo-Romance generally.

4.2 THE DISTRIBUTION OF MEANINGFUL PRONOUN SUBJECTS
4.2.1. The indefinite subject PRO

In general, sentences with unspecified or unknowable subjects occur without overt grammatical subjects in most languages: it is only in those languages which require (or once required) verb-second order that the unspecified agent PRO is given lexical expression. French has *on*, German *man*, English (variously) *one*, *we*, *you*, or *they*. The Rhenish Romansh dialects all have some reflex of UNUS. The Ladin dialects of Badiot and Gardena, as noted already, have /ən/, which is possibly a reflex of HOMO. The following examples from Surselvan and Badiot are typical:

Surselvan

(18) a. *ins*   ei alla   fin
         PRO   is at-the end
         'It is finished.'

      b. alla   fin ei -n   *ins*   mai.
         at-the end is -(hiatus breaker) PRO   never
         'It is never over.'

Badiot

(19) a. da   rina a-   *n*   dɛr   na bɛla vidlada
         from R.   has PRO really a   fine   view
         'From Rina, one has a really fine view'

      b. ʃ   *an*   tɛɲ   kunt   ke S, kapɛʃ   *an*   ke S
         if PRO   holds account that S understands PRO   that S
         'If one bears in mind that S, then one understands that S.'

If the presence of a PRO noun were motivated exclusively by the need to keep the finite verb in second position, then this pronoun should not occur in inverted word order: yet it does appear, as shown in (18b) and (19a).

The Engadine dialects infrequently allow /yn/ as PRO, but much more generally seem to follow Italian in having sentences with unspecified or PRO subjects rendered by impersonal reflexives. These impersonal reflexives, however, typically occur with the dummy subject (Puter) *a(d)* or (Vallader) *i(d)*:

Puter

(20) *a* s   dess   procurer ch' el possa as   schmuanter
         it self should arrange that he can   self move
         libramaing
         freely
         'PRO should arrange that he [the dog] can move freely.'

Vallader

(21) *i* nu s'   ha   seis pos gnanca la   saira
         it not self has his rest even   the evening
         'PRO cannot rest even in the evening.'

In Puter, it seems that the dummy subject with impersonal reflexives is omitted in inverted word order (and thus its presence depends transparently on the verb-second constraint):

(22) a. per la fer   guster *as* stu____ metter aint ün
         for it make taste self must   put   in   a

töch   charn
piece meat
'To make it tasty, PRO must put a piece of meat into it.'

b.   al   muot da l' övin *as* po-___ distinguer üna
     at-the tip   of the egg self can   discern   a
     vschiigna d' ajer
     hole   of air
     'At the tip of the egg, PRO can discern an airhole.'

In Vallader, the dummy subject remains in inverted word order also:

(23)   intuorn las trais *as* fa-   j-
       around the three self make (hiatus breaker)
       a   marenda
       3sg.   snack
       'Around three o'clock, PRO has a snack.'

It has been argued that, in Italian, impersonal *si* has effectively been
reanalysed as a subject pronoun parallel to German *man*, French *on*.
Some of the same arguments could be made for the reanalysis of
Engadine (*a*)*s*. Thus, the impersonal 'reflexive' occurs with intransitive
verbs, as in (20) and (22a). Moreover, this reflexive disconcertingly co-
occurs with object pronouns throughout Italian and in the northern
Italian dialects, as it also does in the following Puter example:

(24)   ün   da quels dis   scu cha *s* ils   vezza be   in
       one of those days like that self them sees only in
       valledas otas
       valleys high
       'One of those days that PRO sees only in high valleys.'

(In Venetian, as in Puter, the impersonal reflexive precedes the object
pronoun clitic: *se li vede* 'they are seen'. In standard Italian, the
impersonal reflexive follows: *li si vede*.)

On the other hand, the Engadine dialects consistently invert subject
noun phrases and verbs after sentence-initial constituents: no such
inversion of the reflexive and the verb ever occurs, as the sentences in (22)
and (23) well illustrate. For this reason, the impersonal reflexive pronoun
is analysed as an object clitic here.

In the southern Ladin dialects of Fassa, Moena, Ampezzo, and
Livinallongo, as well as in Friulian, PRO is sometimes rendered by the
3rd plural form of the verb, but more generally, by the originally reflexive
pronoun *si*. In terms of its syntactic distribution within Friulian, this
morpheme should be reckoned a subject pronominal clitic, which either

precedes the object clitics preverbally or displaces them into postverbal position, and obligatorily displaces the 'true' reflexive object clitic into postverbal position (Gregor 1975: 114; Marchetti 1952: 141, Benincà 1989: 572):

(25) a. *si*   lis   pajave
        PRO   them   paid
        'PRO paid for them.'

     b. *si*   sintivi- le
        PRO   heard   her
        'PRO heard her.'

(26) a. *si*   ciata si   a   jessi
        PRO   finds self to   be
        'PRO finds oneself to be . . . '

     b. *s*   inacuarzi si
        PRO   perceives self
        'PRO recognizes.'

The fact that *si* as the indefinite or impersonal subject PRO precedes all object pronouns might seem to be compatible with an analysis of impersonal *si* as a syntactically reanalysed subject. But the fact that it can displace other object pronouns into postverbal position (as in (25b) and (26)), suggests that it is competing for the same syntactic slot as the latter, and is thus better analysed as an object clitic. Note finally, that in the Rhaeto-Romance dialects which have been under predominantly standard Italian influence, the impersonal reflexive does not occur with a dummy subject (a fact which seems to suggest that the reflexive functions as a subject), but that in many non-Rhaeto-Romance northern Italian dialects, the impersonal reflexive does co-occur with the dummy subject (which seems to suggest that it functions as an object).

A stronger argument for analysing impersonal *se* as a subject pronoun could perhaps be made in such dialects as Ampezzan. Here, the impersonal reflexive co-occurs with, and precedes, all object pronoun clitics, including the homophonous true reflexive.

The fact that impersonal *se* occupies a different syntactic slot from the true reflexive is graphically illustrated by sentences like

(27) dara ɔtes se   se frastona ra testa par monàdes
     some times PRO self breaks the head over trivia
     'Sometimes PRO agonizes over trivia.'

(Appollonio 1930: 45)

There are, then, a number of lexical and syntactic isoglosses within Rhaeto-Romance for the representation of the indefinite subject PRO:

Rhenish Romansh and northern Ladin employ a subject pronoun derived from UNUS or HOMO (as do the non-Rhaeto-Romance Lombard and Abruzzese dialects), while the Engadine Romansh dialects, the southern Ladin dialects, and Friulian, like Italian, use the impersonal reflexive. Among those dialects which use the impersonal reflexive, the Engadine dialects use a dummy pronoun. Finally, in Puter, the dummy pronoun appears only when called for by the verb-second constraint.

4.2.2 Personal pronouns

In all Rhaeto-Romance dialects with the exception of Surselvan (and, to a lesser extent, the other Romansh dialects), there are two series of subject pronouns: stressed and atonic. Subject to certain qualifications, it can be stated that:

> Where there is only the stressed series, these pronouns are obligatory; where there are two, the atonic pronouns are obligatory.

Pending analysis of the atonic pronouns, then, all the Rhaeto-Romance dialects are alike in requiring personal pronoun subjects, and thus in this respect are typical 'type A' or 'non-pro-drop' languages like English, French, or German. In fact, they share this property with other northern Italian dialects. On Genoese, see Browne and Vattuone (1975); on Florentine, Piedmontese, and Trentino, see Brandi and Cordin (1981) and Bracco, Brandi and Cordin (1985); on Paduan, Benincà (1982); on Venetian dialects, Benincà and Vanelli (1982); on Friulian and Ladin, Vanelli (1984a, b) and Benincà (1989). On northern Italian dialects in general, see Renzi and Vanelli (1982), Rizzi (1986), and Benincà (1986).

Surselvan requires personal pronoun subjects in all contexts save one: in inverted word order, the second person pronouns, both singular and plural, may drop. This is not quite the distribution of personal-pronoun subjects in the neighbouring Swiss German dialects, where only the 2nd *singular* pronoun is omitted in inverted word order.

The remaining Romansh dialects share this waiver, but go somewhat further: in inverted word order, atonic subject pronouns are treated as suffixes on the verb, and appear or are omitted in conformity with the three-syllable rule, which militates against antepenultimate stress on verbs.

In most Ladin dialects, and in Friulian, the atonic subject pronouns in all but the 2nd singular and third person are represented by a single vowel. This vowel is elided before a vowel-initial verb by what seems to be a general phonological rule, and results in apparent verb-initial order, as in the Badiot examples:

(28) a. ùn   tut   pert a chësc concurs
         have(1pl.) taken part to this competition
         'We have taken part in this competition'
     b. ùn   incé a disposiziun formulars y chertes
         have(1pl.) also at disposition forms   and charts
         'We also have at our disposal forms and charts.'

This (originally phonetically motivated) elision before a vowel has been analogically extended so that elision is possible before all auxiliary verbs:

(29) a. (i) sun   sta   dër cuntenĉ
         (we) are(1pl.) been very glad
         'We were very glad.'
     b. (i) podun punsé a plö   frabiches adüm
         (we) can(1pl.) think to many buildings together
         'We can think of many buildings together.'

The original phonetic motivation for the reduction is still visible, however, in inverted word order, where the atonic pronoun remains as a verbal suffix:

(30) a. plö tert un-s-*e* inĉe pudü jí a udëi ta
         more late have-we also could go to see in
         Stamparia   Athesia
         Press   A.
         'Later we could also go and visit the Athesia Press.'
     b. Da   misdé sun-s-*e* spo jüs a marëna düĉ adüm
         after noon are-we then gone to lunch all together
         'After noon, we all went to lunch together.'

In suffixed position, too, the atonic subject pronoun is subject to phonetic constraints, and cannot appear if its presence would create antepen-ultimate stress on the verb:

(31) ci podésson-____ pa fa por os?
     what could(1pl.)   then do for you-all
     'What could we do for you, then?'

The fact that the presence of the subject pronoun is conditioned in both Romansh and Ladin by purely phonetic factors is one indication of its status as a bound affix on the verb. We will return to this in section 4.3.

In Friulian, the atonic subject pronoun is supposedly obligatory in the positive assertive indicative, if no object pronoun clitic precedes the verb. (There are, however, numerous examples of unconditioned subject elision in actual texts.) Moreover, if the verb is preceded by either the negative marker *no* or an object clitic, or both, the subject pronoun is omitted unless it is 2nd singular. (Marchetti 1952: 145; Gregor 1975: 122). Only the 2nd singular subject pronoun *tu* is never omittable. (This is common to northern Italian dialects – see Renzi and Vanelli 1982.)

The 2nd singular pronoun, unlike all others, can be reinforced by the stressed form in Badiot (Alton and Vittur 1968: 30). The 2nd singular pronoun, unlike all others is obligatorily omitted in inverted word order in Gardenese.

Finally, in the Gorizian dialect of Friulian (as in Lombard), the second person atonic pronouns, both singular *tu* (Lombard -*t*) and plural *o* (Lombard -*v*), appear obligatorily and invariably as *suffixes* on the verb (Frau 1984: 113).

Summing up: the 2nd singular pronoun has a peculiar status in all the Rhaeto-Romance dialects, although its behaviour in Romansh seems to be diametrically opposed to its behaviour in the Italian dialects. In Romansh, as in the neighbouring German dialects, it stands out by virtue of being omittable, while in Ladin and Friulian, as in northern Italian generally, it stands out by virtue of being indispensable.

4.3 DUMMY PRONOUNS

Type A languages like English have meaningless space-filling pronouns which occupy sentence-initial position when the logical subject of the sentence is presented sentence-finally, or is absent. Examples include:

(32) a. *There* is a hole in my bucket. (existential presentative)
    b. *It* is nice that you are here. (extraposed presentative)
    c. *It* is evening. (subjectless)

Type B languages generally lack dummy pronouns like *there* or 'ambient *it*', tolerating verb-initial order.

All Rhaeto-Romance languages, like many northern Italian dialects, and like French, have dummy subject pronouns. This sets them apart from standard Italian, and from the central and southern Italian dialects.

In Romansh, the dummy subject pronoun is distinctively 3rd singular neuter (Surs. and Surm. *i(gl)*, Eng. *i(d)* $\sim$ *a(d)*). In the Ladin and Friulian dialects, it is the 3rd singular masculine *ə(l)*. The following survey is representative:

4.3.2 Ambient *it*

(33) a. *Surselvan*

Igl ei bi
it   is fine
'It is fine (weather).'
ei splunta
it knocks
'There is a knock.'

(The two different forms are allomorphs conditioned by the following segment: *igl* occurs before vowels only.)

b. *Sutselvan*
Gea   dapartut   ear-*i*   sera
already everywhere was-it evening
'It was evening everywhere already.'

(Linder 1987: 69)

c. *Surmeiran*
/*i* na viɲ   bec da   plover/
it not come not from to-rain
'It won't rain.'
d. *Puter*
a plova
it rains
'It is raining.'
e. *Vallader*
i clocca
it knocks
'There is a knock.'
f. *Gardena*
/*i*   *l* a ʃkumɛntʃá a pluvaj/
and it has begun   to rain
'And it began to rain.'
g. *Moena/Fassa*
/*l* ɛra de otober/
it was of October
'It was (in) October)'
h. *Ampezzan*
l é proprio cioudo ancioi
it is really hot   today
i. *Friulian*
A no nevée maj
it not snows never
'It never snows.'

In some of the Italian dialects, the dummy subject is obligatory only before auxiliary verbs. But we know of no Rhaeto-Romance dialect in which 'ambient *it*' ever disappears by virtue of its position in the sentence. Its presence is obligatory irrespective of word order.

4.3.2 Presentative *it* (existential verbs)

Although presentative sentences with the logical subject left to the end are typified by existential sentences, they occur whenever the logical subject is newly introduced. In the following examples, no distinction is made between existential and other presentative sentences which share a fundamental VXS order. The dummy subject, like other subjects, may undergo subject–verb inversion in questions, or in assertive sentences introduced by a topic noun phrase.

(34) a. *Surselvan*
Ei vegn in urezi
it comes a storm
'There is a storm coming.'
Avon casa ei- s-   *i* mats
before house is (hiatus) it boys
'Before the house, some boys are standing.'
b. *Surmeiran*
bi dasper quella paunt er *igl* ina tgeasetta
just next that bridge was it a house-dim.
'Just next to that bridge there was a small house.'

(from Linder 1987: 142)

c. *Puter*
ad eirans var 40 scolars
it were-1pl. about forty students
'There were about forty of us students.'
sün maisa sun-____ eir üna chavagnina de paun e ün curte
on table are also a basket of bread and a knife
'On the table there are also a breadbasket and a knife.'
d. *Vallader*
id es in fuschina ün velo.
it is in shop a bicycle
'There is a bicycle in the shop.'
che es-*a* da tour a man?
what is it from to-take to hand
'What is there to take by hand?'
e. *Gardena*
/*l* nɛn iə ʃta dɛguŋ tɛ caza/

it not is been no-one in house
'There was no-one in the house.'
/tɛ kal paviʃ fɔe- *l* n ajla/
in that village was it a woman
'In that village there was a woman.'

In the Romansh dialects and in the northern Ladin dialects, then, a dummy subject is obligatory with postposed logical subjects. Only in Puter, however, does this dummy subject ever disappear when the verb-second constraint is satisfied by some other means.

A peculiarity of Surselvan is that presentative sentences whose main verb is *not* existential do permit omission of the dummy pronoun subject in sentences with TVX order. In such sentences, the verb may either agree with the postposed subject or occur in the default 3rd singular (neuter) form – as though still agreeing with an invisible dummy subject:

(35) a. denton vegnan-____ reparti   dalla mumma
        after   come (3pl.) distributed (3pl.) by   mom
        ils   regals
        the presents (3p.)
        'Afterwards the presents are distributed by mom.'

     b. en emprema lingia ei-____   vegniu   examinau
        in first   line   is   come (3n.sg.) examined (3n.sg.)
        il   stan tecnic   dils   vehichels
        the state technical (3m.sg.) of-the vehicles
        'First, the technical condition of the vehicles was examined.'

     c. tier   9   persunas ei-____   vegniu   ordinau
        among nine persons   is   come (3n.sg.) ordered (3n.sg.)
        ina controlla   dil   saun
        a   control (f.sg.) of-the health
        'Nine people had to undergo a health examination.'

In each of these sentences, the logical subject (italicized) is clearly postposed, rather than inverted with the verb. The position where a dummy subject would be expected is marked with an underlined space.

In the southern Ladin dialects, the dummy subject is obligatory with the verb 'to be', and otherwise optional, irrespective of word order, in presentative or existential sentences:

Fassa
(36) a. /n   owta *l* era um pɛre e   una mɛre/
        one time it was a   father and a   mother
        'Once there was a father and a mother.'

b. /po *l* e veɲu   na pitʃola/
    then it is come (m.sg.) a   little-girl (f.sg.)
    'Then there came a little girl.'

c. /se___ vɛŋ   el salvaŋ, el me maɲa, me e   te/
    if   comes the monster he me eats,   me and you
    'If the monster comes, he will eat me, and you too.'

Moena

(37) a. /___ veɲiva pju   nef/
        came   more snow
        'There came more snow.'

b. /no lontan da   alo *l* ɛra la pɛtsa de n   awter/
    not far   from there it was the plot   of an other
    'Not far from there was the plot of another.'

Ampezzan

(38) a. agnére   *l* é sta   ra   sagra inz'el nosc paes.
        yesterday it is been the sagra in   our   village
        'Yesterday was the village feast in our village.'

b. *l* èa tanta   zente
    it was so-many people
    'There were so many people.'

In all Friulian dialects but Gorizian, any type of postposed or inverted lexical subject requires a corresponding subject clitic, and regular agreement of the verb:

Central Friulian

(38) a. *al* e vignuːt un gran teremot
       he is come   a   great earthquake
       'There came a great earthquake.'

b. *a*   vigniːvin   i   benedeːs kavaliːrs
    they came (3pl.) the blessed   silkworms

c. *e*   rive   la   skose des   ondis
    she arrives the   shock of-the eleven
    'There arrives the eleven o'clock shock.'

(from Frau 1984)

Dummy subjects with extraposed sentences:

(39) a. *Surselvan*
      igl ei buca ver   che   S
      it   is not   true   that   S

b. *Surmeiran*
    i vign rachinto, tgi   S
    it is   told   that   S

   c. *Puter*

      ais- *e* permiss   da der il tribut a l' imperatur?
      is it permitted to give the tribute to the Emperor?

   d. *Vallader*

      id es sgüra   meglder da tour quels plü gross
      it is certainly better to take the big ones

   e. *Gardena*

      /l iə baŋ vajra, ke/ S
      it is very true   that S

In the southern Ladin dialects again, the dummy subject is possible, but not apparently necessary, with extraposed sentential subjects:

Ampezzan

(40) a. e *lo* mèo che viene anche io?
       is he better that come also   I
       'Is it better if I come too?'

    b. suzede   che chel che zerca d'imbroià i
       happens that he   that seeks to-confuse the (m.pl.)
       òutre, tanta   òtes el s' imbroia el
       others so-many times he self confuses him
       'It happens that he who seeks to confuse others, so
       many times confuses only himself.'

Fassa

(41) a. /el pɛr   donka ke abjedɛ reʒoŋ vo/
       it seems then   that have reason you-all
       'It seems, then that you are right.'

    b. /e *l* posibol ke tu no te staes pɛzo/
       is it possible that you not you be   worse
       'Is it possible that you are not worse?'

    c. /somea k   el rue   doman/
       seems that he arrives tomorrow
       'It seems that he arrives tomorrow.'

    d. /se kon partir/
       self must leave
       'It is necessary to leave.'

(Examples (41c) and (41d) are field data from Pozzo di Fassa.)
In all typical Friulian varieties, all extraposed sentential subjects require dummy subject pronouns. Note the unexpected *feminine* dummy subject in (42b):

(42) a. /al pareve   ke no l ves sintuːt nuje/
       he appeared that not he had heard nothing
       'It appeared that he had heard nothing.'

    b. /ma e   je vere ke/ S
       but she is true that S
       'But it is true that S.'
    c. /al pararés   k   al ves   di neveá/
       he would-seem that he would of to-snow
       'It looks like snow.'

4.4 THE AFFIX STATUS OF SUBJECT PRONOUNS

Considerable evidence throughout the Rhaeto-Romance dialects, and throughout the dialects of northern Italy, supports the view that atonic subject pronouns are not fully independent noun phrases, but clitics which are well on the way to becoming further reduced to the status of bound affixes on the verb.

As an intermediate category between noun phrases and affixes, clitics exhibit the properties of both bound affixes, and of independent words. The only property of independent words which obligatory atonic subject pronouns still have, in fact, seems to be that they undergo subject–verb inversion in questions (see Brandi and Cordin 1981), who explicitly invoke this criterion of wordhood in their study of these clitics in the northern Italian dialects of Trent and Florence). Thus, for example, in Friulian (Marchetti 1952: 143), we observe a paradigm:

(43) a. Jo o feveli
      b. O feveli jo
         'I speak' (assertive)
(44) a. Jo feveli-o?
      b. Feveli-o jo?
         'Do I speak?' (interrogative)

The full pronoun *jo* occurs on either the left or the right margin of the verbal complex in both statements and questions. In its word-order distribution, at least, it still reflects its origins as a dislocated constituent. The obligatory subject marker *o*, on the other hand, is sensitive to whether the sentence is an assertion or a question. This kind of sensitivity to syntactic information is characteristic of clitics in Romance, and distinguishes them from bound affixes, whose status as prefixes or suffixes is not subject to perturbation. (Compare Vanelli 1984a: 283n., Linder 1987: 94–5, for the northern Italian distribution of this feature.)

Crucially, in non-standard French (Lambrecht 1981) and in some varieties of Florentine, Venetian, and Friulian, even this last vestige of word status is missing. Subject pronouns are always prefixes, irrespective of sentential mood in non-standard French and in these dialects:

Non-standard French
(45) Où tu vas ?
    'Where are you going?'

(Lambrecht 1981)

Florentine
(46) a. O   che tu   vuoi?
       what that you want
       'What do you want?'

Venetian
    b. kosa ti   vol
       what you want
       'What do you want?'

In the Gorizian dialect of Friulian, on the other hand, second person subject pronouns are invariably suffixes:

(47) /tu   pjardis-   tu/
     you   lose (2sg.) you
     'You lose; Do you lose?'

(Frau 1984: 113)

In all other respects, subject markers pattern like bound agreement-marking morphemes, in the majority of the northern Italian dialects. Most obviously, they co-occur not only with pronominal, but also with lexical subject nominal expressions:

Friulian
(48) a. un om   *al* veve doi fis
       a   man he had two sons
       'A man had two sons.'
    b. la   strade *e* va   ju   a plomp
       the road she goes down steeply
       'The road goes down steeply.'
    c. nisun   *l* a   timp di ciala
       nobody he has time to look
       'Nobody has the time to look.'

The obligatory occurrence of a subject clitic even with a noun phrase subject like *nisun* 'nobody' is significant: it excludes the possibility that lexical subjects in examples like (48) can be analysed synchronically as left-dislocated constituents followed by a resumptive pronoun.

    Among the remaining Rhaeto-Romance dialects, we observe the same possibility in at least Sutselvan (Linder 1987: 162):

(49) a. Se Magun han- *i*   bears via   ena femna
      on M.   have they many seen a   woman
      'On Magun, many people saw a woman.'

    b. Mo igl lungatg da la dunnetta   san- *i*   nigns
      but the language of the woman(dim.) know they none
      'But no one knows the language of the little woman.'

The following sentences from Trentino and Fiorentino show the same pattern:

(50) a. *Trentino*
      Nisun *l* ha dit niente.
      no-one he has said nothing
      'No-one said anything.'

    b. *Florentine*
      Nessun *gl* ha detto nulla
      no-one he has said nothing
      'No-one said anything.'

The examples of (50) derive from Brandi and Cordin (1981), as does the argument that cases of clitic doubling such as those of (48), (49), and (50) cannot be examples of resumptive topicalization.

In the same way that obligatory subject pronouns co-occur with lexical NPs, they also co-occur with the relative pronoun {che}, as in the Friulian phrases of (51):

(51) a. dut ce   che   *al* e gno
      all   that which he is mine
      'all that which is mine'

    b. /Mario, ke   al e ɲo barba/
      M.   that he is my uncle
      'Mario, my uncle'

This, too, argues against *NP + clitic* sequences being examples of left dislocation and resumptive topicalization.

Resumptive topicalization may well be their diachronic source, however, and we can adduce syntactic and morphological reasons for this view. First, as noted, the word order of the optional full pronouns in languages like Friulian still reflects this status. So too does their morphology. Vanelli (1984a: 285) points out that the free and optional pronouns tend to be similar to the *oblique* or disjunctive forms, and probably therefore derive from them historically. Finally, other Rhaeto-Romance dialects like Fassan and Ampezzan, and northern Italian dialects like Venetian and Lombard do not allow subject clitic pronouns to co-occur with some or all of these non-topicalizable NP subjects. For example, consider the Fassan and Ampezzan sentences of (52):

(52) a.   *Fassan*
/nessuɲ____ a maɲa la supa/
nobody   has eaten the soup
  b.   *Ampezzan*
/dute____ proa algo/
everybody tries something

The absence of the clitic in (52) contrasts with its presence in the Ampezzan sentences below:

  c.   duta ra me biancheria *r*   e fata   de bona tera
all   the my linen   she is made of fine   cloth
'All my linen is made of fine cloth.'
  d.   chel contadin *l* a   bona tera inz i   so ciampe
that farmer   he has good earth in the his fields
'That farmer has good soil in his fields.'

(Appollonio 1930)

This restriction may also reflect the origin of clitic subject markers as resumptive pronouns.

In direct questions, the subject clitic generally follows the verb, as in the following northern Italian dialect examples:

(53) a.   *Bolognese*
dove e l al professaur?
where is he the professor
'Where is the professor?'
  b.   *Romagnol*
cosa dira   l la mama
what will-say he the mom
'What will mom say?'
(note the lack of agreement of the clitic)
  c.   *Ampezzan*
louráe-lo, to   barba?
worked-he your uncle
'Did your uncle work?'

The co-occurrence of clitic subjects with full lexical NP subjects is common throughout northern Italian. Moreover, all of these dialects have at least a few contexts where the clitic subject can or must be omitted. One such context is following the interrogative pronoun and complementizer *ke*, in both content questions and headless relative clauses:

(54) a. *Romagnol*
/ki k_____ ven kun te/
who that   comes   with   you
'Who's coming with you?'

b. *Friulian*
/kuj ku_____ ven kun te/
'Who's coming with you?'

c. *Ampezzan*
/ci k_____ preʃa,   vade   pjan/
who that   hastens   go (3sg.subj.)   slow
'Let whoever is in haste go slow.'

Another systematic restriction which provides some hints about the origins of the *NP + clitic* construction is manifest in Badiot, Marebban, and Gardenese (among the Ladin dialects), and all Romansh dialects with the exception of Surselvan. These languages allow clitic subject pronouns only in postverbal position. They may co-occur with sentence final lexical subject NP only in inverted (or rather, presentative) word order.

Badiot Ladin
(55) a. Da doman   e   *les*   stades   oshorades les vatges
of   morning   are   they   become   fed   the   cows
'In the morning, the cows are fed.'

b. tagn   d'agn a   *la*   pa   osta fomena?
how-many years has she then your wife
'How old is your wife, then?'

                                 (Pizzinini and Plangg 1966)

The co-occurrence of clitic pronouns with lexical noun phrase subjects is not attested in regular word order in the Romansh dialects. But it occurs frequently in inverted word order at least in Vallader, co-occurring both with proper nouns and with disjunctive or stressed personal pronouns:

(56) a. sta   *la*   Mengia jent   a   chasa?
stays she Mengia gladly at house
'Does Mengia stay at home gladly?'

b. lavur *la*   svelt Mengia?
works she fast   Mengia
'Does Mengia work quickly?'

c. quellas pigliain-   *a*   no
those   take (1pl.) we we
'*We*'ll take those.'

In his careful survey of the written literature, Linder (1987: 146–52) shows traces of this 'clitic doubling' in inverted order in all other Romansh dialects with the exception of Surselvan.

Within Rhaeto-Romance, then, we can distinguish at least four degrees of freedom in subject clitic doubling.

(a) *no* clitic doubling whatever: Surselvan;
(b) clitic doubling only in inverted word order: Sutselvan, Surmeiran, Vallader, Puter, Badiot, Marebban, Gardenese;
(c) clitic doubling only with topicalizable NP: Fassan, Ampezzan (like Lombard, Venetian);
(d) clitic doubling with all NP: Friulian (like Trentino, Florentine), Sutselvan (in inverted word order).

In addition, the numerous cases already documented of *desinential enlargement* throughout Rhaeto-Romance probably reflect an earlier stage of clitic doubling. That is, examples like Pontresina Puter

(57) nus curr- insa
      we   run   (1pl.)

undoubtedly are congealed from a source like

(58) *nus curr- in-   s-   a
       we   run   (1pl.) we   we

We have so far given one major argument against resumptive topicalization as the synchronically motivated structure of *NP + clitic* sequences: frequently, the NPs which co-occur with clitics are not candidates for topic status. Another argument against this analysis is that – like agreement markers in general, and under the same conditions – clitics frequently *fail to mark agreement with the NP which they supposedly resume*. By the same token, unlike lexical pronouns, they fail to mark the gender of the NP for which they stand.

Roughly speaking, agreement between subject and predicate, or between object and predicate, operates obligatorily from left to right but only optionally in the opposite direction (further details in 4.5). Again, we can model the contrast in English:

(59) a. Two mice are (*is) hiding in your drawer.
          (subject precedes agreement-marking verb)
      b. There's (are) two mice hiding in your drawer.
          (subject follows agreement-marking verb)

'Grammatical' English, of course, demands agreement with even a postposed subject in sentences like (59b), but, as even a purist will admit, (59b) is possible with unmarked singular agreement, and (59a) is not.

(For a discussion of the phenomenon in Swiss Romansh, see Linder 1982; for Italian, see Rohlfs 1949: 448). Some examples from northern Italian:

(60) a. *Fassan*
    l e veɲu   la   vivano
    he is come (m.sg.) the witch (f.sg.)
    'There came the witch.'

                                    (Elwert 1943)

    b. *Moena*
       chi e *lo* po   i   ozitegn
       who is he then the Occitans (m.pl.)
       'Who are the Occitans?'

                                    (Plangg 1982)

    c. *Badiot*
      da doman   vegn   *l* oshoré   les vatges
      of morning becomes he fed (m.sg.) the cows (f.pl.)
      'The cows are fed in the morning.'

                        (Pizzinini and Plangg 1966)

    d. *Florentine*
      gl e venuto   delle ragazze
      he is come (m.sg.) some girls (f.pl.)
      'There came some girls.'

                      (Brandi and Cordin 1981)

    e. *Genoese*
      u vene   a   Katajning
      he comes the Catherine
      'Catherine is coming.'

                    (Browne and Vattuone 1975)

    f. *Ampezzan*
      agnere   *l* e sta   ra   sagra   inz el   nosc paes.
      yesterday he is been the feast (f.sg.) in   the   our county
      'Yesterday we had our county feast.'

                          (Appollonio 1930)

    g. *Friulian*
      al era una volta una fameja
      he was one time a   family (f.sg.)
      'There was once a family.'

                            (Iliescu 1972)

(Example (60g), it should be noted, is marginal in Friulian, in which the general pattern is one of full agreement between the clitic and the noun phrase it coccurs with.)

h. *Romagnol*
e   chenta   una   turtureina
he   sings   a   turtle-dove (f.sg.)
'A turtle dove is singing.'

(Gregor 1972)

Paradoxically, non-agreement in the examples of (60) can be motivated if the morphemes in question are analysed as agreement markers; it is anomalous if they are analysed as referential (anaphoric or cataphoric) pronouns. (This is in keeping with the general tendency for grammaticalized elements to become semantically bleached.)

The third way in which obligatory subject pronouns differ from 'true' or referential subject NPs with argument status is in their position relative to the negative morpheme {no}. Subject NPs invariably precede this morpheme: obligatory subject pronouns in at least some dialects (among them Fassan, Paduan, Trentino, Friulian) either obligatorily or conditionally follow it. Thus, Fassan

(61)   El   no *l* se   fida
'He   doesn't   dare'

motivates the structure proposed by Brandi and Cordin, where the obligatory subject marker, italicized in the example, is part of the verbal inflection.

In Florentine, the negation precedes 2nd singular, but can follow third person feminine pronoun subjects. We will return to this repeatedly signalled anomalous status of the 2nd singular pronoun in the following section.

The potential for permutation, Brandi and Cordin argue, following Rizzi (1986), provides further evidence for the constituency of subject pronouns within the verbal complex. This argument, however, could be accepted only if the order of morphemes within a word were subject to rearrangement, while the order of words within a phrase were fixed. If anything, the opposite seems to be the case (see Perlmutter 1971: 100).

Fourth, obligatory subject pronouns seem to resist co-ordination reduction. The prevailing pattern is illustrated by the following examples from Friulian:

(62) a.   *al* vent   dut   e   *al* va   lontan
he   sells   everything   and   he   goes   far-away

b.   quant   ch   *al* vigni   a   se   e   *al* cognosse
when   that   he   came   to   himself   and   he   recognized
l   predi
the   priest

By way of contrast, English, although a type A language, exhibits co-ordination reduction in sentences like the normal translations of (62):

(63) a. he sells everything and ____ goes far away.
     b. when he came to himself and ____ recognized the priest.

Compare the entirely similar behaviour of Surselvan Romansh:

(64) a. Ins   selegra   ed____ ei satisfatgs ...
        PRO rejoices and   is satisfied
        'We rejoice and are satisfied ... '
     b. auters savessen   e____ duessen imitar quella initiativa
        others should-know and   should imitate that   initiative
        'Others should be able to, and indeed should in fact, imitate this initiative.'

Curiously, Lambrecht (1981) notes that while standard French is like English and Surselvan, non-standard French agrees with northern Italian (for a detailed comparison of spoken colloquial French and northern Italian, see Renzi 1989):

(65) a. il mange et ____ boit comme un cochon (standard)
     b. i mange et i boit comme un cochon (non-standard)

Bound morphemes *may* be deleted under identity in co-ordinate constructions (see Kiparsky 1968; Haiman 1983), but this is much more constrained than deletion of independent words. The failure of co-ordination reduction in (62), as in (65) provides further evidence in support of the sub-lexical status of obligatory subject pronouns. (For the same argument in Trentino, see Brandi and Cordin 1981, duly repeated in Bouchard 1982: 407; Rizzi 1986: 402. Slightly different data for Paduan are cited in Benincà 1986.)

Summing up: in spite of what is often said in general surveys, (see Rohlfs 1949: 169, 174; 1986: 146), obligatory subject pronouns are not *entirely* obligatory, but may or must be omitted with certain kinds of subject NP.

Subject clitics are also impossible in Friulian in the presence of certain object or negative clitics. The rules vary greatly from dialect to dialect. In some dialects, obligatory subject markers are not used in persons other than 2nd singular when either object pronouns or the negative particle *no* precede the verb (Marchetti 1952: 145). In others, all subject pronouns except 2nd singular may be omitted when the verb is preceded by any object or reflexive clitic (Gregor 1975: 107). The textual data from Romagnol provided in Gregor (1972) seem to support a similar constraint in that dialect, and Lambrecht (1981) notes that non-standard French also allows subject clitic pronouns to be absent where an object pronoun also precedes the verb. Illustrative of this mutual exclusion are Friulian examples such as those of (66):

(66) a. denant del   ciar___ si e viodut un sflandor
        in-front of-the cart   self is seen   a   flash
        'A flash of light appeared before the cart.'

    b. so pari___ lu   viot.
       his father him saw
       'His father saw him.'

It is this mutual exclusion, rather than co-ordination reduction, which accounts for the absence of obligatory subject-marking pronouns in examples such as those of (67):

(67) a. *e* veve squasi 35 agn e   di zovine___ si   jere
        she had about 35 years and of young   self was
        fate ciacara
        made to-talk
        'She was about thirty-five, and had gotten herself talked about in her youth.'

    b. *al* clame un servidor e___ j   domande ce   ch al ere
       he calls a   servant and him asks   what that it was
       'He calls a servant and asks him what was the matter.'

This sensitivity to the presence of prefixed verbal clitics suggests that obligatory subject markers belong in the verbal clitic complex. To analyse them in this way makes it possible to state a relatively simple 'clitic constraint' at least for Friulian, and possibly Romagnol and non-standard French as well:

(68) All finite verbs must occur with at least one prefixed clitic in statements.

Note that (68) (like constraints on the distribution of Genoese *u* and Paduan *a*) may still reflect, in a rather obvious way, a correlation between word order and the verb-second constraint. In an earlier stage of the language, where all the present clitics were free-standing words, the presence of any one of them would keep the verb from sentence-initial position. (On the other hand, it must be admitted that there are arguments which go the other way. For example, it seems that in Paduan, 2nd singular is always obligatory, but third person forms may or must be omitted in the presence of a full NP (which may be a disjunctive personal pronoun, an interrogative pronoun, a relative pronoun, or a lexical NP – see Benincà 1983). Here, the sensitivity of the obligatory subject morpheme to the presence of full subject NP would seem to argue for its status as an independent NP.)

There are, then, numerous reasons for believing that subject marking 'pronouns' are really inflectional or agreement markers in the northern Italian dialects today, and well on the way to achieving the same status in non-standard French.

One last observation: while there is dialect variation in the degree of subject clisis which the dialects have undergone, all the dialects seem to agree on some rather special treatment of the 2nd singular. This is the subject pronoun which has advanced the furthest in reduction to clitic status (see Renzi and Vanelli 1982). In Friulian and in Paduan, it alone can never be omitted; in Florentine (which permits the absence of 1st singular) and Trentino (which permits the absence of first person, and 2nd plural), it is one of the many which can never be omitted; in Florentine, it is one of the many which follows the negative prefix. A unified explanation for this peculiar status of the 2nd singular pronoun is attempted in the following section.

4.4.1. The degeneration of subject pronouns

The degeneration of personal pronouns into agreement-marking affixes on finite verbs is commonly attested, and constitutes a paradigmatic instance of grammaticalization. A comparison of the Rhaeto-Romance and other northern Italian dialects allows a detailed reconstruction of the probable stages in this process.

The familiar distinction between Perlmutter's 'type A' languages like standard French, and 'type B' or 'pro-drop' languages like standard Italian (Perlmutter 1971: ch. 5) is not exhaustive. There are 'intermediate languages' of two different sorts.

Haiman (1974) dealt with languages like Icelandic, medieval French and German, and even modern German, arguing that in these languages, or in particular constructions within these languages, the superficial subject pronouns characteristic of type A languages appeared only when they were required to keep the finite verb in principal clauses in second position. The pattern can be illustrated with a vestigial contrast in modern English:

(69) a. *There* are three books on the table.
b. On the table (there) are three books.

Among the Rhaeto-Romance dialects, various constructions in Puter and Surselvan offer productive parallels: the dummy subject *igl* 'it' disappears in inverted word order. It may also be that the disappearance of the second-person subject pronoun throughout Romansh in inverted word order is an example of this conditioning by word order.

A strong claim about type A languages is that only those languages which have or have had the V/2 constraint ever become 'type A'. The present-day independence of word order and the appearance of superficial subject pronouns (most pronounced in French and English) must then be viewed as the outcome of a number of historical changes.

That superficial pronoun subjects are motivated by word-order requirements is an old idea: Haiman (1974) cites Beneš (1962), who explicitly correlates the appearance of 'dummy *es*' with the requirements of verb-second order in modern German. Kuen (1957: 302) notes that medieval French and German manuscripts supply subject pronouns before the attested loss of personal subject-marking desinences on the verb, and refers to Thurneysen (1892) for the idea that V/2 required the presence of a subject pronoun 'when no other sentential constituent stands before the verb' (1957: 304). In his classic survey of personal-pronoun subjects in the Lombard dialects, Spiess (1956: 5n.) cites Darmesteter (1897: sect. 390), who notes that in medieval French, the personal-pronoun subject was spelled out 'only when the verb or object pronoun would otherwise stand at the head of the clause'. For more recent works which cite an extensive prior literature on this correlation, see Harris (1978) for French, and Breivik (1983) for Germanic languages.

Recent generative studies of northern Italian dialects, notably Brandi and Cordin (1981), have drawn attention to another class of 'intermediate languages'. Brandi and Cordin showed that in the dialects of Florence and Trento, there is subject pronoun *doubling*. The same phenomenon can be observed in the dialects of Padua (Benincà 1982), Genoa (Browne and Vattuone 1975), Fassa (Elwert 1943), Badiot Ladin (Pizzinini and Plangg 1966), Ampezzo (Appollonio 1930), Bologna (Kuen 1957), Ravenna (Gregor 1972), and the Friuli (Marchetti 1952: 143 *et passim*, Benincà 1989), as we have already noted in the preceding section. For general surveys, see Rohlfs (1949: 169–79), Spiess (1956), Kuen (1957), Benincà and Vanelli (1982, 1985), Renzi and Vanelli (1982), Vanelli (1984a, b), and Benincà (1986).

Subject pronoun doubling means that all inflected verbs (including, in many dialects, impersonal, semantically subjectless meteorological verbs) occur with obligatory subject pronouns. The distribution of these subject pronouns corresponds roughly to the distribution of subject pronouns in type A languages.

(70)   *Florentine*
    a. (Te) tu parli   (Brandi and Cordin, 1981)
       you you speak
    b. *(Te) _____ parli
       you   speak
(71)   *Paduan*
    a. (Ti) te vien   (Benincà 1983)
       you you come
    b. *(Ti) _____vien
       you   come
(72)   *Friulian*
    a. (Jo) o feveli   (Marchetti 1952)
       I   I say
    b. *(Jo) _____ feveli
       I   say
(73)   *Fassa*
    a. (El) no l se fida   (Elwert 1943)
       he not he self trusts
       'He does not dare.'
    b. (El) no _____ se fida
(74)   *Romagnol*
    a. (Me) a voj ben   (Gregor 1972)
       I   I want well
       'I am fond (of . . .)'
    b. *(Me) _____ voj ben

From the description given by Browne and Vattuone (1975), it seems that Genoese/Zeneyze is intermediate in both senses: superficial subjects are only obligatory in certain constructions, but in those constructions, they resemble the superficial pronouns of type A languages. Thus, Zeneyze personal pronouns, like standard Italian personal pronouns, are likely to occur in subject position only under contrastive stress. As far as these pronouns are concerned, Zeneyze is a type B language. However, there exists a most uncharacteristic (for a type B language) dummy pronoun *u*, roughly corresponding to English 'there', German *es*, and the like, which gives Zeneyze a type A look:

(75) U vene u Zorzu
    he comes the George
    'George is coming.' (thetic)

A similar construction is of course, attested in all the languages exemplified in (70)–(74), along with other indices of their apparent type

A status. What Browne and Vattuone call '*u*-insertion' occurs only in thetic sentences, *where the entire sentence conveys new information* (1975: 138). Such sentences, which we have been calling presentative, are characterized by VX order.

There seems to be a similar distribution of the dummy pronoun *a* in Paduan, see Benincà (1983: 34): '*a* would seem to mark syntactically the so-called "entirely new phrase" which indicates that there is nothing in topic position, that is, that there is no pragmatic *topic*.' In Paduan also, such sentences have VX order. The dummy pronoun is, however, always optional.

Finally, Florentine and Trentino also require a dummy subject with VX order, but only when the verb in question is a form of 'be'.

As the sentence fragments above very clearly demonstrate, the verb may in addition occur with optional pronominal subjects of the disjunctive series. The latter, like subject pronouns in type B languages, seem to occur only when they are focused.

So, are these northern Italian dialects type A or type B languages? They seem to be both, and the answer we choose depends on which set of pronouns we are looking at.

Brandi and Cordin (1981) show that in Florentine and Trentino, in a number of ways, the obligatory subject pronouns are syntactically part of the INFL or AGR node, rather than true subject markers. Other arguments can be added to theirs for the other northern Italian dialects: the synchronic status of obligatory subject markers in all the languages under discussion here is that of bound clitics rather than nominal arguments (see also Rizzi 1986). Typologically, then, the northern Italian dialects are impeccably and consistently type B languages, just as is the standard language. There is no need to complicate the type A/type B distinction or the pro-drop parameter. With this triumphant conclusion, Brandi and Cordin are content to consider the matter closed.

However, from a diachronic perspective, these dialects seem to be counterexamples to the strong claim made in Haiman (1974). Bound clitics are not – at least not diachronically – generated *ex nihilo*. At some previous stage in the languages, they must have been 'full' pronouns, with argument status (see Meillet 1921; Meinhof 1936; Bally 1942; and Givón 1976, 1979; Vanelli 1984a, b, 1987). If their linear distribution at that time resembled their distribution now, then at some earlier time the northern Italian dialects *were* type A languages.

And presently, at least, these dialects exhibit standard Italian word order: crucially, there is no verb-second constraint except in Romansh and northern Ladin. Nevertheless, these dialects are not counterexamples to the hypothesis of Haiman (1974): or at least, no more than are modern French, German, or Danish. Back in the thirteenth century, word order in attested northern Italian dialects was similar to that of medieval French, and so was the appearance of superficial pronoun subjects: word order was V/2, and personal-pronoun subjects appeared only when their absence would have led to V-initial word order (Spiess 1956: 17). The correlation between word order and the appearance of the subject pronoun is still transparent in Genoese and Paduan, where *u* or *a* occurs typically at the beginning of sentences with VX order. It is somewhat less transparently recoverable in languages like non-standard French, Friulian, and Romagnol, which exhibit a 'one preverbal clitic constraint'. In some way, subject pronoun doubling was the outcome of V/2 ordering, just as the type A language phenomenon was the outcome of this ordering. What is not yet clear is how this change occurred, and what factors favoured it in northern Italy.

Granting the plausible syntactic change of grammaticalization

(76) pronoun # V > clitic + V

which has been defended and illustrated in many languages, there are various indications that this change originated in two favoured environments: left-dislocated topicalized constructions, and inverted word order.

The first construction, as exemplified by

(77) a. My old man, he rides with the Angels. (Givón 1976)
      b. The one-l lama, he's a priest.

is suggested by the vestigial constraints on clitic doubling which we have already noted in a number of northern Italian dialects. We will say no more about them here.

The second construction, as exemplified by

(78) Are you ready?

is not usually thought of as a seedbed for the reinterpretation of (76), and requires further justification.

Most significant is the fact that 2nd singular pronouns are further reduced than other atonic pronouns – a fact which follows from the overwhelming predominance of second-person subjects in interrogative sentences.

Ettmayer (1903: 50n.) provides evidence that the interrogative or inverted paradigm in many northern Italian dialects was restructured on the basis of the 2nd singular. In Verona, Vicenza, and Trento, 2nd singular interrogative *ʃe-tu* 'are you' was reinterpreted as

(79) ʃe- ____ - t(e)
    be 2sg. inter.

Proof of this reinterpretation is provided by the analogical extension of the -*t(e)* suffix to other persons and numbers as a sign of the interrogative:

(80) 1sg. ʃon-te 'am I'
    1pl. ʃen-te 'are we'

This restructuring demonstrates that in inverted word order, the 2nd singular pronoun is reduced to the point that it is not perceived as a pronoun at all.

Essentially the same phenomenon is attested in Germanic languages, among them English. The common -*t* enlargement in the 2nd singular verbal paradigm (ME *has-t, go-est*; modern German -*st*) is not inherited. It derives plausibly from a reinterpretation of the inverted form, where original *verb + 2sg. desinence ≠ 2sg. pronoun* is reinterpreted as *verb + (enlarged) 2sg. desinence*. The reduced morpheme *t(u)* still maintains a vestigial presence as a pronoun. This ghostly survival may help to account for '2 deletion' (Baur 1969: 30; Haiman 1971; Bayer 1984; Cooper and Engdahl 1989) in Germanic inversions like

(81) a. Hast ____ killed the Jabberwock?
    b. *Zurich German*
      Woane gaasch ____?
      whither go-2sg.
      'Where are you going?'

                                  (Baur 1969: 29)

which are totally productive in impeccably type A languages like German, and in the Rhaeto-Romance dialects of Switzerland (see table 4.1, below). But mainly, the reduced morpheme is now simply part of the agreement marker, and, as such, co-occurs with full pronominal 2nd singular subjects. Most probably, ME 2sg. -*est*, still vestigially attested in archaic forms like

(82) a. Thou watches-t
    b. Thou shal-t

and the like, exemplify the exact same subject doubling as the northern Italian dialects exhibit in the sentences of (70)–(74), and that here, too, the 2nd singular has led the way (and no other pronoun as yet has followed).

Finally, it is tempting to speculate that the French liaison /t/ of inverted word order, now limited to the 3rd singular, is not an etymologically motivated restoration of Lat. 3sg. *-t*, but a relic of the same reinterpretation process. Note in particular the non-standard example from Lambrecht (1981):

(83) *i* l a- ti pu attraper le gendarme le voleur?
he him has ? been-able to-catch the cop the thief

Whatever the original source of *-ti*, example (83) shows an extension of it. A 2nd singular source is at least as plausible as a hypercorrect 'restoration' of a final consonant which has been absent from the spoken language for several hundred years.

Reduction originates in the inverted word order, and we do not know why: nevertheless, the data allow us to state an implicational relationship like

(84) If a language has a special series of atonic subject pronouns in direct order, it also has them in inverted word order.

Many of the Italian Rhaeto-Romance dialects, as we have seen, are similar to other northern Italian dialects like Romagnol, Genoese, Paduan, and Trentino, in allowing clitic doubling. The Swiss dialects and some of the Ladin dialects, on the other hand, are typically described in the prescriptive grammars as standard type A languages like French: one subject pronoun and only one is necessary for every finite verb. (Like medieval French, the latter dialects are still subject to the verb-second constraint: see Nay 1965 for Surselvan, Thöni 1969 for Surmeiran, Scheitlin 1962 for Puter, and Arquint 1964 for Vallader Romansh; Benincà 1985 for Badiot, Gardenese, and Marebban).

However, with the exception of Surselvan, each of these latter dialects *does* allow clitic doubling, but *only* in inverted word order. The standard grammars state that atonic subject pronouns in these Rhaeto-Romance languages exist in complementary distribution with the tonic forms:

tonic pronoun ♯ V ∼ V + atonic pronoun

It was Linder (1987: 4–12) who showed that the relationship between the two is more interesting. Atonic subject pronouns do occur preverbally, and are here still in complementary distribution with the tonic forms and other lexical NPs like the relative pronoun. Postverbally, however, atonic pronouns may co-occur with full subject pronouns in Vallader, and also marginally in Puter, as in

(85) a. *Puter*
chantains -a (nus)
sing-1pl. we we

Table 4.1 Postverbal atonic subject pronouns

	Surmeiran	Puter	Vallader	Fassan	Paduan	Friulian
Singular						
1	a	i	a	–	i	o
2	–	–	–	te	to	tu
3m.	l	e	l	el	lo	al
f.	la	e	la	(a)la	la	A
n.	i	e	a			
Plural						
1	a	a	a	–	i	o
2	–	–	–	–	u	o
3m.	iʎ	e	a	i	li	a
f.				(a)les	le	–

    b. *Vallader*
       pigliain- a (no)
       take-1pl. we we

Here, reduction of form has plainly led to reduction of syntactic function: the erstwhile pronoun has lost its status, and functions only as a verbal ending. It is important to notice that this status reduction has occurred – at this point – only in inverted word order. Preverbally, the fact that atonic and tonic pronouns are mutually exclusive suggests that both are viewed as members of the same syntactic category.

In each of the dialects where cliticization of the subject pronouns is confined to inverted word order, the 2nd singular pronoun is typically zero in inverted word order. In the dialects where cliticization is general, the second-person pronouns are non-null. The correlation is brought out in table 4.1, where three 'inverted cliticization' languages are contrasted with 'generalized cliticization' languages like Fassan, Paduan, and Friulian. (The non-Rhaeto-Romance Paduan is included in order to emphasize that 'generalized cliticization' is an areal phenomenon that extends beyond RR.)

On the one hand, we have the Romansh dialects of Switzerland, together with Badiot, Marebban, and Gardenese, which are characterized by the following typological features:

(a) V/2 order;
(b) null second person pronouns in inverted word order;
(c) clitic doubling in inverted word order (Surselvan excepted).

On the other, we have the remaining Ladin dialects, and Friulian, which (like most of northern Italian dialects) are characterized by the following:

(a) toleration of V/1, V/3 orders;
(b) non-null second person pronouns in inverted word order;
(c) clitic doubling in both direct and inverted word order.

These are not the first structural or typological features which serve to split, rather than to define, a Rhaeto-Romance unity.

We have argued that there is a causal correlation between features (b) and (c): both arise when postverbal pronouns lose their status as independent noun phrases. Is there a causal connection between these two features and (a)? Clearly, there could be: the V/2 constraint requires independent noun phrases in preverbal position only.

Finally, what is the origin, within these dialects, of the V/2 constraint itself? There is evidence that it is very old. Spiess (1956) demonstrates the existence of V/2 in at least one northern Italian dialect, Lombard, since the thirteenth century. But here the authors must confess to some disagreement. Following Helty (1975), Haiman sees German influence on Romansh, Badiot, Marebban, and Gardenese, as long-lasting and decisive. (He also attributes the historically attested replacement of clitic pronouns by full tonic pronouns in Surselvan over the last two hundred years to German influence.) Benincà sees V/2 as an independent common northern Italian medieval pattern (see Benincà 1985).

4.5 AGREEMENT

In the syntax of most Romance languages, the following situation is the norm. Within a noun phrase, modifiers agree with their heads; within a sentence, predicative adjectives agree with their subjects, in both number and gender, and verbs agree with their subjects in person and number, irrespective of the relative order of subject and agreement-marking predicate; the perfect participles of transitive verbs agree only with (preceding) clitic object pronouns, in number and gender.

The above specifications describe the default agreement system in Romance and it is hardly worthwhile to exemplify this system in yet another series of dialects. The following discussion will therefore deal only with systematic and interesting exceptions to this in Rhaeto-Romance dialects. These exceptions are of several kinds:

(a) In Surselvan, which manifests traces of a three-gender system in its adjectival morphology, subject–predicate agreement often seems to fail. Although lexical subjects can only be masculine or feminine, predicate adjectives are sometimes *neuter*; and, although lexical subjects may be plural, predicate verbs are sometimes *singular*. Typically, but not always, agreement failure occurs where the subject follows the agree-ment-marking predicate. A major question is whether the Surselvan phenomena are any different, from a purely syntactic point of view, from similar behaviour attested throughout Romance and beyond. Our answer to this question will be 'no'.

(b) In most of the Ladin dialects, and in some Friulian, modifiers often fail to agree with their heads in number. Although the heads may be plural, modifiers are often *singular*. Typically, this failure of agreement occurs only when the heads are *feminine* plural. The question arises whether apparent agreement failure is a morpho-syntactic phenom-enon, or best described as a phonological fact. Our answer will be that it is syntactic for all varieties but Friulian, where it seems to be purely phonological.

(c) In Romansh and Ladin, perfect participles of transitive verbs often fail to agree with preceding relative-pronoun objects, and with preceding reflexive pronouns. The question is the syntactic status of these syntactically inert-seeming morphemes: are they nouns or something else? Our conclusion will be that relative-pronoun objects are comple-mentizers in all Rhaeto-Romance dialects but Friulian, where their status is ambiguous. Reflexive pronouns are noun phrases in Engadine Romansh and Friulian, but verbal prefixes without nominal status in Surselvan and Ladin.

In no case, irrespective of the analysis adopted, are we dealing with syntactic behaviour which is both common to, and peculiar to, all the Rhaeto-Romance dialects.

4.5.1 Surselvan predicate agreement

The survival of the -US/-UM distinction in Surselvan as a distinction between predicate and attributive adjectives appears full-fledged in our earliest continuous texts, and is unique within Romance. Masculine singular nouns occur with predicate adjectives in inherited-US, but with attributive adjectives in inherited -UM:

(86) a. il   hotel ei veni   -us   nazionalisa -us
        the hotel is become (m.sg.) nationalized (m.sg.)
        the hotel has been nationalized.'
     b. il   hotel nazionalisa -u
        the hotel nationalized (m.sg.)
        'the nationalized hotel'

In cases where final -UM caused umlaut of the preceding vowel, the attributive/predicate contrast is doubly marked:

(87) a. il   um   ei bun -s
      the man is good (m.sg.)
      'The man is good.'
  b. in bien- ____   um
     a   good (m.sg.) man

(In this case, the -US/-UM distinction is still maintained in Sutselvan also. Although final /-s/ and final /-m/ have both disappeared here, a fully phonologized contrast survives between vowels which were umlauted before following *-UM, and those which were not umlauted before following *-US. See chapter 2, p. 146.)

The -US/-UM distinction in Latin was not only one of case, but of gender: -US was masculine singular nominative, while -UM was masculine singular accusative, or neuter singular (nominative or accusative). Although there are no common nouns in Surselvan which are neuter, there are a handful of personal and demonstrative pronouns which are. There is thus a possible distinction among predicative adjectives between those which agree with common nouns like /um/ 'man' and those which agree with neuter pronouns like /iʎ/ ~ /ej/ 'it', or /kwej/ 'that':

(88) a. il   um   ei bun- s
      the man is good (m.sg.)
  b. quei ei bien- ____
      that is good (n.sg.)

Given the syntactic ambiguity of the -UM form, the question naturally arises whether adjectives which occur in this form are to be construed as *attributive* adjectives on possibly null heads, or as *neuter* forms. Either analysis is plausible in the case of possessive pronouns.

Possessive pronominal adjectives occur in both attributive and predicative forms:

(89) a. il   cavagl ei me- s
      the horse is my (m.sg.)
      'The horse is mine.'
  b. (il) mi- u   cavagl
      the my (m.sg.) horse
      'my horse'

Consequently, when a possessive pronominal adjective occurs in the -UM form, it can only be because it agrees with a neuter subject, as in (90):

(90) quei ei mi- u
      that is mine (n.sg.)

Possessive pronouns, however, occur in only the -UM form (for non-feminine singulars) or the -A form (for feminine singulars):

(91) la   mi- a
      the my   (f.sg.)
      'mine'
(92) il   mi -u
      the my ?
      'mine' (m.sg.)

The -UM form of (92) is identical with the masculine singular form of (89), and with the neuter singular form of (90). It is impossible to tell whether the form of (92) is due to the fact that all possessive pronouns are treated as possessive pronominal adjectives with null heads, or that all non-feminine possessive pronouns are treated as neuter. The more likely analysis is the former: possessive pronouns in Surselvan, as in other dialects, will be analysed as possessive pronominal adjectives with null heads.

A faint echo of the inherited -US/-UM contrast survives in Vallader masculine singular possessive pronominal adjectives, which retain the reflex of -US (e.g. /mes/ 'my') for the *attributive* form, and the reflex of -UM (e.g. /miw/ 'my') for the *predicative* form, and for the possessive pronoun (see chapter 2, p. 147). (The essential arbitrariness of the reinterpretation, accusative > attributive, in Surselvan ('explained' in chapter 2, p. 146) is highlighted by the coexisting accusative > predicate in Vallader. Both dialects agree, however, in treating possessive pronouns in the same way.)

In Surselvan, reflexes of -US occur only on predicative adjectives. This means that we can identify as predicative adjectives some forms whose status in English at least is unclear. For example, it is not certain whether appositional adjectives in English are 'really' attributive, predicative, or some other type of adjective:

(93) *Red* with embarrassment, George tried to look unconcerned.

In Surselvan, such adjectives are unambiguously predicative:

(94) a. igl um   schischeva, malsaun -s,   in letg.
        the man   lay,   *ill*,   (m.sg.) in bed
     b. el meina   persul -s   omisdus hotels
        he manages *alone* (m.sg.) both   hotels
        'He manages both hotels alone.'

Again, predicative adjectives continue to be treated as such even when their underlying subjects are subjects of infinitives:

(95) Il   Segner fa   attent -s   Job che S
      the Lord   makes   aware (m.sg.) Job that S
      'The Lord makes Job aware that . . .'

Failure of predicative adjective agreement may be of two kinds. In the first case, failure may simply highlight a universal fact. In the second, failure may be dialect-specific. An example of the first kind of failure is the behaviour of adjectives in the superlative degree. From English alone, we might be tempted to analyse each of the following underlined adjectives as predicatives:

(96) a. He is *good*.
      b. You are *better*.
      c. I am *the best*.

In fact, superlatives like the one in (96c) can function as noun phrases (as in 'save the best for last'), which suggests that they may be attributives with null heads. Surselvan data support this analysis, as witness the translations of (96):

(97) a. El ei bun-s. (predicative)
      b. Ti eis meglier-s (predicative)
      c. Jeu sun il meglier-____ (attributive)

The apparent failure of predicative /-s/ agreement in (97c) is actually no failure at all: superlative adjectives are actually attributive, with an understood head like 'one'.

(Ideally, it should be possible to confirm this analysis of superlatives by contrasting them with elatives, which in languages like Italian have the same morphological form as superlatives, but mean 'extremely . . . ' rather than 'the most . . . '. Unfortunately, elatives in Surselvan occur only as prenominal – that is, attributive – modifiers, whose form is distinct in any case from that of superlative adjectives: they occur, as do Italian elatives, with the derivational suffix *-isim*, e.g. /in bɛlisim di/ 'an extremely beautiful day'.)

The second class of agreement failure appears at least to be genuine: predicative adjectives fail to agree with masculine singular subjects, and appear in the *neuter singular*, rather than the masculine singular, form. A sub-category of these cases appears unproblematic: the predicative adjective agrees not with the (generally postverbal) 'true' subject, but with a preceding neuter dummy subject /iʎ/ ∼ /ej/, which can be variously translated by the English dummy subjects 'it' or 'there'. Note that in the same way, the predicate verb agrees in number with this dummy subject:

(98) a. igl ei sta- u   zacons   (existential sentence)
       it is been(n.sg.) several (m.pl.)
       'There have been several.'
       (Not: *igl ein (3pl.) sta-i (m.pl.) zacons)

   b. igl ei i   -u   sur il pas San Gliezi
      it is gone (n.sg.) on the pass St   Lucius
                                              (impersonal passive)
      'We all went over the St Lucius pass.'

   c. ei vegn pri -u   ina collecta
      it comes taken (n.sg.) a   collection
                                              (impersonal passive)
      'A collection was taken.'

   d. il   davos temps eis -i seforma -u   ina opposiziun
      the last time is it formed (n.sg.) an opposition
                                              (presentative)
      'Lately there has formed an opposition.'

   e. aschia eis -i aunc resussi -u   da fa   enzatgei
      thus   is it also succeeded (n.sg.) of to-do something
                                              (extraposed subject)
      'Thus, it was possible to do something.'

   f. Quest' jamna eis -i vegni -u   debatta -u
      this   week is it come (n.sg.) debated (n.sg.)
      durant uras ed uras sur d'in meglier
      for   hours and hours over of-a better
      schurmetg dil   luvrer.   (impersonal passive)
      protection of-the worker.
      'This week there was debate for hours and hours concerning
      better workers' protection.'

   g. Malgrad sedutas da notg eis -i buca pusseivel
      despite sessions of night is it not possible
      - ____ da metter tut   sut tetg
      (n.sg.) of to-put everything under roof
                                       (extraposed sentential subject)
      'In spite of night sessions, it was not possible to complete
      everything.'

Dummy pronouns occur in all the Rhaeto-Romance dialects: the only difference is that in these other dialects, they are masculine, rather than neuter, singular. Agreement is almost invariably with the dummy pronoun rather than the postposed subject, except that *verbs* still are able to agree in number with the 'true' rather than the dummy subject. An example of this from Old Surselvan is the passage from Wendenzen's (1701) *Life of Jesus*:

(99) a. pertgiei ei   vegni -en   a   vegnir   ils   gis . . . .
       because it (3sg.) come (3pl.) to   come   the days (3pl.)
       'For there will come the days . . .'

Examples like (99a) can be easily compared to English examples like (b) and (c):

   b. There *are* no problems with your proposal.
   c. There'*s* no problems with your proposal.

Although the existential verb should agree with the true subject 'problems' in number, (99c) is perfectly acceptable, indicating that agreement *can* be with the dummy pronoun 'there'.

We have seen that the original functional motivation for the dummy subject in Surselvan, as in other verb-second languages, may have been to keep the finite verb from occupying sentence-initial position. The clearest evidence in favour of this functional hypothesis is that the dummy pronoun is optional post-verbally (that is, in sentences with postposed or presentative subjects, whose initial position is taken by some adverbial constituent):

(100) a. Alla   radunonza ei vegni- u   in giuvnatsch
       to-the   meeting   is come (n.sg.) a   churl
       'To the meeting (there) came a churl.'
   b. En quei ei exponi- u   ils premis
       in   that is displayed (n.sg.) the prizes
       'In that (there) were displayed the prizes.'
   c. En emprem lingia ei vegni- u   examina-
       in first   line   is come (n.sg.) examined
       u   il   stat   technic   dils   vehichels.
       (n.sg.) the state technical (m.sg.) of-the vehicles
       'First examined was the technical condition of the vehicles.'
   d. Tier   nof persunas ei vegni- u   ordina-
       among nine persons is come (n.sg.) ordered
       u   ina controlla   dil   saun.
       (n.sg.) a   checkup (f.sg.) of-the health
       'For nine persons there was ordered a medical checkup.'
   e. plinavon   ei vegni- u   retratg- _____
       furthermore is come   (n.sg.) withdrawn (n.sg.)

> sil   plaz sjat permissiuns   da karar
> on-the spot seven permissions (f.pl.) of to-drive
> 'Furthermore, there were withdrawn on the spot seven
> driving licences.'
>
> f. Cheu vegn   baghia- u   ina casa
>   here comes built (n.sg.) a   house (f.sg.)
>   'Here a house is being built.'

$$\text{(from Stimm 1976: 48)}$$

If the agreement of the predicate verb and perfect participle in (100) is with a dummy subject /iʎ/, as it is in the examples of (98), then this dummy subject is optionally deleted when it occurs postverbally, but causes predicate agreement before it vanishes.

Alternatively, by a less abstract hypothesis, verbs and participles agree only with *preceding*, and never with following subjects. The default, or unmarked, form of the verb is 3rd singular, and of the predicative adjective, neuter singular. (In the other Rhaeto-Romance and Italian dialects which have sentences analogous to (100), the default form of the adjective is masculine singular.) According to the second, less abstract, hypothesis, word order alone, and not the presence of a dummy subject, determines the form of the agreement-marking predicates, whether these are verbal or adjectival.

In favour of the minimalist hypothesis are sentences which differ minimally from those of (100):

(101) a. Alla   radunonza ei *in giuvnatsch* vegni- us.
         to-the meeting   is a churl   come (m.sg.)
         'To the meeting, a churl came.'

   b. L'jamna vargada ei *il   Cussagl   dils stans*
      the-week past   is the regional council
      s-occupa- us   cun il   niev concept da traffic.
      occupied (m.sg.) with the new concept of traffic
      'Last week, the Council was occupied with the new traffic proposal.'

   c. Cheu vegn   *la   casa   dil Desax* baghia- da.
      here comes the house of Desax built (f.sg.)
      'Here the Desax house is being built.'

$$\text{(Stimm 1976)}$$

   d. Aschia ei *igl alzament dil   tscheins d'aua*
      thus   is the raising   of-the tax   of-water
      buca vegni- us   sut las rodas.
      not come (m.sg.) under the wheels
      'Thus the (question of) raising the water tax was not discussed.'

In these sentences, it seems that word order is the crucial feature which distinguishes them from the corresponding sentences of (100): while in (100), the postposed subject follows the predicative adjective, in (101) the subject precedes the predicative adjective, and agreement therefore occurs.

The minimalist hypothesis is in fact the one proposed by Meyer-Lübke, Rohlfs, and Linder to account for similar facts in Romance and Greek, standard Italian, and Rhaeto-Romance in particular (Meyer-Luebke 1899: sect. 344; Rohlfs 1949: II, 448; Linder 1982: 161). Thus, in literary Italian (which coincides with regional spoken varieties, but not with the written standard of today:

(102) a. Venne   alquanti soldati   (Cellini)
       came (3sg.)   some   soldiers (3pl.)
       'There came some soldiers.'

    b. Manca   osterie   in Milano?   (Manzoni)
       is-lacking   hostels (pl.) in Milan
       'Are hostels lacking in Milan?'

Moreover, the same pattern of word-order dictated agreement seems to arise in other Rhaeto-Romance dialects. In Puter:

(103) a. In mincha cas   nun es gnieu-____   invulo-____
       in every   case not is   come (m.sg.) stolen (m.sg.)
       üngüns raps.
       any   raps.
       'In any case, no money was stolen.'

    b. Hoz   gniva   fümanto   our muntanellas.
       today was (sg.) smoked (m.sg.) out marmots (f.pl.)
       'Today, marmots were smoked out.'

In Badiot, agreement is with the preceding pronoun – which may itself agree or fail to agree in number and gender with the postposed true subject of the sentence:

(104) a. [da doman veɲ- l   oʃore- ____   les vatces]
       of morning comes he (m.sg.) milked (m.sg.) the cows (f.pl.)
       'In the morning, the cows are milked.'

    b. in sabeda   e- l gnü   inauguré   ____   na
       on Saturday is it come (m.sg.) inaugurated (m.sg) an
       mostra   de operes
       exhibition (f.sg.) of works
       'On Saturday, there was inaugurated an exhibition of works.' (no leftwards agreement)

(105) a. [da doman e   les sta- des   oʃora- des
        of   morning are they been (f.pl.) milked (f.pl.)
        les   vaces]
        the   cows
        'In the morning, the cows were milked.'

    b. da   süa man é inc'e nasciü- des   pitöres
       from his hand is also born (f.pl.) pictures (f.pl.)
       pur   scenars
       purely scenic
       'From his hand there also issued purely representational
       pictures.' (leftwards agreement occurs)

So, too, leftwards agreement seems to be an option in Gardena:

(106) a. y   sce l- e ven fat- es   trei plazes
        and thus it is come made (f.pl.) three beaches
        'And so, there were made three beaches.'

    b. Tl 1987 ie uni- da cumplete-da   la   Brockhaus
       in 1987 is come (f.s) completed (f.s.) the Brockhaus
       Enzyklopädie
       Encyclopedia (f.sg.)
       'In 1987 was completed the Brockhaus Encyclopedia.'
       (leftwards agreement occurs)

(107) a. l ie uni - ____ teni - ____ na funzion   te dlieja
        it is come (m.sg.) held (m.sg.) a function (f.sg.) in church
        'There was held a function in the church.'

    b. da   chësta union ne ie l nasciu- ____ degun
       from this   union not is it born (m.sg.) no
       mutons
       children (m.pl.)
       'From this union, no children were born.' (no leftwards
       agreement occurs)

In Fassa, agreement is with the preceding pronoun, which apparently
always is masculine singular, irrespective of the number and gender of
the true postposed subject:

(108) a. /l e veɲu- ____ la   vivanɔ/
        he is come (m.sg.) the fairy (f.sg.)
        'The fairy came.'

    b. /po l e veɲu- ____ na pitʃola/
       then he is come (m.sg.) one little-one (f.sg.)
       'Then there came a little girl.'

Nevertheless, there is evidence that the minimal hypothesis (leftwards agreement is optional, rightwards agreement is obligatory) cannot be maintained in its simplest form. In Surselvan, in the Engadine dialects, and in regional or literary Italian, subject noun phrases which have been (vacuously) fronted by left-dislocation fail to induce agreement:

(109) *Surselvan*
    a. caschiel   vegn   magliau- _____ bia
       cheese (m.sg.) comes eaten   (n.sg.) much
       'Cheese, much is eaten of.'
    b. damondas era (ei) vegni- u   fatg   neginas
       questions was it come (n.sg.) made (n.sg.) none (f.pl.)
       'Questions there were none.'

(Stimm 1976: 45)

(110) *Puter*
    a. plövgias   es- a gnü- _____   bleras
       rains (f.pl.) is it come (m.sg.) many (f.pl.)
       'Rains there were many.'
    b. /catʃaders na   mankeva   kweSt ɔn/
       hunters   not lacked (3sg.) this   year
       'Hunters there were plenty of this year.'

(Linder 1982: 160)

(111) *Italian*
    a. Ascoltatori non ne   mancava
       listeners   not of-them lacked (3sg.)
       'Listeners were not lacking.'
    b. soldati non ne   verrà   certamente
       soldiers not of-them will-have (3sg.) certainly
       'Soldiers there certainly will not be.'

(Rohlfs 1949: II, 448; 1969: 20)

In (109)–(111), the thematized subject precedes the agreement-marking predicate word – in fact standing at the head of the sentence in which it occurs – but fails to induce agreement. Moreover, in at least (109) and (110), agreement is apparently with a dummy subject which is present.

Further arguing against the minimal word-order hypothesis (at least in its most general form) is the fact that in the sentences of (101) (which originally suggested the hypothesis), the subject does indeed precede the predicative adjective which agrees with it in number and gender. But it *follows* the verb, which nevertheless agrees with it in person and number. Note the impossibility, in Surselvan, of sentences like (112):

(112) *Alla radunonza *ei*   dus giuvnatschs vegni
       to-the meeting   is (3sg.) two churls   come (m.pl.)

By the order-determines-agreement hypothesis, the copula should fail to agree with the subject, while the perfect participle should agree. So, there are cases where agreement should occur but does not, and cases where agreement should not occur, and yet it does.

Sentence (112) constitutes evidence of a more abstract analysis: whether or not a predicate element agrees with the subject is determined in deep structure by the position of the subject before subject–verb inversion and topicalization apply. Some revision of this sort is necessary in order to account not only for (112) but for the simplest cases of sentences where either of these two word-order-changing transformations apply. In general, agreement is not affected by subject–verb inversion in questions, or by topicalization, as examples like the following make clear:

(113) a. Vegn- an   els?
         come (3pl.) they (m.pl.)
         'Are they coming?'
      b. Bial- as   sun   las flurs   da sta
         beautiful (f.pl.) are (3pl.) the flowers (f.pl.) of summer

Another possible analysis of problematic sentences like (100) is that word order is in this case irrelevant: what we think of as 'postposed subjects' in existential or presentative sentences are not subjects at all, or perhaps, not quite subjects. In fact, these sentences have no subjects, and their morphological predicates occur in the default 3rd singular neuter inflection, irrespective of where the presentative 'subjects' occur. (The fact that leftwards agreement is possible in a number of the Ladin dialects may be a reflection of the indeterminate status of such presentative logical subjects which are teetering on the verge of acquiring true grammatical subjecthood.)

Comparative and typological evidence exists which supports this view. In general, subject status is reserved for noun phrases which package old or given information. In some languages, like Surselvan for example, *indefinite* noun phrases in general fail to qualify for subject status. In other languages, like non-standard French, constraints on permissible subjecthood may be even stricter: Lambrecht (1981) argues that *lexical* noun phrases of any type fail to qualify, and that sentences which are common in English, and prescribed by normative grammars in French, like 'John left', simply do not occur.

Most spectacular in their subjectlessness are sentences which seem to be topicalized inversions of structures like NP_1 *be* NP_2, such as (114):

(114) Casey was the last one up.

The distribution of Surselvan predicative *-s* suggests that inversions of (114), such as (115),

(115) The last one up was Casey.

are subjectless: NP$_2$ 'the last one up', although the sentence topic, is a predicate complement, and as such clearly cannot occasion subject–verb agreement. On the other hand NP$_1$ 'Casey', is a postposed expression exactly like the postposed non-subjects of (100), and thus also cannot cause agreement. Surselvan thus offers wild-looking sentences like (116):

(116) a. Quella   che a   dau   ora quei cudisch ei
          the-one (f.sg.) who has given out that book   is
          sta- u   Dr Helena de Lerber.
          been (n.sg.) Dr H.L. (f.sg.)
          'The one who published that book was Dr. Helena de Lerber.'
       b. il   quart (m.sg.) ei sta- u   Giachen Martin
          the fourth   is been (n.sg.) G.   M.
          'Fourth was Giachen Martin.'

These examples are drawn from Stimm (1976: 52), where many others of the same type are given.

In all of the sentences we have discussed so far with unexpected neuter singular predicate agreement, a dummy neuter subject pronoun was always possible. This encouraged the speculation that 3rd singular neuter inflection in morphological predicates was not a default or unmarked value for person, number, and gender, but the result of actual agreement. However, in the last class of cases we discuss, no dummy pronoun is ever possible. If the predicate occurs in 3rd singular neuter form, it is not by agreeing with /iʎ/ in the following examples (from Stimm 1976: 43):

(117) a. caschiel (m.sg.) ei bien (n.sg.)
          'Cheese is good.'
       b. aua frestga (f.sg.) ei bien (n.sg.) avunda
          'Fresh water is good enough.'
       c. mo extrems (m.pl.) ei (3sg.) buca sanadeivel (n.sg.)
          'Only extremes is not healthy.'
       d. cigarettas (f.pl.) ei (3sg.) nuscheivel (n.sg.)
          'Cigarettes is harmful.'

Stimm argued that what distinguished the subjects of (117) was that they occurred without articles and (citing Kühner-Gerth on Classical Greek) that such generic noun phrases, in which 'the subject is viewed not as a definite object, but as a general concept' fail to occasion agreement. We suspect that the apparent noun phrase subjects of (117) fail to occasion agreement for the same reason that 'the three little pigs' or 'bacon and eggs' fail to cause agreement in the English sentences

(118) a. 'The three little pigs' is (*are) Nina's favourite fairy tale.
   b. Bacon and eggs sounds (*sound) good.
   c. Too many carrots is (*are) too many carrots, even if you're Bugs Bunny.

They fail to cause agreement because they are *titles*: of stories, possible meals, or scenarios in general. The scenarios they name are single things, and it is with those single things that the predicate agrees.

In their treatment of titles, languages may disagree. Stimm notes that the construction, while common to Surselvan and Classical Greek, is extremely rare in Latin. It seems to be rare also in languages like German and Russian, where story titles which happen to be plural noun phrases almost always occasion plural number agreement. English may be somewhere in the middle of this typological continuum: in spite of structures like (118), English tolerates proverbs like (119),

(119) Too many cooks (pl.) *spoil* (pl.) the broth.

where a thoroughgoing Surselvan approach would insist on

(120) 'Too many cooks' *spoils* the broth.

From a typological perspective, then, the failure of number and gender agreement in Surselvan finds congeners in many other languages which are far more distantly related to it than Ladin or Friulian.

What is unique to the dialect is simply the morphological fact that the -US/-UM distinction marks not only gender, but a contrast between predicate and attributive adjectives. How this transformation of an inherited category could have come about is a fascinating question. Unfortunately, the textual attestation we have shows us no development. Instead, the state of affairs described above seems to have been completely stable since ca 1600. Masculine singular subjects took predicate -*s* adjectives; neuter pronouns like {ei} took predicate neuter singular predicative adjectives:

(121) a. Bab eis ei (n.sg.) bucca pusseiuel (n.sg.) ca quei calisch vomig navent da mei?
   'Father is it not possible that this cup go away from me?'
                                                          (Alig *Epistolas* 1674)
   b. Per quei ch ei (n.sg.) vegnig cunplaneu (n.sg.) quei plaid
      for that that it   come   fulfilled   that word

'So that this prophecy may be fulfilled.'

(ibid.)

and subjectless sentences or sentences with postposed presentational 'subjects' occurred with predicates in the default 3rd singular and neuter form:

(122) enten ina da quellas era 4 Pelagrins
'In one of these (ships) was 4 pilgrims.'

(*Cudisch dilg viadi*, ca 1600)

4.5.2 Modifier-head agreement in Ladin

In the unmarked or default Romance case, articles, quantifiers, and adjectives agree in number and gender with the head noun in a noun phrase. This was the situation inherited from Latin, at least. There are a number of northern Italian dialects, however, in which *plurality* is marked only once within noun phrases *whose heads are feminine plural*. This situation seems to be characteristic of almost all Ladin dialects, with the exception of Badiot. (Friulian seems to have this feature also, but, as we shall argue, does not.) Nevertheless, it is not an exclusively Ladin feature. (Rohlfs 1949: II, 47 indicates Bagnone, Villafranca, Isolaccia, Livigno, Val Colla, Mesolcina, and Bergell outside the Ladin area of Rhaeto-Romance with this same feature of 'lazy agreement'.)

In Fassa, Elwert claimed that only the last word within the noun phrase marks number (Elwert 1943: 113), whether this word is the head noun, as in (123) and (125), or the adjective, as in (124):

(123) la (f.sg.) bɛla (f.sg.) fɔmɛnes (f.pl.)
'the beautiful women'
(124) la (f.sg.) spala (f.sg.) lɛrʝes (f.pl.)
'wide shoulders'
(125) la (f.sg.) setemɛnes (f.pl.)
'the weeks'

(Possibly related is the fact that in a cluster of perfect participles, only the last need be marked for number and gender:

(126) e   stat (m.sg.) deʃed-eda (f.sg.) fin   meza net
am   stayed   awake   until midnight
'I have stayed awake until midnight.'

(Elwert 1943: 152).)

In modern Fassa, as in modern Gardena and Ampezzan, we have found another pattern of lazy agreement:

The Ladin lazy agreement rule

In noun phrases with feminine plural heads, the head noun always marks plurality. Prenominal modifiers consistently fail to mark plurality, but postnominal modifiers always do.

For example, we have failed to encounter examples like (124) above (in which plurality is marked on the last word in the noun phrase, but not necessarily the head noun), while meeting with examples like:

(127) a. l   autra   valedes   ladines
         the (f.sg.) other (f.sg.) valleys (f.pl.) ladins (f.pl.)
         'the other Ladin valleys'
      b. la   monz   autes   de Fasha
         the (f.sg.) mountains (f.pl.) high (f.pl.) of Fassa
         'the high mountains of Fassa'

In Gardena, we encounter exactly the same pattern (the first three examples, from Gartner 1879, are reproduced in his phonetic transcription: the last three, from written sources, reproduce the conventional orthography):

(128) a. [noʃta/ (f.sg.) /ɹalinəs] (f.pl.)
         'our chickens'
      b. [la/ (f.sg.) /ɹaməs/ (f.pl.) /kuətʃnəs] (f.pl.)
         'The red legs'
      c. [dutta/ (f.sg.) /la/ (f.sg.) /kreaturəs] (f.pl.)
         'all the animals'
      d. de bela   ëures   liegres
         of beautiful (f.sg.) hours (f.pl.) joyful (f.pl.)
         'beautiful joyful hours'
      e. duta   la   paroles   feminines
         all (f.sg.) the (f.sg.) words (f.pl.) feminine (f.pl.)
         'all the feminine words'
      f. nosta   bela   montes   ladines
         our (f.sg.) beautiful (f.sg.) mountains (f.pl.) ladin (f.pl.)
         'our beautiful ladin mountains'

Appollonio claimed that in Ampezzan, as in Fassa, only the last member of a feminine noun phrase is marked for number (Appollonio 1930: 27):

(129) a. ra (f.sg.) bela (f.sg.) toses (f.pl.)
         'the beautiful girls'
      b. ra (f.sg.) tosa (f.sg.) beles (f.pl.)
         'the beautiful girls'

Again, we have failed to encounter forms like (129b): the head noun is always marked for plurality. On the other hand, postnominal modifiers never fail to agree with the preceding head noun in number as in (130):

(130) a. ra   vales   ladines
        the (f.sg.) valleys (f.pl.) ladins (f.pl.)
    b. outra   robes   interessantes
        other (f.sg.) things (f.pl.) interesting (f.pl.)
        'other interesting things'

Note that as an incidental consequence of the lazy agreement rule of Ladin the definite article in Fassa, Gardena, and Ampezzan *can never* occur in the feminine plural form. Indeed, Gartner (1879: 88) notes as a feature of the morphology of Gardena that the feminine singular and the feminine plural article are the same, namely /la/. On the other hand, in Ampezzan, not only the definite article, but also the demonstrative adjectives, and all possessive pronominal adjectives except in the 1st plural and 2nd plural occur in only one feminine form: the singular.

There are two closely related reasons, it seems to us, that this syncretism of number should be treated as a syntactic, rather than a purely morpho-phonological fact. The first is that *adjectives* in the noun phrase in Gardena, Fassa and Ampezzan mark plurality depending on their position in the noun phrase: this alternation implies that there is a productive rule in these dialects for marking, or failing to mark plurality. Given that articles in the Ladin noun phrase are obligatorily followed by other elements, their failure to mark plurality is automatically predicted by this already productive rule.

The second reason is that there is a class of determiners in Ampezzan which can occur alone. This is the class of possessive pronominal adjectives, which, when followed by a head noun, is totally invariable, and fails to mark either number or gender. However, the possessive pronominal adjective may also occur alone, both as a predicative adjective, and as a possessive pronoun. When it does, it is fully marked for number and gender:

(131) a. mɛ ɟato   'my cat' (m.sg.)   *but*
     b. el mɛ   'mine'
(132) a. mɛ parola 'my word' (f.sg.) *but*
     b. ra mɛa   'mine'
(133) a. mɛ ɟatɛ   'my cats' (m.pl.) *but*
     b. i miei   'mine'
(134) a. mɛ parole 'my words' (f.pl.) *but*
     b. ra mees   'mine'

(see Appollonio 1930: 48). It seems, then, that the productive rule of plural marking applies to determiners as well as to other prenominal modifiers. It is only because Ladin (like English, but unlike Romansh) happens not to permit articles to appear as the surface structure heads or final elements of noun phrases, that they consistently fail to mark plurality.

Finally, we note that in Friulian what seems to be 'lazy agreement' is a process of a different kind. Again, it involves the feminine plural, but it seems to be phonologically determined. In some Friulian dialects, only the last word of the noun phrase has a full *-is* (f.pl.) ending. The other elements of the noun phrase occur not in the feminine singular (with the suffix *-A*), but with the distinctive suffix *-i*, which is identical with the feminine plural, minus the final /s/. Corresponding to the singular expressions in (135):

(135) a. la bjele femine
      b. la femine bjele
         'the beautiful woman'

possible plurals are

(136) a. li bjeli feminis
      b. li femini bjelis

but never

(137) c. *la bjele feminis
      d. *la femine bjelis

It seems that phonological reduction alone is responsible for what looks like a 'weak declension' of the plural in Friulian: a set of desinences which are distinct from both the singular and plural full forms.

4.5.3 Verb–object agreement

4.5.3.1 Relative pronouns as objects

In the 'standard' agreement model represented by French and Italian, perfect participles do not agree with following lexical noun phrases:

(138) a. J' ai   commis (m.sg.) une faute (f.sg.)
         I have committed   a   mistake
      b. Ho   fatto (m.sg.) molti sbagli (m.pl.)
         I-have made   many   mistakes

In French, they do agree with both preceding pronominal object pronoun clitics and with relative pronouns in number and gender. On the basis of this criterion, the relative pronoun *que* could be said to function as a noun phrase in French:

(139) a. les fautes (f.pl.) *que* nous avons commis-es (f.pl.)
       'the mistakes that we have made'
    b. nous les (f.pl.) avons fait-es (f.pl.)
       'we have made them'

Italian tolerates only agreement with preceding object clitics, as in (139b):

(140) a. li   ho   fatti
       them (m.pl.) I-have made (m.pl.)

The equivalent of (139a) is not completely ungrammatical, at least for some speakers, but has the same status as agreement with any other (following) full noun phrase, as shown in the following specimens:

    b. gli errori   che   ho   fatto (??fatti)
       the errors (m.pl.) that I-have made (m.sg.)
    c. ho   fatto   (?? fatti) molti errori
       I-have made (m.sg.)   many errors (m.pl.)

In general, the Rhaeto-Romance languages manifest asymmetry in the status they accord the relative pronoun: the appropriate agreement targets agree with the relative pronoun when it functions as a subject, but they do not agree with it when it functions as an object. This asymmetry is independent of whether the languages in question are heavily committed to object agreeement or not.

Friulian seems to be more committed to verb–object agreement than the other Rhaeto-Romance languages. Verb–object agreement is completely optional in a number of cases which in French and standard Italian are distinguished.

In the first case, past participles of transitive verbs can agree even with following lexical object noun phrases:

(141) a. /kwalkidun al a   *kopa- s*   i   servidors/
      someone   he has killed (m.pl.) the servants (m.pl.)
      'Someone has killed the servants.'
      (Also possible: *kopá* (m.sg.))
    b. /vevin *mitud- is*   ju   lis bisacis/
      had   put   (m.pl.) down the knapsacks (m.pl.)
      'They had put down their knapsacks.'
      (Also possible: mituːt (m.sg.))

    c. /al a *lasa- de* la sostanse/
      he has left (f.sg.) the property (f.sg.)
      (Also possible: lasaːt (m.sg.))

On the other hand, as in the following examples, the past participle does not generally agree with even the preceding relative pronoun:

(142) a. /i sbaʎos   k i aj *fat*/
        the mistakes (m.pl.) that I have made (m.sg.)
        'the mistakes I have made'
        (Also possible: *fats* (m.pl.))
     b. /la frute   k i aj *koɲusuːt* jer/
        the girl (f.sg.) that I have met (m.sg.) yesterday
        'the girl I met yesterday'
        (Also possible: *konjusude* (f.sg.))
     c. /lis pwartis   k o vin *batuːt*/
        the doors (f.pl.) that we have hit (m.sg.)
        'the doors we have knocked on'
        (Also possible: *batudis* (f.pl.))
     d. /la kurtise   k al veve *pjarduːt*/
        the knife (f.sg.) that he had lost (m.sg.)
        (Also possible: *pjardude* (f.sg.))

But agreement is obligatory between an adjective and the relative pronoun:

(143) une robe   k o riten   impwartant-e
      a thing (f.sg.) that I consider important (f.sg.)
      'something that I consider important'

Other Rhaeto-Romance languages seem alike in never allowing perfect participles to mark number and gender agreement with a preceding object relative pronoun. Thus:

    Puter
(144) la chanzun (f.sg.) ch' avais chanto (m.sg.)
      'the song that you all have sung'

                                         (Scheitlin 1980: 119)

    Vallader
(145) las schoccas (f.pl.) cha no vain surgni (m.sg.)
      the coats   that we have received
      'the coats we have received'
    Fassan
(146) /ki doj (m.pl.) ke e kompra (m.sg.)/ (Elwert 1943)
      these two   that have bought
      'these two that I have bought'

Ampezzan

(147) ra   parola (f.sg.) che te   m' as   dito (m.sg.)
      the word   that you me have said
      'the words you said to me'

(Appollonio 27)

Gardenese

(148) la   burta cosses   che la   ustoria de nosc
      the   ugly   things (f.pl.) that the history of our
      secul a   purta- ____ a   nosta Tiëra
      century has brought (m.sg.) to our   country
      'the ugly things history has brought upon our country'

However, when the relative pronoun replaces the subject noun phrase, it regularly causes the normal agreement targets to agree with it, as the following examples will illustrate:

Gardenese

(149) la   strutures   che ie uni-   des   frabiche- des
      the structures   that is come (f.pl.) built   (f.pl.)
      'the structures that have been built'

Badiot

(150) chësta mostra   che é resta-   da
      this   exhibition (f.sg.) that is remained (f.sg.)
      davert- a
      open   (f. sg.)
      'this exhibition, which has remained open'

Fassan

(151) zirca 500 familie   che é doenta- de   soz-
      about 500 families that are become (f.pl.) associates
      e   de la   Sociazion
      (f.pl.) of the Society
      'approximately 500 families that have become members of the society'

It seems almost as if the relative pronoun – in so far as agreement provides a diagnostic – is schizophrenic in Rhaeto-Romance. Let us say that the ability to transmit features of number and gender to a following verb, adjective, or participle defines a noun phrase. Then, we can say:

When occupying subject position, the relative pronoun functions as an ordinary noun phrase. When occupying object position, it functions as an extra-sentential complementizer or some other inert constituent.

This schizophrenic analysis is compatible with the fact that relative pronouns in many northern Italian dialects (not to mention French) seem to 'mark nominative and accusative case' – typologically an aberration in languages which have basically given up marking case productively. The so-called nominative case is actually a relative pronoun, while the so-called accusative is actually a complementizer. The analysis is also compatible with the fact we have already noted in Friulian that the 'same relative pronoun' may co-occur with subject marking clitics, but is mutually exclusive with object pronoun clitics (see Haiman 1990).

4.5.3.2 Reflexive pronouns as objects

In the following discussion, we will be examining two properties of reflexive pronouns: their ability to transmit features of gender and number to following perfect participles, and their mobility.

(a) Feature transmission

Where the perfect auxiliary is 'be' the perfect participle agrees with the subject irrespective of the presence of a reflexive morpheme. Therefore, the criterion of feature transmission is significant only in cases where the perfect auxiliary is 'have'.

In both Friulian and Surselvan, the reflexive verbs can choose either 'have' or 'be' as auxiliary, and the past participle agrees in gender and number with the (lexical or intended) subject when the auxiliary is 'be', while there is no agreement when the auxiliary is 'have':

> *Friulian*
> (152) a. /e   se   a   kopaːt/
>   she self has killed (m.sg.)
>   'She killed herself.'
>   b. /e   se   je kopade/
>   she self is killed (f.sg.)
>   'She killed herself.'
> (153) a. jeu hai se- smarvigliau- _____
>   I   have self marvelled (no agreement)
>   'I was surprised.'
>   b. jeu sun se- smarvigliau- s
>   I   am   self marvelled   (m.sg.)
>   'I was surprised.'

This used to be the pattern in Tuscan and Italian until the eighteenth to nineteenth century, and is still fairly common (with different preferences depending on the person of the verb) in northern Italian dialects and in parts of Ladin.

In Surmeiran, the only possible auxiliary is 'have'. As in Surselvan and Friulian, there is no agreement of the perfect participle in this case (Thöni 1969: 52).

A striking difference between the Engadine dialects (which, like Surmeiran, employ only the transitive verb 'have' as the reflexive auxiliary) and all other Rhaeto-Romance dialects, is that in Engadine, the reflexive does trigger agreement of the following perfect participle:

> *Puter*
> (154) /ils mats s   ɛm   lavo-   s/
>   the boys self have washed (m.pl.)
>   'The boys have washed.'

This syntactic feature connects the Engadine dialects with varieties of Trentino. In these dialects, the reflexive pronoun behaves like an object clitic pronoun. In most of Rhaeto-Romance, it is inert with respect to agreement.

To conclude: if the ability to transmit features is a criterion for NP-hood, the reflexive pronoun is NP-like in the Engadine dialects only.

(b) Mobility

In all the Rhaeto-Romance dialects with the exception of Surselvan and Surmeiran, the reflexive pronoun is clearly a member of the set of object pronoun clitics, at least as far as the criterion of mobility is concerned. In Surselvan, the reflexive pronoun has been entirely reduced to affix status. Nothing, not even a perfect auxiliary, may separate the invariable prefix *se* from the verb. In Surmeiran, the reflexive pronoun may either precede or follow the perfect auxiliary, as in (155):

> (155) a. ia *ma*   *va*   tratg   aint
>   I   myself have   dressed in
>   b. ia *va*   *ma*   tratg   aint
>   I   have   myself dressed in
>   'I have dressed.'

The first pattern is characteristic of most Rhaeto-Romance, while the second is Surselvan. While Surmeiran allows both, it seems to prefer the Surselvan pattern (Thöni 1969: 52).

One other way in which both Surmeiran and the Engadine dialects approach the Surselvan pattern is in the relative immobility of the reflexive object marking pronoun in the imperative mood. In most

Rhaeto-Romance dialects, object pronouns in general either precede or follow the verb, depending on its mood: typically, they precede the verb except in the imperative (see Elwert 1943: 139, for Fassan; Appollonio 1930: 45, for Ampezzan; Scheitlin 1962: 86 for Puter).

In Surmeiran and Vallader, the object pronoun clitics follow this pattern, but the reflexive pronoun does not: irrespective of verbal mood it tends to *precede* the verb except in the case of the 2nd singular reflexive. Thus

> *Surmeiran*
>
> (156) a. dagn-   igls
>   give (1pl.)   them
>   'let's give them'

but

> b. ans   tiragn   aint
>   ourselves   dress (1pl.) in
>   'let's get dressed'
>
> *Vallader*
>
> (157) a. scriva'-   m
>   write (2pl.) me
>   'write me, you all!'

but

> b. ans   cuffortain
>   ourselves   comfort (1pl.)
>   'let's take heart'

Only the 2nd singular reflexive pronoun retains the mobility to respond to different moods of the verb by assuming different positions:

> *Surmeiran*
>
> (158) teira- t   aint
>   dress   yourself   in
>   'Get dressed!'
>
> *Vallader*
>
> (159) cufforta- t
>   comfort   yourself
>   'Take heart!'

If relative mobility and separability constitute criteria for NP-hood, reflexive pronouns are least NP-like in Surselvan, and most NP-like in Puter and the Italian dialects, with Vallader and Surmeiran lying somewhere in between.

Appendix: some irregular verbs

The forms of irregular verbs are learned individually. They are highly conservative, and resist analogical levelling. Some idea of the range of phonological and morphological variation within Rhaeto-Romance may be given by considering the paradigms of a handful of these irregular verbs. With the exception of 'must', all items are shared throughout Rhaeto-Romance. All of them are also shared far beyond, within the Romance family.

Sources for Swiss Romansh in general include: Decurtins (1958), a general survey; for Surselvan, Nay (1965), Tekavčić (1974); for Surmeiran, Thöni (1969); for Puter, Scheitlin (1962), Ganzoni (1977); for Vallader, Arquint (1964), Ganzoni (1983); for Ladin varieties, Kramer (1976); for Fassa, Elwert (1943); for Badiot, Pizzinini and Plangg (1966), and Alton and Vittur (1968); for Gardena, Gartner (1879); for Moena, Heilmann (1955); for Ampezzan, Appollonio (1930); for Friulian, Marchetti (1952), Francescato (1966), Rizzolatti (1981), Frau (1984).

The alternation symbol '∼' is reserved for paradigmatic alternation within the same dialect. When two or more forms are listed without such a tilde, they represent forms from different (sub) dialects.

The grammatical categories listed are infinitive, present indicative, imperative, gerund, perfect participle, subjunctive present, imperfect indicative, imperfect subjunctive, and past. For most dialects and most verbs, full paradigms are required only in the present indicative.

Note that in dialects where the subjunctive is a primary desinence, a number of verbs have alternate stem forms depending on whether they are stressed. The stressed stem form is given first.

In Badiot Ladin, the subjunctive differs from the present indicative only when the stem is stressed: that is, in the singular, and the 3rd plural.

Full paradigms are given only in the imperative and present indicative. In most of the other tenses and moods, either the stem is constant (as in the imperfect indicative or subjunctive), or occurs in only two forms depending on mobile stress (as in the present subjunctive). Such constant or regularly predictable stems are followed by a dash.

In Friulian, the past definite is given only in the 1st singular form. The other forms are however predictable, given the pattern on page 89. The 2nd plural indicative form is given as -*éjs*, the 2nd plural imperative as -éjt, but the /é/ has different outcomes in the various dialects (*é:* ~ *iə* ~ *éj*). The stressed vowel of Friulian infinitives is generally shortened – in the varieties where -r is dropped in this precise morphological context – by a rule which shortens all word-final long vowels.

Table A.1 'be'

	Surselvan	Surmeiran	Puter	Vallader	Fassa	Gardena	Badiot	Friulian
Inf.	ɛsər	ɛsər	ɛsər	ɛsər	eser	veʃter	eʃter	jɛsi sɛj
Pres.	sun ejs ej ɛsɛn sɛs ejn	suŋ iʃt ɜ iʃɛn iʃɛs ɛn	sun ɛʃt ɛs ɛsɛns ɛsɛs sun	sun ɛʃt ajs ɛʃɛn ɛʃɛt sun	soŋ es e sjoŋ sjede e	soŋ ies ie soŋ sɛjs ie	suŋ es e suŋ se(j)s e	soj sɛːs soːs e siŋ sɛjs soŋ
Imp.	sɛjɛs sɛjɛs	sɛjɛs sɛjɛs	sajɛʃt sajɛs	sajɛʃt sajɛt	sies siá	sibes sɛjze	siːs sides ʃtéde sé(j)ze	jɛsi (sta) jɛsit stejt sint
Ger.	ɛsən(d)	sjond ɛsənd	sjan	sjon(d)	(sjaŋ)		ʃtan	
Perf.	ʃtaw	ʃto	ʃto	ʃtat	ʃtat	ʃtat	ʃte	staːt
Subj.	sejj-	sej-	saj-	saj-	sie-~	ʃib- siː-	sid-~ s-	sed-~ se-
I.I.	ɛr- fuv-	er-	dejr-	dejr-	er-	fo-	fo-	(j)er-
I.S.	fus-	fis	fys	fys	fos	fos-	fə- fos-	fos-
Past	—	—	fyt	fyt	—	—	—	foj

Note: Initial /d/ in the imperfect in the Engadine dialects is a reflex of INDE.

Table A.2 'can'

	Surselvan	Surmeiran	Puter	Vallader	Fassa	Gardena	Badiot	Friulian
Inf.	pude	pudɛkr	pudɛr	pudajr	poder	pudaj	podej	podé
Pres.	pos	pos	pos	pos	pose	pos	po	pwes
	pos	poʃt	pouʃt	poʃt	pos	poses	pos	pwɛdis
	po	po	po	po	pel	po	po	pwes
								po
	pudɛjn	pudaɲ	pudɛns	pudajn	podoŋ	pudoŋ	poduŋ	podiŋ
	pudɛjs	pudets	pudɛs	pudajvet	podede	pudajs	podejs	podejs
	pon	pon	pawn	pon	pel	po	po	pwɛdiɲ
Imp.		poses	poseʃt	poseʃt				
		poses	posɛs	posɛst				
Ger.	pudɛnt	pudond	pujand	pujond	podaŋ	pudaŋ	pudoŋ	podínt
Perf.	pudew	pudia	pudia	pudy	podu	pedu	pudy	podú:t
						pudu		
Subj.	pos- ~ pud-	pos-	pos-	pos-	pos- ~ ?pod-	pos- ~ pud-	poj-	pwɛd-
I.I.	pudev-	pudev-	pudɛv-	pudajv-	pode-	pudov-	pudo-	podɛv-
I.S.			pudɛs-	pudɛs-	podes-	pudas-	podɛs-	podɛv-
Past	—	—	pudet-	pudet-	—	—	—	—

Note: Because of the great dialect variation in the expression of this word, the Friulian paradigm here represents central Friulian only.

Table A.3 'come'

	Surselvan	Surmeiran	Puter	Vallader	Fassa	Gardena	Badiot	Friulian
Inf.	veɲi	nɛkr	ɲir	ɲir	veɲir	uni	ɲi	viɲi
Pres.	veɲel	viɲ	vɛɲ	vɛɲ	veɲe	vɛɲɛ	vɛɲ	vɛɲ
	vɛɲs	viɲst	vɛɲʃt	vaɲʃt	veɲes	vɛɲes	veɲes	vɛɲs
	vɛɲ	viɲ	vɛn	vaɲn	veɲ	vɛɲ	vɛɲ	vɛɲ
	veɲin	niɲ	ɲins	ɲin	veɲoɲ	uɲoɲ	ɲuɲ	viɲiɲ
	veɲis	nits	ɲis	ɲivet	veɲide	uɲajs	ɲi:s	viɲi:s
	vɛɲan	veɲan	vɛɲen	vɛɲen	veɲ	vɛɲ	vɛɲ	vɛɲin
Imp.	new	vea	vɛ	vɛ	(d)jej	viɛ	vi	vɛɲ
	veɲi	ni	ɲi	ɲit	veɲi	unide	ɲide	viɲi:t
Ger.	viɲen(t)	ɲon(d)	ɲin(d)	ɲon(d)	—	uɲaɲ		viɲint
Per.	veɲiw	nie	ɲie	ɲy	veɲu	uni	ɲy	viɲu:t
Subj.	vɛɲ-	vea-	vɛɲ-	ɲi-		vɛɲ-	veɲes-	vɛɲi
		ni-		vɛɲ-				
		viɲ-						
I.I.	veɲiv-	niv-	ɲiv-	ɲiv-	veɲi-	univ-	ɲɔ-	viɲiv-
I.S.		nis-	ɲis-	ɲis-	veɲis-	unis-	ɲis-	viɲis-
Past		—	ɲit-	ɲit-	ɲit-	—	—	viɲi

Table A.4 'give'

	Surselvan	Surmeiran	Puter	Vallader	Fassa	Gardena	Friulian
Inf.	da	dar	der	dar	dɛr	de	da
Pres.	dun	duŋ	dun	dun	dae	de	doj
	das	dast	dɛʃt	daʃt	dɛs	des	das
	dat	dat	dɔ	da	dɛʃ	da	da
	dajn	daɲ	dɛns	dajn	daʒoŋ	daʒoŋ	diŋ
	dajs	dets	dɛs	dajvet	daʒede	daʒajs	dajs
	datən	datən	dɛm	dan	dɛʃ	da	daŋ
Imp.	daj	do	do	da	da	da	da
	dej	dɛ(t)	dɛ	dat	daʒede	daʒade	dajt
Ger.	dent	dont	dand	don(d)	daŋ	daʒaŋ	dant
Perf.	daw	do	do	dat	dat	dat	da:t
Subj.	dɛt-		dɛt-	dɛt-		dɛb-~ daʒ-	dɛj-
I.I.	dev-	dav-	dɛv-	dajv-	daʒe-	daʒo-	dav-
	dav-						dev-
I.S.		des-	des-	des-	daʒes-	daʒes-	das-
							des-
Past	—	—	dɛt-	dɛt-	—	—	dej

Table A.5 'go'

	Surselvan	Surmeiran	Puter	Vallader	Fassa	Gardena	Badiot	Friulian
Inf.	ir	ɛkr	ir	ir	ʒir	ʒi	ʒi	lá/ʒi
Pres.	mɔn	viɲ	vɛɲ	vɛɲ	vae	vɛdɛ	vad(e)	voj
	vas	vast	vɛʃt	vaʃt	ves	vɛs	vas	vas
	va	vɔ	vɔ	va	va	va	va	va
	mejn	ɟaɲ	ɟɛns	ɟajn	ʒɔŋ	ʒɔŋ	ʒuŋ	liŋ/niŋ ʒiŋ
	mejs	ɟets	ɟɛs	ɟajvet	ʒide	ʒajs	ʒi:s	lajs/ʒi:s
	van	vɔn	vɛm	van	va	va	va	vaŋ
Imp	va	vɔ	vo	va	va	va	va	va
	mej	ɟe	ɟɛ	it	ʒi	ʒide	ʒide	lajt/ʒi:t
Ger.		ɟon	ɟand	ɟond		ʒaŋ		lant/ʒint
Per.	iw	iə	iə	i	ʒit	ʒit	ʒy	ʒu:t/la:t
Subj.	mɔnd-~ mej-	ɟej-	ɟaj-	ɟaj-	ʒi-	vɛdɛ-	vajs-	vad-
I.I.	mav-	ɟev-	ɟev-	ɟajv-	va-~ ʔʒi-	ʒiv-	ʒɛ-	lav-/ʒɛv-
I.S.		ɟɛs-	ɟɛs-	ɟɛs-	ʒis-	ʒis-	ʒis-	las-/ʒɛs-
Past			ɟet-	ɟet-				lej/ʒej

Table A.6 'have'

	Surselvan	Surmeiran	Puter	Vallader	Fassa	Gardena	Badiot	Friulian
Inf.	ave	avɛkr	avɛr	avajr	aer	avaj	avɛj	(a)vé
Pres.	aj	vo/va	(d)ɛ	(n)a	ɛ	ɛ	a	aj
	as	ast	ɛʃt	aʃt	ɛs	ɛs	as	as
	a	o/o	ɔ	a	a	a	a	a
	vejn	van	vɛns	vajn	oŋ	oŋ	uŋ	viŋ
	vejs	vets	vɛs	vajvet	ɛde	ɛjs	ɛjs	vejs
	an	ɔn	ɛm	an	a	a	a	aŋ
Imp.	ajies	vejies	ɛjɛʃt	ajeʃt	abjes	ɛbes	a:js	ve
	vejes	sejes	ʃɛs	ajet	abjá	əjze	ede	vejt
Ger.	avɛn(d)	avɛn(d)	avjand	evjond				vint
Perf.	ju	jɛi	jɛi	ɲy	abu	abu	alby	vu:t
Subj.	aj-	vɛj-	ɛj-	naj-	abj-	ɛb-	ais-	veb-
	av-							
I.I.	(ə)vev-	vev-	əvev-	vajv-	aé-	ov-	aa-	vev-
I.S.	vɛs-	vɛs-	əvɛs-	vɛs-	aes-	ɛs-	es-	ves-
								vares-
Past			əvɛt-	(ə)vɛt-				vej

Note: The initial consonants /n/ and /d/ in the 1st singular indicative in Puter and Vallader are (like the /d/ in the imperfect of 'be' in Vallader) reflexes of INDE, surviving elsewhere in the language as the partitive pronoun.

Table A.7 'know'

	Surselvan	Surmeiran	Vallader	Fassa	Gardena	Badiot	Friulian
Inf.	save	savɛkr	savajr	saer	savaj	svɛj	savé
Pres.	saj	sa	sa	se	se	sa	saj
	sas	sast	saʃt	sɛs	sɛs	sas	sa(s)
	sa	so	sa	sa	sa	sas	sa
	savejn	savaɲ	savajn	saoɲ	savoɲ	savuŋ	saviŋ
	savejs	savets	savajvat	saede	savajs	savejs	savejs
	san	son	san	sa	sa	sa	saŋ
Imp.	sapies	sapcas	sapcaʃt		sɛbɛs	sa	sepis
	savejs	sapcas	sapcat		savajze	savede	savejt
Ger.			savjon		savaɲ		savint
Perf.	səviw	savie	savy	sapu	sapu	salpy	savú:t
				savu	savu		
Subj.	sap-	sapc-	sapc-	(sapj-)		sajs-	sep-
	sav-						
I.I.	savev-	savev-	savajv-	sae-	savov-	cas-	saves-
I.S.	saves-	saves-	saves-	saes-	savas-	saves-	saves-
Past	—	—	savet-	—	—	—	savej

Table A.8 'make'

	Surselvan	Surmeiran	Puter	Vallader	Fassa	Gardena	Badiot	Friulian
Inf.	fa	far	fɛr	fa	fɛr	fe	fa	fa
Pres.	fɛtʃəl	fatʃ	fatʃ	fɛtʃ	fae	feʒe	feʒi	faːʃ
	fas	fast	fɛʃt	faʃt	fes	feʒes	feʒes	faːs
	fa	fɔ	fɔ	fa	fɛʃ	feʃ	feʃ	faːʃ
	fəɟɛjn	fəʃaɲ	fɛns	fajn	faʒoɲ	faʒoɲ	faʒuɲ	faziɲ
	fəɟejs	fəʃets	fɛs	fajvat	faʒede	faʒajs	faʒejs	fazejs
	fan	fɔn	fɛm	fan	fɛʃ	feʃ	feʃ	fāziɲ
Imp.	faj	fɔ	fɔ	fa	fa	fe	fa	faːs
	fəɟej	fəʒɛ	fɛ	fat	faʒe	faʒadɛ feʒɛ	faʒede	fazejt
Ger.		faʒond	fan	fon(d)		faʒaɲ		fazint
Perf.	fac	fac	fat fats fatʃ	fat	fat	fat	fat	fat
Subj.	fɛtʃ- ~ fəɟ-	fɛtʃ-	fatʃ-	fɛtʃ-	fa- ~ faʒ-	feʒes-		faz-
I.I.	fəɟev-	fəɟev-	fev-	fajv-	faʒe-	faʒov-	faʒɔ-	fazev-
I.S.		fəɟes-	fes-	fes-	fazes-	faʒas-	fazes-	fazes-
Past	—	—	fɛt-	fɛt-	—	—	—	fes/fazéj

Table A.9 'must'

	Surselvan	Surmeiran	Puter	Vallader
Inf.	ʃtue	ʃtuɛkr	ʃtuver	ʃtuvajr
Pres.	ʃtɔj	ʃtɔ	ʃtøʎ	ʃtoʎ
	ʃtos	ʃtas(t)	ʃtuʃt	ʃtoʃt
	ʃtɔ	ʃtɔ	ʃtu	ʃto
	ʃtuejn	ʃtuaɲ	ʃtuens	ʃtuvajn
	ʃtuejs	ʃtuajs	ʃtues	ʃtuvajvet
	ʃtɔn	ʃtɔn	ʃtøʎam	ʃton
Ger.		ʃtuvjan	ʃtuvjan	ʃtuvjon
Perf.		ʃtuiə	ʃtuviʃ	ʃtuvy
				ʃty
Subj.	ʃtop-	ʃtɔpc-	ʃtøʎ- ~ ʃtopc-	ʃtøʎ- ~ ʃtopc-
I.I.		ʃtuev-	ʃtuev-	ʃtuvajv-
I.S.		ʃtuɛs-	ʃtuɛs-	ʃtuves-
Past	—	—	ʃtuvet-	ʃtuvɛt-

Note: This verb marks a recognized lexical boundary: Romansh dialects shared or borrowed a French word (M. Fr. *estovoir* < EST OPUS); Ladin, a German word (*müssen*); and Friulian, an Italian word (*bisogna*, itself ultimately a Germanic borrowing). Friulian and some Ladin also developed CONVENIT. Only cognates of *estovoir* are listed here.

Table A.10 'say'

	Surselvan	Surmeiran	Puter	Vallader	Fassa	Gardena	Friulian
Inf.	dir	dɛkr	dir	dir	dir	di	di
Pres.	dicəl	dej	di(ʃ)	di	die	diʒɛ	diʃ
	dias	dejʃt	diʃt	diʃt	dis	diʒɛs	dis
	di	dej	diʃ	diʃ	diʃ	diʃ	diʃ
	ʒejn	ʒaɲ	dʒɛns	dʒajn	diʒoɲ	diʒoɲ	diziɲ
	ʒejs	ʒets	dʒɛs	dʒajvet	diʒɛde	diʒajs	dizers
	dien	dejen	dien	diʒen	diʃ	diʃ	diziɲ
Imp.	di	dej	di	di	di	di	di:s
	ʒaj	ʒe	dʒe	dit	diʒe	diʒadɛ	dizejt
Ger.		ʒond	dʒan	dʒond		diʒaɲ	dizint
Perf.	dɛc	ʒɛtʃ	dit	dit	dit	dit	dit
		dɛc					
		zɛt					
Subj.	dic-~	ʒej-	di-		di-~		diz-
	ʒə-				ʔdiʒ-		
I.I.	ʒev-	ʒev-	dʒɛv-	dʒajv-	diʒe-	diʒo-	dizev-
I.S.	ʒes-	ʒes-	dʒes-	dʒes-	diʒes-	diʒas-	dizes-
Past	—	—	dʒɛt-	dʒɛt-	—	—	dizej

Table A.11 'should'

	Sursilvan	Surmeiran	Puter	Vallader	Gardena	Badiot	Friulian
Inf.	due	dueɕr	dover	dəvajr	duvaj	dovej dasaj	dové
Pres.	duej duejs duej duejn duejs duejn				da doŋ dajs da		dɛrf devis dɛrf dovín dovéjs déviɲ
Perf.	duju				dasu du		dovurt
Subj.	duejr- ~ du-						devi-
I.I.					dov-	dɔ-	dovev-
I.S.		dues-	des-	des	des-	dɛs-	doves-

Note: The imperfect subjunctive does duty for the present in Surmeiran, Puter, and Vallader.
The Gardena forms are rare, being mostly replaced by the German borrowing /mɛsaj/, while in Friulian /vè di/ 'to have to' is the more common form.

Table A.12 'stay'

	Surselvan	Surmeiran	Puter	Vallader	Fassa	Gardena	Friulian
Inf.	ʃta	ʃtar	ʃter	ʃtar	ʃter	ʃte	sta
Pres.	ʃtun ʃtas ʃta ʃtejn ʃtejs ʃtaten	ʃtun ʃtaʃt ʃtat ʃtaɲ ʃtets ʃtaten	ʃtun ʃteʃt ʃtɔ ʃtens ʃtes ʃten	ʃtun ʃtaʃt ʃta ʃtajn ʃtajvet ʃtan	ʃtae ʃtes ʃteʃ ʃtaʒoɲ ʃtaʒede ʃteʃ	ʃte ʃtes ʃta ʃtaʒoɲ ʃtaʒajs ʃta	stoj staːs sta stiɲ stajs stan
Imp.	ʃtaj ʃtej	ʃto ʃte(t)	ʃto ʃte	ʃta ʃtat	ʃta ʃtaʒe	ʃta ʃtaʒade	sta stajt
Ger.		ʃto	ʃto	ʃtond		ʃtaʒaɲ	stant
Perf.	ʃtaw			ʃtat	ʃtat	ʃtat	start
Subj.	ʃtɛt- ~ ʃtə-	ʃtet-	ʃtet-	ʃtet-		ʃteb- ~ ʃtej-	stedi- stej-
I.I.	ʃtav- ʃtev-	ʃtav-	ʃtev-	ʃtajv-	ʃtaʒe-		stav- stev-
I.S.		ʃtɛs-	ʃtes-	ʃtes-	ʃtaʒes-		stas- stes-
Past.	—	—	ʃtet-	ʃtet-	—	—	stej

Table A.13 'want'

	Surselvan	Surmeiran	Puter	Vallader	Fassa	Gardena	Badiot	Friulian
Inf.	(vu)le	(vu)lekr	vuler	(vu)lajr	voler	ulɛj	orɛj	ole
Pres.	vi	vi	vøʎ	vøʎ	voj	en	o	wej
	vul	vot	vowʃt	voːʃt	ves	ses	os	uːs
	vul	vot	vowl	voːl	vel	uel	o	uːl
	lejn	laŋ	vulɛns	lajn	voloŋ	uloŋ	oruŋ	oliŋ
	lejs	lets	vulɛs	lajvet	volede	ulajs	orɛjs	olɛjs
	vulen	votɛn	vøʎan	voʎan	vel	uel	o	wɛliŋ
Imp.	veʎas		vøʎaʃt	vøʎaʃt		uebes		olejt
	vulejes		vøʎas	vøʎat		ulade		
Ger.		vulen	vuʎand	vuʎond		ulaŋ		olint
Perf.		lie	vulie	vuʎy	volu	ulu	ory	oluːt
Subj.	veʎ- ~ vul-	viʎ-	voʎ-	voʎ-	vo- ~ ʔvol-	ueb- ~	ojs- / ul-	wel-
I.I.		lev-	vulɛv-	lajv-	vole-	ulo-	-cro	olev-
I.S.		les-	vulɛs-	les-	voles-	ules-	ores-	oles-
Past		—	vulet-	vulet-	(vu)lɛt-			olej

References

Adams, M. 1987, 'Old French, null subjects, and verb second Phenomena', unpublished dissertation, UCLA.

Alcock, A. 1970, *The History of the South Tyrol Question*, London: Michael Joseph.

Alton, J. 1881, *Proverbi, tradizioni ed anneddoti delle valli Ladine orientali*, Innsbruck: Accademica Wagner.

Alton, J. and F. Vittur, 1968, *L Ladin dla Val Badia*, Brixen: A. Weger.

Andersen, H. 1972, 'Diphthongization', *Language* 48: 11–50.

Appollonio, B. 1930, *Grammatica del dialetto ampezzano*, Trento: Arti Grafiche Tridentum.

Arquint, J. 1964, *Vierv Ladin*, Tusan: Lia Rumantscha.

—— 1979, *Zur Syntax des Partizipiums der Vergangenheit im Bündnerromanischen mit Ausblicken auf die Romania.* (Romania Raetica 3), Chur: Società Retorumantscha.

Ascoli, G.I. 1873, *Saggi Ladini* (Archivio Glottologico Italiano I), Turin: Ermanno Loescher.

—— 1882–5, 'L'Italia dialettale', *Archivio Glottologico Italiano* 8: 98–128.

—— 1883, 'Annotazioni sistematiche al Barlaam e Giosafat soprasilvano'. *Archivio Glottologico Italiano* VII: 406–602.

ASLEF = Atlante storico-linguistico-etnografico friulano, directed by G.B. Pellegrini, vol. 6, Padua: Udine 1972–86 (distributed by Max Niemeyer, Tübingen)

Bally, C. 1942, *Linguistique générale et linguistique française*, Bern: Francke.

Battisti, C. 1908, 'Die Nonsberger Mundart', *Sitzungsberichte der Akademie der Wissenschaften, Wien: Philosophisch-Historische Klasse* 160: 3.

—— 1931, *Popoli e lingue nell'Alto Adige*, Firenze: Bemporad.

—— 1937, *Storia della 'questione ladina'*, Firenze: Le Monnier.

Baur, A. 1969, *Grüezi mitenand*, Winterthur: Gemsberg.

Bayer, J. 1984, 'COMP in Bavarian Syntax', *The Linguistic Review* 3: 209–74.

Belardi, W. 1965, 'Sulle nasali velare e dentale finali di parola nel Badiotto del nord', *Istituto Universitario di Napoli: Sezione linguistica: Annali* 6: 187–98.

Bender, B., G. Francescato and Z. Saltzmann, 1952, 'Friulian phonology', *Word* 8: 216–23.

Beneš, E. 1962, 'Die deutsche Wortfolge von der Mitteilungsperspektive her betrachtet', *Philologica Pragensia* 2: 6–19.

Benincà, P. 1982, 'Il clitico "a" nel dialetto Padovano', in *Studi linguistici in onore di G.B. Pellegrini*, Pisa: Pacini, 25–35.

—— 1985, 'L'interferenza sintattica: di un aspetto della sintassi ladina considerato di origine tedesca', *Quaderni Patavini di Linguistica* 5: 3–17.

—— 1986, 'Punti di sintassi comparata dei dialetti italiani settentrionali', in G. Holtus and K. Ringger (eds) *Raetia antiqua et moderna: W. Theodor Elwert zum 80. Geburtstag*, Tübingen: Niemeyer, 457–79.

—— 1989, 'Friaulisch: Interne Sprachgeschichte. I: Grammatik. Evoluzione della grammatica'. *LRL* 3: 563–85.

Benincà, P. and L. Vanelli, 1976, 'Morfologia del verbo friulano: il presente indicativo', *Lingua e Contesto* 1: 1–62.

—— 1978, 'Il plurale friulano: contributo allo studio del plurale romanzo', *Revue de Linguistique Romane* 167–8: 241–91.

—— 1982, 'Appunti di sintassi veneta', in M. Cortelazzo (ed.) *Guida ai dialetti veneti*, Padua: Cleup, vol. 5, 7–38.

—— 1985, 'Italiano, veneto, friulano: fenomeni sintattici a confronto', *Rivista Italiana di Dialettologia*, Bologna: Clueb, vol. 8, 166–94.

Benincà-Ferraboschi, P. 1973, 'Osservazioni sull' "unita lessicale ladina" ', in G. Pellegrini (ed.) *Studi Linguistici Friulani*, Udine: Società Filologica Friulana, vol. 3, 121–32.

Bezzola, R.R. 1979, *Litteratura dals Rumauntschs e Ladins*, Cuoira: Lia Rumantscha.

Billigmeier, R. 1979, *A Crisis in Swiss Pluralism* (Contributions to the Sociology of Language, 26). The Hague: Mouton.

Boehmer, E. 1871, 'Prädicatscasus im Rätoromanischen', *Romanische Studien* 2: 210–26.

Bolinger, D. 1967, 'Adjectives in English: attribution and predication', *Lingua* 18: 1–37.

Bonjour, E., H.S. Offler, and G.R. Potter, 1952, *A Short History of Switzerland*, Oxford: Clarendon Press.

Bouchard, M. 1982, 'On the content of empty categories', unpublished doctoral dissertation, MIT.

Bracco, C., L. Brandi, and P. Cordin, 1985, 'Sulla posizione soggetto in italiano e in alcuni dialetti dell'Italia Centro-settentrionale', in A. Franchi De Bellis and L. M. Savoia (eds) *Sintassi e morfologia della lingua italiana d'uso, Atti del 17. congresso della Società di Linguistica Italiana*, Roma: Bulzoni, 185–209.

Brandi, L. and P. Cordin, 1981, 'Dialetti e italiano: un confronto sul parametro del soggetto nullo', *Rivista di Grammatica Generativa* 6: 33–87.

Breivik, L. 1983, *Existential 'there'*, Bergen: Department of English, University of Bergen.

Browne, W. and B. Vattuone, 1975, 'Theme-rheme structure and Zeneyze clitics', *Linguistic Inquiry* 6: 136–40.

Caduff, L. 1952, *Essai sur la phonétique du parler rhétoroman de la vallée de Tavetsch*, Bern: Francke.

Cavigelli, P. 1969, *Die Germanisierung von Bonaduz in geschichtlicher und sprachlicher Schau*, Frauenfeld: Huber.

Chomsky, N. 1957, *Syntactic Structures*, The Hague: Mouton.

Cooper, R. and E. Engdahl, 1989, 'Null subjects in Zürich German'. Paper presented at the sixth workshop on Comparative Germanic Syntax, Lund.

Craffonara, L. 1971–2, 'Le parlate di San Vigilio di Marebbe, di San Martino e La Villa in Val Badia', dissertation, University of Padua.

—— 1976, 'Rätoromanisch', *Der Schlern* 50: 472–82.

Darmesteter, A. 1897, *Cours de grammaire historique de la langue française*, vol. 4: *Syntaxe*, Paris: Delagrave.

D'Aronco, G. 1982, *Nuova antologia della letteratura friulana*, Udine: Ribis.

Decurtins, A. 1958, *Zur Morphologie der unregelmässigen Verben im Bündnerromanischen* (Romanica Helvetica, 62), Bern: Francke.

—— 1965, 'Das Rätoromanisch und die Sprachforschung', *Vox Romanica* 23/2: 256–304.

Decurtins, C. (ed.) 1883, 'Quattro testi soprasilvani', *Archivio Glottologico Italiano* 7: 149–364.

Di Giovine, P. 1987, 'Sull'origine del morfema di plurale {ŝ} nei sostantivi e aggetivi maschili badioti uscenti in vocale tonica', *L'Italia dialettale* 50: 23–71.

Dizionario etimologico storico friulano, vols. 1–2, A-Ezz, Udine: Casamassima 1984–7.

Ebneter, T. 1973, *Das bündnerromanische Futur* (Romanica Helvetica 85), Bern: Francke.

—— 1982, 'Far en romanche', in *Studi linguistici in onore di G.B. Pellegrini*, Pisa: Pacini, 183–92.

Eggenberger, J. 1961, *Das Subjektspronomen im Althochdeutsch: ein syntaktischer Beitrag zur Frühgeschichte des deutschen Schrifttums*, Chur: S. Sulser.

Elcock, W. 1960, *The Romance Languages*. London: Faber & Faber.

Elwert, W. 1943, *Die Mundart des Fassa-Tals* (Wörter und Sachen, new series, 2), Heidelberg: Winter.

—— (ed.) 1976, *Rätoromanisches Colloquium, Mainz* (Romanica Aenipontana, 10). Innsbruck: Institut für romanische Philologie der Leopold-Franzens-Universität.

Ettmayer, K. 1902, 'Lombardisch–ladinisches aus Südtirol', *Romanische Forschungen* 13: 321–672.

—— 1903, *Bergamaskische Alpenmundarten*, Leipzig: Reisland.

—— 1919, 'Zur Kenntnis des Altladinischen', *Zeitschrift für romanische Philologie* 39: 1–18.

Fernow, C.L. 1808, *Römische Studien*, vol. 3, Zurich: Gessner.

Filzi, M. 1914, 'Contributo alla sintassi dei dialetti italiani', *Studi Romanzi* 11: 5–14.

Flöss, E. 1990, 'Ladino, italiano, e tedesco nella produzione scritta di alunni di scuola media della Val Badia: ricerca sulla tipologia degli errori', dissertation, University of Padua.

Foulet, L. 1930, *Petite syntaxe de l'ancien Français*, Paris: Champion.

Francescato, G. 1956, 'Saggio statistico sul friulano a Udine', *Ce fastu?* 32: 39–59.

—— 1959, 'A case of coexistence of phonemic systems', *Lingua* 8: 78–86.

—— 1962, 'Il dialetto di Erto', *Zeitschrift für romanische Philologie* 86: 492–525.

—— 1963, 'I dittonghi induriti in friulano', in *Weltoffene Romanistik. Festschrift A. Kuhn zum 60. Geburtstag*, Innsbruck: University of Innsbruck (also in G. Francescato, *Studi linguistici sul friulano*, Florence: Olschki, 146–51).

—— 1966, *Dialettologia friulana*, Udine: Società Filologica Friulana.

—— 1970, *Studi linguistici sul friulano*, Firenze: Olschki.

Francescato, G. and G. Salimbeni, 1976, *Storia, lingua, e società in Friuli*, Udine: Casamassima.

Frau, G. 1984, *I dialetti del Friuli*, Udine: Società Filologica Friulana.

—— 1989, 'Friaulisch: Interne Sprachgeschichte; II: Lexik. Evoluzione del lessico', *LRL* 3: 586–96.

Frei, B., O. Menghin, E. Meyer and E. Risch (eds) 1971, *Der heutige Stand der Räterforschung in geschichtlicher, sprachlicher, und archäologischer Sicht*, Basel: Schriftenreihe des Rätischen Museums, Chur.

Gamillscheg, E. 1935, *Romania Germanica*, vol. II, Berlin: de Gruyter.

—— 1962, 'Zur Entstehungsgeschichte des Alpenromanischen', *Gesammelte Aufsätze* 2: 161–90.

Ganzoni, G. 1977, *Grammatica Ladina: Grammatica sistematica del rumantsch d'Engiadin'Ota*, Samedan: Lia Rumantscha.

—— 1983, *Grammatica Ladina. Grammatica sistematica dal rumantsch d'Engiadina Bassa*, Samedan: Lia Rumantscha.

Gartner, T. 1879, *Die Gredner Mundart*, Linz, privately published (reprinted 1974, Walluf-Nendeln: Saendig).

—— 1883, *Rätoromanische Grammatik*, Heilbronn: Henninger.

—— 1892, 'Die Mundart von Erto', *Zeitschrift für romanische Philologie* 16: 183–209.

—— 1910, *Handbuch der rätoromanischen Sprache und Literatur*, Halle: Max Niemeyer.

Gazdaru, D. 1962, 'Un conflicto "dialectologico" del siglo pasado', *Orbis* 11: 61–74.

Ghetta, F. and G. Plangg, 1987, 'Un proclama in ladino del 1631', *Mondo Ladino* 11: 281–93.

Givón, T. 1976, 'Topic, pronoun and grammatical agreement', in Charles Li (ed.) *Subject and Topic*, New York: Academic Press, 149–88.

—— 1979, *On Understanding Grammar*, New York: Academic Press.

Goebl, H. 1987, 'Drei ältere kartographische Zeugnisse zum Dolomitenladinischen', *Ladinia* 11: 113–46.

Grad, A. 1969, 'Contributo al problema della palatalizzazione delle guturali C, G davanti ad A in friulano', in *Atti del Congresso internazionale di linguistica e tradizioni popolari*, Gorizia, Udine, Tolmezzo: Società Filologica Friulana, 101–6.

Greenberg, J. 1966, *Universals of Language, with Special Reference to Feature Hierarchies*, The Hague: Mouton.

Gregor, D. 1972, *Romagnol: Language and literature*, New York: Oleander.

—— 1975, *Friulan: Language and literature*, New York: Oleander.

—— 1982, *Romontsch: Language and literature*, New York: Oleander.

Grisch, M. 1939, *Die Mundart von Surmeir*, (Romanica Helvetica 12), Paris: Droz.

Gruell, J. 1969, 'Entwicklung und Bestand der Rätoromanen in den Alpen', *Mitteilungen der Österreichischen geographischen Gesellschaft* 107.

Haiman, J. 1971, 'Targets and paradigmatic borrowing in Romansch', *Language* 47: 797–808.

—— 1972, 'Phonological targets and unmarked structures', *Language* 48: 365–78.

—— 1974, 'Targets and syntactic change', The Hague: Mouton.

—— 1983, 'On some origins of switch-reference marking', in J. Haiman and P. Munro (eds) *Switch Reference and Universal Grammar*, Amsterdam: Benjamins, 105–28.

—— 1985, *Natural Syntax*, Cambridge: Cambridge University Press.

—— 1990, 'Schizophrenic complementizers', in W. Croft, K. Denning, and S.

Kemmer (eds.) *Studies in Typology and Diachrony for Joseph Greenberg*, Amsterdam: Benjamins, 79–94.

Hall, R. 1974, *External History of the Romance Languages*, New York: Elsevier.

Harris, M. 1978, *The Evolution of French Syntax: a Comparative Approach*, London: Longmans.

—— 1986, 'The historical development of *si* clauses in Romance', in E. Traugott, A. Ter Meulen, J. Reilly, and C. Ferguson (eds) *On Conditionals*, Cambridge: Cambridge University Press, 265–84.

Heilmann, L. 1955, *La parlata di Moena*, Bologna: Zanichelli.

—— 1958, 'Testi dialettali moenesi in trascrizione fonetica', *Quaderni del'Istituto di Glottologia dell'Università di Bologna* 3: 53–80.

Heinz, S. and U. Wandruszka (eds) 1982, *Fakten und Theorien. Festschrift für Helmut Stimm*, Tübingen: Narr.

Heller, K. 1968, 'Untersuchungen zur rätoromanischen Verbalsyntax', unpublished dissertation, University of Innsbruck.

Helty, G. 1975, 'Westfrankische Superstrateinflüsse auf die Galloromanische Syntax', *Romanische Forschungen* 87: 413–27.

Hetzron, R. 1975, 'On presentative sentences: or, why the ideal word order is VSO(P)', in C. Li (ed.) *Word order and word order change*, Austin: University of Texas Press, 346–88.

Heuberger, R. 1932, *Rätien im Altertum und Frühmittelalter*, reprinted 1981, Aalen: Scientia.

Holtus, G. and K. Ringger (eds) 1986, *Raetia antiqua et moderna: W. Theodor Elwert zum 80. Geburtstag*, Tübingen: Niemeyer.

Holtus, G., M. Metzeltin and Ch. Schmitt (eds) 1989, *Lexikon der romanistischen Linguistik*, vol. III, Tübingen: Niemeyer.

Hubschmid, J. 1956, 'Vorindogermanische und jüngere Wortschichten in den romanischen Mundarten der Ostalpen', *Zeitschrift für romanische Philologie* 66: 1–94.

—— 1951, *Alpenwörter romanischen und vorromanischen Ursprungs*, Bern: Francke.

Huonder, J. 1901, 'Der Vokalismus der Mundart von Disentis', *Romanische Forschungen* 11: 431–566.

Iliescu, M. 1968–9, 'Esquisse d'une phonologie frioulane', *Revue Roumaine de Linguistique* 13: 277–85; 14: 273–88.

—— 1972, *Le friulan (à partir des dialectes parlés en Roumanie)*, The Hague: Mouton.

—— 1982, 'Typologie du verbe frioulan', in *Studi linguistici in onore di G.B. Pellegrini*, Pisa: Pacini, 193–204.

Iliescu, M. and H. Siller Runggaldier, 1985, *Rätoromanische Bibliographie*, Innsbruck: AMAE.

Jaberg, K. 1939, 'Considérations sur quelques caractères généraux du romanche', in *Mélanges de linguistique offerts à Charles Bally*, Geneva: Georg, 283–92.

Jaberg, K. and J. Jud, 1928–40, *Sprach- und Sachatlas Italiens und der Südschweiz*, Zofingen: Ringier.

Joppi, V. (ed.) 1878, 'Testi inediti friulani dei secoli XIV al XIX', *Archivio Glottologico Italiano* 4: 185–342.

Jud, J. 1911, 'Dalla storia delle parole lombardo-ladine', *Bulletin de dialectologie romaine* 3: 1–18; 63–86.

—— 1919, 'Zur Geschichte der bündnerromanischen Kirchensprache', reprinted 1973 in his *Romanische Sprachgeschichte und Sprachgeographie*, Zürich: Atlantis, 161–211.

Kamprath, C. 1985, 'The syllabification of consonantal glides: post-peak distinctions', *New England Linguistic Society* 16.

—— 1986, 'Suprasegmental structures in a Raeto-Romansh dialect: a case study in metrical and lexical phonology', unpublished dissertation, University of Texas at Austin.

Kayne, R. 1975, *French Syntax*, Cambridge, MA: MIT Press.

—— 1984, *Connectedness and Binary Branching*, Dordrecht: Foris.

—— 1985, 'L'Accord du participe passé en français et en italien', *Modèles linguistiques* 7: 73–89.

—— 1989, 'Facets of Romance past participle agreement', in P. Benincà (ed.) *Dialect Variation and the Theory of Grammar*, Dordrecht: Foris, 85–103.

Kemmer, S. 1988, 'The middle voice: a typological and diachronic study', unpublished doctoral dissertation, University of California, San Diego.

Kiparsky, P. 1968, 'Tense and mood in Indo-European', *Foundations of Language* 4: 30–56.

Kramer, H. 1963/4, 'Die Dolomiten-Ladiner unter der Österreichischen Monarchie', *Südtiroler Kulturinstitut: Jarhrbuch* 3/4: 88–144.

Kramer, J. 1972a, 'Abbozzo di una fonematica del surselvano letterario', *Revue Roumaine de linguistique* 17: 345–59.

—— 1972b. 'Klaus Peter Schneider: die Mundart von Ramosch', *Archiv für das Studium der neueren Sprachen und Litteraturen* 208: 431–3.

—— 1976, *Historische Grammatik des Dolomitenladinischen: Formenlehre*, Gerbrunn bei Würzburg: Lehmann.

—— 1977, *Historische grammatik des Dolomitenladinischen: Lautlehre*, Gerbrunn bei Würzburg: Lehmann.

Krasnovskaia, N. A. 1971, *Friuly*, Moscow: Akademia Nauk. (It. transl. *I Friulani*, Udine, 1980, Ribis.)

Kuen, H. 1937, 'Die ladinischer Dolomiten Mundarten in der Forschung der letzten 10 Jahre', *Zeitschrift für romanische Philologie* 57: 481–520.

—— 1957, 'Die Gewohnheit der mehrfachen Bezeichnung des Subjekts in der Romania und die Gründe ihres Aufkommens', in G. Reichenkron, M. Wandruszka, and J. Wilhelm (eds.) *Syntactica und Stylistica, Festschrift für E. Gamillscheg zum 70. Geburtstag*, Tübingen: Niemeyer, 293–326.

—— 1968, 'Einheit und Mannigfaltigkeit des Raetoromanischen', in K. Baldinger (ed.) *Festschrift W. von Wartburg zum 80. Geburtstag*, Tübingen: Niemeyer, 47–69.

Kuryłowicz, J. 1949, 'La Nature des procès dits analogiques', *Acta Linguistica* 5: 121–38.

Lambrecht, K. 1981, *Topic, Antitopic, and Verbal Agreement in Non-standard French*, Amsterdam: Benjamins.

Leonard, C. 1962, 'Proto-Raeto-Romance and French', *Language* 40: 23–32.

—— 1964, 'A reconstruction of Proto-Lucanian', *Orbis* 18: 439–84.

—— 1972, 'The vocalism of Proto-Raeto-Romance', *Orbis* 21: 61–100.

—— 1978, *Umlaut in Romance*, Grossen-Linden: Hoffmann.

Lepsky, G. 1964, 'Fonematica Veneziana', *L'Italia Dialettale* 15: 1–22.

Linder, K. 1982, 'Die Nichtübereinstimmung von finitem Verb und nachgestelltem Subjekt bei (Genus und) Numerus im Rätoromanischen Graubündens', in S. Heinz and U. Wandruszka (eds) *Fakten und Theorien: Festschrift für Helmut Stimm*, Tübingen: Narr, 147–62.

—— 1987, *Grammatische Untersuchungen zur Charakteristik des Rätoromanischen in Graubünden*, Tübingen: Niemeyer.

Liver, R. 1989, 'Bündnerromanisch: Interne Sprachgeschichte, II: Lexik', *LRL* 3: 789–803.

Longworth, P. 1974, *The Rise and Fall of Venice*, London: Constable.

Luedtke, H. 1955, 'Zur Lautlehre des Bündnerromanischen', *Vox Romanica* 14: 225.

—— 1957, 'Inchiesta sul confine dialettale fra il veneto e il friulano', *Orbis* 6: 122–5.

—— 1962, 'Zur sprachlichen Stellung des Münstertals', *Orbis* 11: 111–15.

—— 1965, 'Die lateinischen Endungen -um/-in/-unt und ihre romanischen Ergebnisse', in I. Iordan (ed.) *Omagiu lui Alexandru Rosetti*, Bucuresti: 487–99.

Lutta, M. 1923, *Der Dialekt von Bergün und seine Stellung innerhalb der rätoromanischen Mundarten Graubündens (Zeitschrift für romanische Philologie, 71)*, Halle: Niemeyer.

Luzi, J. 1904, 'Die sutselvischen Dialekte: Lautlehre', *Romanische Forschungen* 16: 757–846.

Marchetti, G. 1952, *Lineamenti di grammatica friulana*, Udine: Società Filologica Friulana.

Meillet, A. 1921, 'L'évolution des formes grammaticales', in *Linguistique historique et liguistique générale*, Paris: Champion, 130–49.

Meinhof, C. 1936, *Die Entstehung flektierender Sprachen*, Berlin: Reimer.

Meyer, E. 1971, 'Die geschichtlichen Nachrichten über die Räter und ihre Wohnsitze', in B. Frei, *et al.* (eds) *Der heutige Stand der Räterforschung in geschichtlicher, sprachlicher, und archäologischer Sicht*, Basel: Schriftenreihe des Räteischen Museums, Chur, 5–11.

Meyer-Lübke, W. 1899, *Grammatik der romanischen Sprachen*, reprinted 1972, Hildesheim: Georg Olms.

—— 1935, *Romanisches etymologisches Wörterbuch*, 3rd edn, Heidelberg: Carl Winter.

Migliorini, B. and T. Griffith, 1984, *The Italian Language*, London: Faber & Faber.

Nay, S. 1965, *Bien di, bien onn. Praktisches Lehrbuch der rätoromanischen Sprache (deutsch–surselvisch)*, 3rd edn, Disentis: Lia Rumantscha.

Nazzi Matalon, Z. 1977, *Mari lenghe. Gramatiche Furlane*, Gurize-Pordenon-Udin: Institut di Studis Furlans.

Palla, L. 1988, 'Processi di tedeschizzazione e di italianizzazione dei ladini dolomitici nel periodo della grande guerra e dell'annessione all'Italia', *Ladinia* 12: 159–90.

Pellegrini, G. 1970, 'La classificazione delle lingue romanze e i dialetti italiani', *Forum Italicum* 4: 211–37.

—— 1972a, *Saggi sul ladino dolomitico e sul friulano*, Bari: Adriatica editrice.

—— 1972b, *Introduzione all'ASLEF*, Udine (distributed by Niemeyer, Tübingen).

—— 1975, 'Noterelle linguistiche slavo-friulane', *Annali dell'Istituto Orientale di Napoli – Slavistica* 18: 129–54.

—— 1982, *Studi linguistici in onore di G. B. Pellegrini*, Pisa: Pacini.

—— 1985, 'Reti e Retico. In *L'Etrusco e le lingue dell' Italia antica'*, *Atti del Convegno della Società Italiana di Glottologia*, Pisa: Giardini.

—— 1987a, 'The sociolinguistic position of central Rhaeto-Romance', *Romance*

Philology 40: 287–300.

Pellegrini, G. and C. Marcato, 1988, *Terminologia agricola friulana*, Udine: Società Filologica Friulana.

Pellegrini, G. and A. Zamboni, 1982, *Flora popolare friulana*, Udine: Casamassima.

Pellegrini, R. 1987b, *Tra linguistica e letteratura: per una storia degli usi scritti del friulano*, Udine: Casamassima.

Pellis, U. 1910–11, *Il sonziaco. Annuario dell'I.R. Ginnasio Superiore di Capodistria*, Trieste: Hermanstorfer.

Perlmutter, D. 1971, *Deep and Surface Structure Constraints in Syntax*, New York: Holt Rinehart, Winston.

Pfister, M. 1986, 'Die Bedeutung des Bündnerromanischen, Zentralladinischen, und Friaulischen für die Rekonstruktion altoberitalienischer Sprachschichten', in G. Holtus and K. Ringger (eds) *Raetia antiqua et moderna: W. Theodor Elwert zum 80. Geburtstag*, Tübingen: Niemeyer, 167–82.

Pirona, G., E. Carletti and G. B. Corgnali, 1935, *Il nuovo Pirona: vocabolario friulano*, Udine: Società filologica friulana.

Pizzinini, A. and G. Plangg, 1966, *Parores ladines* (Romanica Aenipontana 3), Innsbruck: Institut für romanische Philologie der Leopold-Franzens-Universität.

Plangg, G. 1969, 'Zum Sprachtypus des ladinischen und seiner Nachbarn', *Der Schlern* 43: 159–76.

—— 1973, *Sprachgestalt als Folge und Fügung (Zeitschrift für romanische Philologie*, 133) Tübingen: Niemeyer.

—— 1982, 'Emphatische Konstrukte im Zentralladinischen', *Studi linguistici in onore di G. B. Pellegrini*, Pisa: Pacini, 305–17.

Planta, J. 1776, *An Account of the Romansh Language* (reprinted 1972), Menston: Scolar Press.

Planta, R. von 1926, *Birkicht und Vokalmetathese. Festschrift Gauchat*.

Politzer, R. 1967, *Beitrag zur Phonologie der Nonsberger Mundart* (Romanica Aenipontana 2), Innsbruck: Institut für romanische Philologie der Leopold-Franzens-Universität.

—— 1972, 'Final -s in Romania', in J. Anderson and J. Creore (eds) *Readings in Romance Linguistics*, The Hague: Mouton, 414–22.

Prader-Schucany, S. 1970, *Romanisch Bünden als selbständige Sprachlandschaft* (Romanica Helvetica 60), Bern: Francke.

Prati, A. 1936, 'Spiegazioni di nomi di luoghi del Friuli', *Revue de linguistique romane* 12: 44–143.

Pulgram, E. 1958, *The tongues of Italy*, Cambridge, MA: Harvard University Press.

Pult, J. 1897, *Le parler de Sent*, Lausanne.

Redfern, J. 1971, *A Lexical Study of Raeto-Romance and Contiguous Italian Dialect Areas* (Janua Linguarum, Series Practica 120), The Hague: Mouton.

Renzi, L. 1985 *Nuova introduzione alla filologia romanza*, Bologna: Il Mulino.

—— 1989, 'I pronomi soggetto: un caso di parentela tipologica tra fiorentino e francese, e un capitolo poco noto di storia della lingua italiana', ms., University of Padua.

Renzi, L. and L. Vanelli, 1982, 'I pronomi soggetto in alcune varietà romanze', *Studi linguistici in onore di G. B. Pellegrini*, Pisa: Pacini, 121–45.

Repetti, L. and E. Tuttle, 1987, 'The evolution of Latin PL, BL, and CL, GL in

Western Romance', *Studi Mediolatini e Volgari* 33: 54–115.

Richebuono, G. 1985, 'Aus der Geschichte der Ladiner der fünf Dolomitentaler', *Informationsschrift* 40: 13–99 (Autonome Provinz Bozen, Südtirol).

da Rieti, G. 1904, *Grammatica teorico-pratica per imparare la lingua romancia*, St Gallen: Cavelti-Hangartner.

Risch, E. 1971, 'Die Räter als sprachliches Problem', in Frei *et al.* (eds) *Der heutige Stand der Räterforschung in geschichtlicher, sprachlicher, und archäologischer Sicht*, Basel: Schriftenreihe des Rätischen Museums, Chur, 12–21.

Rizzi, L. 1986, 'On the status of subject clitics in Romance', in O. Jaeggli and C. Silva-Corvalan (eds) *Studies in Romance Linguistics*, Dordrecht: Foris, 391–419.

Rizzolatti, P. 1981, *Elementi di linguistica friulana*, Udine: Società Filologica Friulana.

Roberge, Y. 1989, 'Predication in Romontsch', *Probus* 1,2: 225–9.

Rohlfs, G. 1949, *Historische Grammatik der italienischen Sprache*, 3 vols (reprinted 1972), Bern: Francke.

—— 1966–9, *Grammatica storica della lingua italiana e dei suoi dialetti*, vol. I: *Fonetica* (1966), vol. II: *Morfologia* (1968), vol. III: *Sintassi e formazione delle parole* (1969) (updated and revised version of Rohlfs 1949), Torino: Einaudi.

—— 1971, *Romanische Sprachgeographie*. Munich: Beck.

—— 1972, 'La posizione linguistica del ladino', in his *Studi e ricerche su lingua e dialetti d'Italia*, Firenze: Sansoni, 125–31.

—— 1975, *Rätoromanisch*, Munich: Beck.

—— 1986, 'Die Sonderstellung des Rätoromanischen', in G. Holtus and K. Ringer (eds) *Raetia antiqua et moderna: W. Theodor Elwert zum 80. Geburtstag*. Tübingen: Niemeyer, 501–11.

Rusinow, D. 1969, *Italy's Austrian Heritage 1919–1946*, Oxford: Clarendon Press.

Sabatini, F. 1965, 'Sull'origine dei plurali italiani: il tipo in -*i*', *Studi Linguistici Italiani* 5: 5–39.

Schane, S. 1971, 'The phoneme revisited', *Language* 47: 3.

Scheitlin, W. 1962, *Il pled Puter*, Samedan: Union dals Grischs.

—— 1980, *Il pled Puter*, 3rd edn, Samedan: Union dals Grischs.

Schlieben-Lange, B. 1971, *Okzitanische und katalanische Verbprobleme*, Tübingen: Niemeyer.

Schmidt, H. 1951/2, 'Zur Geschichte der rätoromanischen Deklination', *Vox Romanica* 12: 21–81.

Schneller, C. 1870, *Die romanischen Volksmundarten in Südtirol*, Wiesbaden: Saendig.

Schorta, A. 1964, *Rätisches Namenbuch*, vol. II: *Etymologien*, Bern: Francke.

Schorta, A. and A. Decurtins (eds), 1939– , *Dicziunari Rumantsch Grischun*, Chur: Societa Retorumantscha.

Schuchardt, H. 1870, *Über einige Fälle bedingten Lautwandels im Churwälschen*, Gotha: Perthes.

Schuerr, F. 1938, *La classificazione dei dialetti italiani*, Leipzig: Keller.

—— 1963, 'Die Alpenromanen', *Vox Romanica* 22: 100–26 (reprinted in his *Probleme und Prinzipien der romanischen Sprachwissenschaft*, Tübingen: Gunter Narr, 325–43).

Sonder, A. and M. Grisch, 1970, *Vocabulari Surmeir*, Chur: Lia Rumantscha.

Spiess, F. 1956, *Die Verwendung des Subjekt-personalpronomens in den lombardischen Mundarten*, Bern: Francke.

Stimm, H. 1973, *Medium und Reflexivkonstruktion im Surselvischen* (Bayerische Akademie der Wissenschaften, Sitzungsbericht Jahrgang 1973, 6) Munich: Verlag der BAdW.

—— 1976, 'Zu einigen syntaktischen Eigenheiten des Surselvischen', in W. Th. Elwert (ed.) *Rätoromanisches Colloquium, Mainz* (Romanica Aenipontana, 10), Innsbruck: Institut für romanische Philologie der Leopold-Franzens-Universität, 31–58.

Tagliavini, C. 1926, 'Il dialetto del Comelico', *Archivum Romanicum* 10: 1–200.

—— 1933, 'Alcuni problemi del lessico ladino centrale', *Revue de linguistique romane* 9: 285–319.

—— 1972, *Le origini delle lingue neolatine*, 6th edn, Bologna: Patron.

Tekavčić, P. 1974, 'Abbozzo del sistema morfosintattico del soprasilvano odierno', *Studia Romanica et Anglica Zagrabiensia* 33–6: 359–488; 37: 5–134.

Thöni, G. 1969, *Rumantsch-Surmeir*, Chur: Lia Rumantscha.

Thurneysen, R. 1892, 'Zur Stellung des Verbums im Altfranzösischen', *Zeitschrift für romanische Philologie* 16: 289–307.

Trumper, J. 1975, 'Obiezioni sistematiche all'uso dei tratti teso/rilassato nell'analisi di sistemi vocalici e di rotazioni vocaliche', *Lingua e contesto* 2: 1–86.

Tuttle, E. 1986, 'Alpine systems of Romance sibilants', in G. Holtus and K. Ringer (eds) *Raetia antiqua et moderna: W. Theodor Elwert zum 80. Geburtstag*, Tübingen: Niemeyer, 315–42.

Ulleland, M. 1965, 'L'*el* ascitizio nella prima singolare del verbo soprasilvano', *Studia Neophilologica* 37: 105–15.

Ulrich, J. (ed.) 1882, *Rhätoromanische Chrestomathie*, Halle: Niemeyer.

Urzi, E. 1961, 'Analisi fonematica della parlata di Ortisei', *Quaderni* 6: 69–87 (Università di Bologna: Istituto di Glottologia).

Vanelli, L. 1979, 'L'allungamento delle vocali in friulano', *Ce fastu?* 55: 66–76.

—— 1984a, 'Pronomi e fenomeni di prostesi vocalica nei dialetti italiani settentrionali', *Revue de linguistique romane* 48: 281–95.

—— 1984b, 'Il sistema dei pronomi soggetto nelle parlate ladine', in D. Messner (ed.) *Das Romanische in den Ostalpen*, Vienna: Verlag der Österreichischen Akademie der Wissenschaften, 147–60.

—— 1985, 'Friulano', in L. Renzi (ed.) *Nuova introduzione alla filologia romanza*, Bologna: Il Mulino, 367–73.

—— 1987, 'I pronomi soggetto nei dialetti italiani settentrionali dal Medioevo ad oggi', *Medioevo Romanzo* 12: 173–211.

Vellemann, A. 1924, *Grammatica teoretica ed istorica della lingua ladina d'Engadin'Ota*, Zurich: Füssli.

Wartburg, W. von 1950, *Die Ausgliederung der romanischen Sprachraume*, Bern: Francke.

—— 1956, 'Die Entstehung des Rätoromanischen und seine Geltung im Land', in his *Von Sprache und Mensch*, Bern: Francke, 23–44.

Watkins, C. 1962, *Indo-European Origins of the Celtic Verb*, Part I: *The Sigmatic Aorist*, Dublin: Institute of Advanced Studies.

Widmer, A. 1959, *Das Personalpronomen im Bündnerromanischen*, (Romanica Helvetica, 67), Bern: Francke.

Zamboni, A. 1980–1, 'Un problema di morfologia romanza: l'ampliamento verbale in -IDIO, -IZO', *Quaderni Patavini di Linguistica* 2: 171–87.

—— 1982–3, 'La morfologia verbale latina in +SC+ e la sua evoluzione romanza: appunti per una nuova via esplicativa', *Quaderni Patavini di Linguistica* 3: 87–138.

—— 1983, 'Note aggiuntive alla questione dei verbi in -ISCO', *Studi di Grammatica Italiana* 12: 232–7.

—— 1984, 'Di alcuni continuatori mediani del germ. SKAIBO "mestolo", "cucchiaio" ', *L'Italia dialettale* 47: 311–15.

Index